C. 5
W9-DGG-997

AN AKKADIAN GRAMMAR

A Translation of Riemschneider's

Lehrbuch des Akkadischen

by

Thomas A. Caldwell, S.J.
John N. Oswalt
John F. X. Sheehan, S.J.

Marquette University Press
Milwaukee, Wisconsin 53233
United States of America

Copyright © 1974, 1975 by
John F. X. Sheehan, S.J.

ISBN 0-87462-444-4

First Edition, 1974
Second Edition, 1976
Third Edition, 1977
Fourth Printing, 1977
Fifth Printing, 1978

All rights reserved. No part of this publication may be reproduced, stored in a retrieval system or transmitted in any form or by any means (electronic, mechanical, photocopying, recording, or otherwise) without the prior written permission of the copyright owner and publisher.

Printed in the United States of America
by
Marquette University Press
Milwaukee, Wisconsin USA

Preface

This grammar, a translation of Riemschneider's *Lehrbuch des Akkadischen* has Parts I and II as shown in Table of Contents consolidated under one cover.

A General Vocabulary for the entire work, Part II, should serve as a useful tool for the beginner.

The publishers and translators will welcome any comments and recommendations from faculty and students using an *Akkadian Grammar* as a text or reference.

Translators' Preface

The appearance of Riemschneider's *Lehrbuch des Akkadischen* in English dress, *An Akkadian Grammar, Parts I and II,* is due to various circumstances.

First, of course, was the bizarre hobby interest of the translators which impelled them to devote much time to the project. With vivid memories of their first year Akkadian studies, they realized how much such a book could mean to beginners whose German, in Seminary or in first year of Graduate School, might present almost as many problems as Akkadian. The translators selected Riemschneider for a plethora of reasons. They were not in total sympathy with all the grammatical theories present in the book. Still, in comparison with any other textbook available, this one is by far the richest in the basics of a good textbook, exercises, and reading lessons.

Lessons 1-18 are complete in themselves with rich vocabularies. Part II of this translation, bound under this cover after Part I, is a general vocabulary. The book is now complete with an index and table of contents. The former shows up some of the inconsistencies of the translators (who moved from Verbs 'I *n*' to Verbs 'Primae *n*' for example), but it should be useful.

This book was originally subsidized both by the Marquette University Jesuit Community and by the Marquette University Theology Department. The translators express their gratitude to these communities.

AN AKKADIAN GRAMMAR

TABLE OF CONTENTS

PARTS I & II

Introduction

The Place of Akkadian Among the Semitic Languages and its Relationship to Sumerian

Akkadian (Babylonian-Assyrian) may be considered the most important of the numerous languages of the Ancient Near East. Akkadian texts have come to us from a time-span of more than two thousand years. They are the chief source of our knowledge of ancient Mesopotamia and her history, economy, culture, literature and religion. Akkadian is also the oldest known Semitic language. Its meaning for comparative Semitics and for the knowledge of languages in general has become clearer and clearer in recent years.

This textbook is intended to make the approach to Akkadian easier for the interested student. Unlike most previous Akkadian textbooks which lay great stress on the learning of the cuneiform script, this book will attempt to introduce the beginner more easily into the grammar of the language through texts in transliteration. (However, the appendix of this English translation includes several texts in Cuneiform.)

The textbook is divided into lessons which treat the grammatical material gradually from the easy to the difficult stages. The author judged that no artificially formed sentences ought to be used as reading passages.

He looked for a collection of texts from which one could easily extract small, united passages suitable for the beginner. Old-Babylonian omen-texts are such a collection. Especially the apodoses of the omens are so written that they are well suited for elementary instruction in Akkadian. Omen-texts form the basis of the first nineteen lessons which are devoted to Old-Babylonian. With these omen-texts, beginning with the twelfth lesson, paragraphs from Hammurabi's Code are used, as well as Old-Babylonian letters and a legal document. In the remaining eight lessons, each of which deals with the grammar of a specific period of the language, the author has used texts which he thought especially well suited to illustrating that grammar. If anyone wishes to look up these texts in their original publications, he can find the references in our listing of sources at the back of the book. He will also find there the changes made by the author (correction of misspellings and completion of broken lines).

A textbook cannot play the role of a chrestomathy for the Akkadian language. Still, the author hopes that his selections will offer the student an insight into some important groups of texts. The decision to ignore cuneiform signs in this book was not overly influenced by the technical difficulties of printing Cuneiform. The author felt that a detour around the boredom of learning Cuneiform should be offered to the student who is interested only in the language. Moreover, it is a fact that the learning of Cuneiform and the reading of cuneiform texts -- especially from the earlier periods -- is much easier if the student already has a real mastery of the grammar. The reason is this: Cuneiform uses word-signs frequently and many of its syllable-signs have several possible phonetic values. Only the advanced student, with the help of his grammatical knowledge, can select the correct reading from a plethora of possibilities by eliminating what is grammatically impossible.

No further justification is required today for the judgment that the study of Akkadian should begin with the oldest possible texts. Only in this way can one attain an understanding of the way the language developed. That means one must begin with Old-Babylonian. (For Old-Assyrian is still badly documented and insufficiently researched; so it is considerably more difficult for the beginner.) Cuneiform is traditionally taught by using normal writing (Neo-Assyrian) of Young-Babylonian texts. Practical considerations are decisive here. Neo-Assyrian signs are somewhat simpler and occur with fewer variants than the Old-Babylonian. They are therefore more easily learned. If one wishes to teach simultaneously the grammar of Old-Babylonian and Cuneiform according to the Neo-Assyrian orthography, only one way is possible. One must transcribe the Old-Babylonian texts into New-Assyrian signs. This method has been often tried, but its value remains open to dispute.

The beginner is advised to give up the idea of learning Cuneiform -- at least for the time being. Only when he has some real mastery of the grammar and can understand texts in transliteration should he begin with the reading of relatively easy cuneiform passages. These texts do not have to be texts in Neo-Assyrian. One can begin immediately with the Old-Babylonian cursive writing. The academic system of Hittite instruction shows that this is possible. For the script of their language the Hittites used a slightly simplified variation of the Old-Babylonian cursive writing. Students began relatively quickly to read the Hittite cuneiform even though Akkadian was completely unknown to them. Preparation for the reading of Old-Babylonian requires that a sign-list be used which is arranged according to the Old-Babylonian forms. The author intends eventually to complement this present book with an Old-Babylonian cuneiform reading book and that will include a sign-list. Until that appears, one who wishes to read Old-Babylonian texts in Cuneiform could read either from Goetze's Omen-Texts (Old-Babylonian Omen-Texts, Yale Oriental Series, 1966 reprint) or Bottéro's Letters From Mari (Archives Royal de Mari: Textes Cuneiformes du Louvre XXII, Paris, 1946. The sign list is by Bottéro and Finet, Repertoire Analytique des Tomes I-V, Paris, 1954.).

If anyone wishes to use the book for self-instruction, this should be his method: he should read the grammatical part of the lesson thoroughly and make a real effort to grasp the examples. Then he should translate the exercises and texts with the help of the glossary. Next he should compare his translation with that given at the back of the book. Finally he should translate the material back into Akkadian. (This instruction applies at least to lessons 1-19.) In this writing the words should not be written syllabically but joined with careful attention to length of vowels and double consonants. The transcription of the exercises (also given at the back of the book) should serve as the model for this exercise. Before the student begins the next lesson, he should repeat the grammatical part of the lesson one more time.

In the writing of this textbook, the author was able to use experience acquired in teaching Cuneiform at the University of Baghdad in 1962-64. He owes thanks to Dr. Lubor Matouš for reading the entire manuscript critically and suggesting numerous corrections. Professor Karl-Heinz Deller gave the author helpful suggestions on handling the grammar of Neo-Assyrian in the twenty-seventh lesson. The author is extremely grateful.

This book could not have been written without the progress made by scholarly research in the past few decades. At this point, the author would like to pay tribute to the two scholars who, in his opinion, have made the greatest contributions to this research: Benno Landsberger and Wolfram von Soden.

K. Riemschneider

The Place of Akkadian Among the Semitic Languages and its Relationship to Sumerian

0.1 The Semitic Languages   Akkadian is the oldest attested Semitic language. As (North-) Eastern Semitic it is contrasted to the Western Semitic languages. The Western Semitic languages are divided into two groups: a northern group including the Canaanite languages (Ugaritic, Amorite, Hebrew and Phoenician) and Aramaic, and a southern group including Arabic and Ethiopic.

Moscati and others: An Introduction to the Comparative Grammar of the Semitic Languages, Wiesbaden, 1964.

0.2 Akkadian   The Semitic language which was spoken in Mesopotamia from the middle of the third millennium B.C. and whose use reaches to the first century A.D. is named after the city Akkad, the capital of the kingdom of Sargon of Akkad (2340-2284). The purely demotic original form of Akkadian has not been handed on to us. The oldest inscriptions which we have show the influence of non-Semitic Sumerian on the Akkadian language.

0.3 Sumerians and Akkadians   The Sumerians are the creators of the oldest developed civilization in Mesopotamia (ca. 3000 B.C.). For the most part, they inhabited southern and central Babylon between the Tigris and Euphrates rivers from the Persian Gulf to what is now modern Baghdad. Around 2600 B.C., Akkadian nomads emigrated into Sumerian territory and began to adopt their sedentary style of life and their culture. With the increasing mingling of the two peoples, the Sumerians were gradually absorbed into the Akkadians. After 1900 B.C. Sumerian was no longer spoken. Still, it continued to serve for centuries along with Akkadian as a literary and liturgical language.

0.4 *Akkadian and Sumerian* Since the Akkadians were culturally dependent on the Sumerians, the gradual mingling of the two peoples led to a definite modification of Akkadian by Sumerian. The Sumerian influence is shown in numerous loan-words in Akkadian, e.g. *ṭuppum*, "clay tablet" from the Sumerian DUB and *ekallum*, "palace," from the Sumerian E-GAL, "great house." The proto-Semitic phonetic structure is heavily modified in Akkadian in the presence of the Dentals, Velars, Pharyngeals and Laryngeals (see 0.12). Likewise the most important syntactic peculiarity of Akkadian, the placing of the predicate at the end of the sentence, can be explained by Sumerian influence. Such word order is otherwise almost never found in the Semitic languages.

Stages of the Language and Dialects

0.5 *The Development of Akkadian* In the two and one half millennia in which Akkadian was used, it changed constantly in grammar and vocabulary. One must distinguish different stages of the language and various dialects. Sources: a) Grammars: The first grammar was published by F. Delitzsch, *Assyrische Grammatik mit Paradigmen, Übungsstücken, Glossar und Litteratur*, Berlin, 1889. It treated Assyrian royal inscriptions and other Young-Babylonian texts (0.9). W. von Soden, *Grundriss der Akkadischen Grammatik*, Analecta Orientalia 33, Rome, 1952, treated all the stages of the language and its dialects. Ungnad's shorter *Grammatik des Akkadischen*, (4th edition edited by Matouš, Munich, 1964) differs from this standard work in some details. One may also compare E. Reiner, *A Linguistic Analysis of Akkadian*, th Hague, 966. b) Dictionaries: W. von Soden, *Akkadisches Handwörterbuch* (abbreviated AHw), Band I (A-L), Wiesbaden, 1959-1965, Band II is coming out in fasicles; . L. Oppenheim and others, *The Assyrian*

Dictionary of the Oriental Institute of the University of Chicago (abbreviated CAD), Chicago and Glückstadt, 1956 ff. Until now nine volumes have appeared: A (first half), B, D, E, G, H, I/J, S and Z.

0.6 Old Akkadian The oldest stage of the language, Old Akkadian, is attested by inscriptions found in Southern Babylon and dating from the twenty-fourth to the twentieth century. Only after this period can Akkadian be clearly separated into two dialects: Babylonian and Assyrian.

> Source-books: I. J. Gelb, Old Akkadian Writing and Grammar, 2nd edition, Chicago, 1961; Glossary of Old Akkadian, Chicago, 1957.

0.7 Babylonian From the twentieth century on, the language of Middle and Southern Babylonia is Babylonian. This language has four discernible stages of development. Old Babylonian (20th to the 16th century) is well attested through a plethora of varied texts: letters, legal documents, codes of law, and omen-texts. This stage of the language is treated in the first nineteen lessons of the textbook. In later development of Babylonian, one can distinguish Middle-Babylonian (15th to 11th century, treated in the twenty-first lesson), Neo-Babylonian (10th to 7th century, treated in the twenty-second lesson), and Late-Babylonian (from the 6th century on, treated also in the twenty-second lesson).

> Source-books: First of all, one should consult the grammars written by von Soden and Ungnad/Matouš which were cited in 0.5. For Middle-Babylonian, one might consult: J. Aro, Studien zur mittelbabylonischen Grammatik, Studia Orientalia 20, Helsinki, 1955; by the same author, Glossar zu den mittelbabylonischen Briefen, Studia Orientalia 22, 1957; for Neo-Babylonian: S. Ylvisaker, Zur babylonischen und assyrischen Grammatik, Leipziger Semitische Studien 5, 6 Leipzig, 1912; also his "Dialectic Differences between Assyrian and Babylonian," Journal of the American Oriental Society 33, 1913, 397-401; E. S. Rimalt, "Wechselbeziehungen zwischen dem Aramäischen und dem Neubabylonischen," Wiener Zeitschrift für die Kunde des Morgenlandes 39, 1932, 99-122.

0.8 Assyrian One can divide the Akkadian dialect of Assyria into three developmental stages: Old Assyrian which (apart from some royal inscriptions) is known to us only from business letters and legal documents of Assyrian merchants working in the eastern portion of Asia Minor in the 19th and 18th centuries (treated in the twenty-fifth lesson), Middle Assyrian (16th to the 11th century, treated in the twenty-sixth lesson), and Neo-Assyrian from the 10th to the 7th century (treated in the twenty-seventh lesson).

> Source-books: There are as yet no detailed and specific books written on the linguistic stages of Assyrian. Still, for Old Assyrian, one may consult: J. Lewy, Studies in Old Assyrian Grammar and Lexicography, Orientalia NS 19, 1950, 1-36; for Middle Assyrian: J. Lewy, Das Verbum in den altassyrischen (by which he means Middle-Assyrian) Gesetzen, Berlin, 1921; for Neo-Assyrian, in addition to the writings by Ylvisaker cited in 0.7, one may also consult K. Deller, "Zur sprachlichen Einordnung der Inschriften Aššurnasirpals II," Orientalia NS 26, 1957, 144-156.

0.9 The Language of Poetry and Literature The language of Old-Babylonian poetry (treated in the twentieth lesson) uses numerous archaic forms and is quite different from the Old-Babylonian of the letters and legal documents. Likewise, the literature of the Neo-Babylonian and Late-Babylonian time, along with a great portion of the Assyrian Royal Inscriptions is written in a special form of the language: Young-Babylonian (treated in the twenty-third lesson). It is quite distinct from the contemporary Neo-Babylonian vernacular.

> Source-books: W. von Soden, "Der hymnisch-epische Dialekt des Akkadischen " Zeitschrift für Assyriologie NF 6, 1931, 163-227, 1933, 90-183.

0.10 Dialects and Written Languages of Mesopotamia's Neighbors Certain dialectical modifications of Akkadian can be recognized in various texts which come from fringe districts of Mesopotamia. One can distinguish for example, between the Old-Babylonian of Babylon (0.7) and the Old-Babylonian dialects of Elam and the territory of Dijala (both of which are east of the Tigris) and Mari, situated at the mid-point of the Euphrates where the modern border between Syria and Iraq is located. Several special forms of written Akkadian arose around the middle of the second millennium with the spread of Babylonian culture into the neighboring districts of Mesopotamia. Akkadian came under the influence of the vernaculars of these areas. These special forms would include the Amarna Letters and the dialects of the Hittite capital Ḫattuša and of Ugarit and Nuzi. These various mutations of the language will not be treated in this textbook.

0.11 Sound-Patterns In addition to the three basic Semitic vowels, *a*, *i*, and *u*, Akkadian also possesses the vowel *e*. All vowels can occur in either a short (*a*, *e*, *i*, *u*) or a long form (*ā*, *ē*, *ī*, *ū*). Long vowels which result from the contraction of two vowels, whether long or short, are written in the transliteration (0,15) with a circumflex (*â*, *ê*, *î*, *û*).

idâk (< °*idūak*), he killed

0.12 Consonants and half-vowels Akkadian has the following consonants: the bilabials *p*, *b*, and *m*; the dentals *t*, *d*, *ṭ*, and *n*; the palatals *k*, *g*, and *q*; the dental fricatives *s*, *z*, and *ṣ*; the palatal-alveolar fricative *š*, the liquids *l* and *r*, the velar *ḫ* and the laryngeal ' (glottal stop); also the half-vowels *w* and *y*. There are some other sounds which occur only in Old-Akkadian: a sibilant whose exact pronunciation cannot be determined (possibly a lateralized dental), which is written in the transliteration *ś*. There is also the pharyngeal ^{c}.

Pronunciation: *s* is sharp as in the English word "set." *z* corresponds to the English "zero;" *š* corresponds to English *sh* as in "sharpen."

' may occur in English as in the "stop" which some speakers feel between the two words "her" and "aunt" in uttering the expression "her aunt." ᶜ really has no corresponding sound in English. One may describe it vaguely as the preceding consonant voiced. More realistically, the sound is identified with the ayin of the Arabic and Hebrew alphabets. The Semitic sounds ṭ, q̣, and ṣ (sometimes described as "emphatic") are velarized, which is to say that they are produced farther back in the mouth than the corresponding sounds t, k, and s.

In opposition to the proto-Semitic Consonantal System (S. Moscati and others, Introduction to the Comparative Grammar of the Semitic Languages Wiesbaden, 1964, pp. 24ff.), the most striking change is the complete disappearance of the inter-dental fricatives t̠, d̠, and ṭ (in Arabic ẓ). These become s, z and ṣ in Akkadian. Coalescing with the laryngeal stop ' are the velar ġ ('5), the pharyngeal ḥ ('3) and ayin and ('4), together with the laryngeal h ('2).

0.13 Language and Script: Sumerian Cuneiform For the writing of their language, the Akkadians used the cuneiform which the Sumerians had invented. For writing material they used small tablets formed out of damp clay and impressed signs on this material by means of a reed-stylus. In the oldest written Sumerian documents, these signs were a kind of picture writing. For example, the sketch of a fish expressed the idea "fish" and the head of an ox served to express the idea "cattle." Unlike the hieroglyphic writing of the Egyptians, the Sumerian signs did not serve as "picture-writing" for very long. In the damp clay, the lines formed with the stylus were easily changed into wedge-shaped (cuneiform) impressions. Since it was difficult to draw curved lines, the convention of two separate impressions made at an angle with one another was developed. This phenomenon, along with the tendency to simplify the complicated pictures, led to a disappearance of the "picture-writing" aspect of the cuneiform signs.

The Sumerian script was originally ideographic (one sign for one word). By broadening the meaning of individual signs, the Sumerians were able to represent grammatical elements and could in this way develop the system into a combination of ideograms and syllabic signs. [Thus, the sign for GAL "great" could also simply represent the syllable -gal-, if necessary.]

> Source-books: A. Falkenstein, *Die Keilschrift* in *Das Sumerische, Handbuch der Orientalistik* 1 Abt. Band II, 1, p. 6ff., Leiden, 1959. R. Labat, *Manuel d'epigraphie akkadienne*, Paris, 1952.

0.14 *The Writing of Akkadian* To express their language the Akkadians used not only the Sumerian ideograms (0.19) but above all the syllabic signs. The phonetic structure of the Akkadian language differs radically from that of the Sumerian. For this reason, the Akkadians could not write their language in the Sumerian script with any degree of precision. For example, if one wished to express one of the emphatic sounds characteristic of Akkadian (ṭ, q̣, ṣ, 0.12), he would have to use syllabic signs which contained *t* or *d*, *k* or *g*, *z* or *s*. The syllable *ṭu* would be written with the sign *du*, *q̣i* with the sign *ki*, *ṣa* with the sign *za*. The resulting ambiguity of the signs was a disadvantage which was removed gradually through the development of certain special signs.

0.15 *Transliteration and Transcription* In order to read a cuneiform text with some ease, we frequently first re-write it in latin letters. Two types of re-writing should be carefully distinguished. A *transliteration* converts the cuneiform text into latin letters sign by sign; all the syllables belonging to one word are connected by short horizontal strokes. Ideograms (0.19) are transcribed in capital letters. A *transcription* (or "normalization") on the other hand, attempts to reproduce more closely the correct pronunciation. The syllables are put together in words without the connecting strokes. The length of the vowels (0.11, 0.22) and the doubling of consonants required by the grammar are noted (even when these are not written in the cuneiform text). The ideograms are converted into their corresponding Akkadian equivalents. For further illustration, one should consult 0.16, 0.19-0.23 and the following example written in a) Cuneiform, b) transliteration, c) transcription and d) literal translation. The meaning of the text is: "A servant will kill his master and take possession of the throne."

a.					
b.	*wa-ar-du-um*	*be-el-šu*	*i-da-ak-ma*	*gišGU.ZA-am*	*i-ṣa-ba-at*
c.	*wardum*	*bēlšu*	*idâkma*	*kussiam*	*iṣabbat*
d.	servant (Nom.)	master, his	he kills and	throne	he seizes

Frequently, even in the transliteration, the ideograms will be replaced by the corresponding Akkadian words: *wa-ar-dum be-el-šu i-da-ak-ma kussiam i-ṣa-ba-at*. The texts of the following lessons are so re-written.

0.16 *Syllable-Signs* The following types of Syllable-signs can occur: Consonant plus Vowel (*du*, *be*, *šu*, *da*, etc.), Vowel plus Consonant (*ar*, *um*, *el*, *ak*, etc.), and Consonant plus Vowel plus Consonant (*bat*, *tar*). However, syllables like *bat* and *tar* can be expressed by combinations of the first two kinds: *ba-at*, for example, is read *bat*, not *ba'at* and *ta-ar* is read *tar* and not *ta'ar*. Therefore, the word *dannum*, strong, could be written with the syllable signs *da-an-nu-um*, *dan-nu-um*, or *dan-num*.

In addition to the three aforementioned types of signs, there are the *a*, *e*, *i*, *u* and *ú* which (when they occur at the beginning of a word or syllable) stand for the glottal stop plus the vowel and are therefore transcribed: 'a, 'e, etc.

Much less frequent (but especially in Neo-Assyrian texts) are some double-syllabled signs used like baba, bada, etc.

0.17 Homophony A syllable can be written with various signs. In order to make clear which of the signs was used in the Cuneiform, the transcriber uses a convention of accents and numbers in the transcription. For example, the syllable gi is expressed either by the sign gi or through another sign which is transcribed as gí or through a third (gì), a fourth (gi_4), a fifth (gi_5), etc.

The accents have nothing to do with the stress of the word (ha-al-qá-at) is read halqat, "is lost" with the stress on the first syllable.

That an occasional sign with a very high number does sometimes occur (for example, $\check{s}e_{20}$) should not lead the reader to the conclusion that homophony plays a great role in Akkadian. The diacritical accents and numbers are used to differentiate signs which occur over the rather enormous time-span of the transmission of the many cuneiform languages. In any unified text-material, i.e., in texts which are closely bound together in time and place of origin as well as content, homophony is quite limited in scope. There would be one or, at the most, two or three possibilities for the writing of a specific syllable. So in Northern Old-Babylonian, še is consistently written with še; the Southern Old-Babylonian texts use še, but more frequently use $\check{s}e_{20}$. The remaining eighteen signs for the vocalic value še do not occur in Old-Babylonian. Some signs occur almost always in certain particular words where they are written out of convention: e.g., u_4 in ūmum, "day," (u_4-mu-um, u_4-ma-am) because u_4 = ud which is the Sumerian word for "day." One can also transcribe it UD-mu-um or in other ways using the Sumerian significance of the sign.

> Source-books: W. von Soden, *Das Akkadische Syllabar*, 2nd ed., Analecta Orientalia 42, Rome, 1967; rare and unspecified vocalic values of individual signs are marked with an *x*; e.g., the sign *in* with the meaning *en* is transcribed *en*$_x$.

0.18 *Polyphony* The reading of Cuneiform is made more difficult by the fact that many signs have several values. The sign for *ut* can also be read as *tam*, *ṭám*, and *per*. The correct reading can be determined only by the context of the word and sentence. Moreover, the Cuneiform does not make clear whether the final sound of a syllable is voiced, voiceless, or emphatic (0.12). The words *im-qú-ut*, "he fell," *im-du-ud*, "he measured," and *ib-lu-uṭ*, "he lived," all end with the same sign. The sign *ut* then is also the sign *uṭ* and *ud*. In like manner, the sign *ak* has also the values *ag* and *aq*. The sign *it* has also the values *id* and *iṭ*. Signs which contain *e* are only occasionally differentiated from those which contain *i*. There are different signs for the pairs *te* and *ti*, *me* and *mi*, *el* and *il*, *en* and *in*. On the other hand, only one sign is available for *ge* and *gi*, *ke* and *ki*, *ep* (*eb*) and *ip* (*ib*), *ek* (*eg*, *eq*) and *ik* (*ig*, *iq*).

0.19 *Word-Signs* The Akkadians took over from the Sumerians not only the syllable-signs, but also the word-signs (Ideograms). But they read these as though they were the corresponding Akkadian word. So the Sumerian sign *lugal*, "king," when it occurs in an Akkadian text, is read as though it were the Akkadian word for king, *šarrum*. *šarrum*, "king," can then be written in Akkadian either with the word-sign LUGAL (or LUGAL-um, 0.21) or it can be written syllabically *ša-ar-ru-um*, *šar-ru-um*, *šar-rum* (0.16).

0.20 **Determinatives** The Akkadians borrowed from the Sumerians the scribal practice of using certain determinatives before and after some classes of nouns. These determinatives indicated to what general group a particular noun belonged, and marked it accordingly. These are not intended to be read, but in the transliteration they are placed above the line before or after the word which they modify. The most important determinatives are:

d (= dinger, Sumerian, "god") Almost always written before the names of gods: ^{d}Marduk = "Marduk."

é (Sum. "house"), occasionally written before buildings or parts of buildings: ^{é}bētum is read $^{(é)}$bētum, "house."

f (= mí, Sum. "woman"), used for the most part in the earlier periods before the names of women: ^{f}Qaqqadānītu = the Qaqqadānītu (fem).

giš (Sum. "wood") often used before implements and objects made of wood: ^{giš}GU.ZA is read $^{(giš)}$kussûm, "throne."

há placed after the word; shows that the word which it follows is plural: UDU^{há} is to be read immerū$^{(há)}$, "sheep."

íd (Sum. "river") before the names of rivers and canals: ^{íd}Banītu = "Banitu River."

itu (Sum. "month") before the names of months: ^{itu}Simānum, "Simān."

kam is placed after numbers which are written with digits and not syllabically: UD 2^{kam} is to be read ūm 2$^{(kam)}$, "the second day."

ki (Sum. "place") is placed after certain city names: KÁ. DINGER.RA^{ki} is to be read Bābili$^{(ki)}$, "Babylon."

kur (Sum. "land, country") before the names of countries: ^{kur}Sangibute = "the Land of Sangibute."

kuš (Sum. "skin") used before objects made of leather: ^{kuš}mašlium, "leather strap."

lú (Sum. "man") often used before names of trades or occupations: ^{lú}e-di-ku, "basket weaver."

m (indicating the number "one") sometimes used before male personal names: ^{m}Ilum-bānî, "(the) Ilum-bani;" in Old-Akkadian and Old-Babylonian texts also used before feminine personal names: ^{m}Mattatum, "(the) Mattatum " (fem.).

meš placed after a word it indicates that the word is plural: LUGAL^{meš} is to be read šarrānū, "kings."

mí (Sum. "woman") used before the names of feminine occupations: ^{mí}šu-gi-tum is to be read $^{\text{(mí)}}$šugītum, "priestess."

sar (Sum. "beet") is often placed after the names of plants: šu-ha-ti-in-ni^{sar} is to be read šuhatinnī$^{\text{(sar)}}$, "a plant."

túg (Sum. "dress") used before clothing material or pieces of clothing: ^{túg}hurdabašše, "loin cloth."

ú (Sum. "plant"), before the names of plants: ^{ú}pū'u, "straw, chaff."

uru (Sum. "city") before the names of cities: ^{uru}Hundur, "Hundur."

In the texts and exercises throughout the book, determinatives are given only when the word to which they belong is written syllabically. It is not given when ideograms are used (0.19), e.g., ^{lu}e-di-ku^{meš} but kussûm and not ^{giš}kussûm for ^{giš}GU.ZA.

0.21 Phonetic Complements The last syllable or the two last syllables of the Akkadian word sometimes will be added to an ideogram in order to make clear the grammatical form (the case) of the word and to make reading easier: LUGAL-rum is read šarrum, "the king" (nom.) LUGAL-am (or LUGAL ra-am) is to be read "the king" (acc.).

In the texts of the following lessons, the ideograms are changed into Akkadian words. To simplify printing, the phonetic complement will not be printed. *LUGAL-am* appears therefore as *šarram* and not as *šarram*^{am} or as *šarram(am)*.

0.22 *Length of Vowels* In the cuneiform writing, the length of a vowel can be shown only after a sign which is consonant-plus-vowel; the corresponding vowel sign is then added (*a*, *e*, *i*, *ú*, or occasionally *u*). This is called *plene* or full writing.

> *i-ma-a-at* = *imât*, he dies
>
> *ša-me-e-em* = *šamêm*, of the sky, heavens
>
> *na-ak-ri-i-ka* = *nakrīka*, of your enemy
>
> *pa-nu-ú-ša* = *panūša*, their front

These indications of the lengthening of vowels are frequently left out of the script and then can be determined only by knowledge of the grammar.

> *i-ma-at* (*imât*)
>
> *na-ak-ri-ka* (*nakrīka*)

At the beginning of a word or syllable the length is not expressed and for that reason can be determined only grammatically: *ēribum*, the one who enters, is written *e-ri-bu-um* and not *e-e-ri-bu-um*.

Sometimes, especially at the end of a sentence, a vowel sign will be used although no long vowel is present:

> *i-la-a-ak* = *illak*, he goes
>
> *šu-ul-mu-u-um* = *šulmum*, health, salvation

Long vowels after the beginning of a syllable are occasionally marked in the Old-Babylonian Hymn of Ištar through *plene* writing:

> *ba-ši-à-a*, *bašiā*, they are created
>
> *nam-ra-i-i*, *namrā'i*, they are fat(tened); the fattened ones

0.23 *Doubling of Consonants* In Cuneiform the doubling of consonants can easily be represented:

i-ṣa-ab-ba-at, he grasps

iṭ-ṭù-ul, he glances

However, with some frequency, only the second consonant will be written so that the consonantal doubling can be determined only from the grammar:

i-ṣa-ba-at, for iṣabbat

i-ṭu-ul, for iṭṭul

0.24 The Writing of the Glottal Stop As an initial sound, the glottal stop (0.12) is not represented. This is largely true when the stop occurs as a medial sound, e.g., iš-al = iš'al, he asked, and ma-li-at = maliat (actually mali'at), it is full. Only in verbs which are Middle Aleph (16.4) are special signs used for the glottal stop:

na-a'-da-at = na'dat, she informed

ì'-id = i'id, pay attention

Remarks on the Exercises and Texts

0.25 The Exercises "Omen-texts" form the foundation of lessons 1-19. Omen-texts are collections of individual omens. For the most part, each of them is quite intelligible in itself, independently of the larger context. More than any other Old-Babylonian group of texts, the omen-texts offer sentences which exemplify the precise grammatical point which a given lesson is studying.

> Source-books: A. L. Oppenheim, Ancient Mesopotamia, Portrait of a Dead Civilization, Chicago, 1964, 206 ff.; D. O. Edzard, Die Altorientlische Reiche I, (Fischer, Weltgeschichte 2), Frankfurt, 1965, 172ff.

0.26 Omens Every omen consists of two parts: the protasis (0.27) which describes a certain set of conditions, and the apodosis (0.28) which predicts the result to follow if the conditions are fulfilled. As an example of a "birth-omen" (0.29) we may cite:

> "If the teeth of the aborted animal protrude..." (protasis); "the days of the King are at an end and another will sit upon his throne." (apodosis)

In the exercises, we shall make use of examples which are protases without the accompanying apodosis and *vice versa*. In the transliteration of the Omens (O), protasis and apodosis are separated by a semicolon. If the apodosis has many parts, each is separated by a comma. This kind of punctuation is only a help to the reader and has no basis in the cuneiform text.

0.27 *Protases* In the protasis of an omen a phenomenon is described which is considered as extraordinary and therefore a portent of the predicted result which is contained in the apodosis. The protasis always has the form of a conditional sentence introduced by the word "if," *šumma* in Akkadian. One can classify the various groups of omen-texts by the nature of the phenomenon treated in the protasis: e.g., birth-omens (0.29), astronomical omens, and omens derived from examining the entrails of various sacrificed animals (0.30). Among the organs examined were the liver, gall bladder and lungs. Samples of these latter are found in 0.31-0.33.

0.28 *Apodoses* The apodoses are generally limited to the result whose occurrence is expected in the near future. Prophecies are rarely of a general nature as sorrow or joy. More common are those which have to do with the Good or Evil of society as a whole, as predictions about the weather (rain, heat, cold), good harvests or bad, plagues of grass-hoppers, calamities, inflation, mass starvation, wars and their consequences (devastation). Other omens treat the destiny of an individual man who is generally described in the "entrails-omen" as "a man," (awīlum) or sometimes as "the owner of the sheep which is sacrificed," (bēl immerim). These deal with life and death. ("The man will die, gored by a bull.") They may deal with good luck and bad. ("A lion will rage within the man's sheepfold.") They may treat of a man's relationship to the government ("The Royal Officials will seal up the man's house.") Most frequently of all, the apodoses deal with the King in his role as leader of the army (victory or defeat of the royal army), in his personal destiny (death or survival from a revolution of his subordinates and palace officials). Some apodoses deal with past events but may also mean that the event under discussion may happen again. "...a liver-omen of Narām Sîn who ruled the world." Very uncommon are apodoses which are formulated as imperatives. ("...drive out the foe.") Sometimes an omen has two or more apodoses: "The flood will come" or a second meaning (šanûm šumšu), "rain, the destruction of booty." What is common to these apodoses is that they are all favorable. The irrigation ditches will be filled by the predicted flood; the rain has a similar meaning for agriculture. The third apososis however, is restricted to the success of a military undertaking: which army will take charge of the spoils of war.

0.29 Omens of Birth The protases of the Old-Babylonian birth-omens deal with abnormal phenomena in new-born sheep. It is certain that only a portion of the depicted cases actually were observed, e.g., the protrusion of the teeth from the mouth of a lamb or the birth of a lamb with one eye. The majority of these omens rest on fantasy and exaggeration, such as the imagining of a lamb in the form of a serpent or with the face of a lion or a wolf, or with lions' paws or from whose mouth there hung the head of another sheep!

0.30 Divination of Entrails Miscarriages and astronomical phenomena which provided the occasion for omen predictions were, of course, limited. If one wanted to be in a position to make omen predictions for the future whenever need arose, one had to be in a position to provide omens artificially. This was possible, for example, through the examination of entrails. The inhabitants of Babylon had noticed very early in their history that the appearance of various organs in animals which had been slaughtered or sacrificed admitted of wide variation. They then attributed a special meaning to this fact. They came to believe that the organs of the sacrificial animal were a mirror of the Cosmos and that they afforded precise answers to direct questions about the future for the initiate who participated in the sacrifice -- if he knew properly how to frame those questions. So they carefully observed the condition of the individual organs and their parts, their color and their texture (which could be changed by various illnesses) and developed a precise terminology by which one could differentiate exactly the parts and the condition of the viscera which were important for divination.

0.31 Terms Used in Liver Omens The priests involved in sacrificial divination studied the liver very carefully. (In Akkadian, amūtum.) The same word is used in Akkadian for "an omen from the liver." The following Akkadian terms for the various parts of the liver are determined with certainty:

naplastum is the left lobe of the liver (lobus sinister).

bāb ekallim, the "palace gate" describes the space between the two lobes of the liver in which the gall bladder rests.

ubānum, finger, means the pyramidal process (processus pyramidalis).

abullum, "city gate" probably means the *porta hepatis*. Two sites which cannot be exactly determined (but which are probably located on the underside of the left lobe of the liver) are described with the words *padānum* (path) and *danānum* (strengthening). The location of the sites named as *nīrum* (yoke) and *ṣibtum* (growth or tumor) cannot be determined with any real certainty.

0.32 *Terms Used in Gall Bladder Omens* In the gall bladder (*martum*, bitterness in Akkadian), one can distinguish the following:

maṣraḫ martim, the entrance of the bile, i.e., the bile duct.

martum qablāša, the center of the gall bladder.

rēš martim, the base of the gall bladder.

appi martim, nose of the bladder, the upperside of the front portion of the gall bladder. In opposition to that is the

išdī martim (or *išid martim*), the underside of the gall bladder.

0.33 *Terms Used in Lung Omens* For the participant in divination, the most important part of the lung (*ḫašûm*) was the *ubān ḫašî qablītum*, the middle finger of the lung. Perhaps by this was meant the *lobus azygos*. Next in importance was the *kišād ḫašîm*, the neck of the lung, perhaps a portion of the windpipe.

0.34 *Symptoms or Indications Found in the Organs* The ancients observed a variety of phenomena on the surface of the liver, the gall bladder and other internal organs. These included cysts and cavities and a number of other changes probably induced by illness. Among the most important were:

kakkum, weapon, and *kakki imittim*, weapon of the right

šēpum, foot

pillurtum, cross

<u>erištum</u>, a wish-mark

<u>ziḫḫum</u>, cyst, pimple

<u>šīlum</u>, cavity, depression

<u>piṭrum</u>, a fissure

<u>pilšum</u>, a hole dug; a breach in a wall

[In the names of some of these, one can observe again the workings of the Babylonian imagination.]

0.35 <u>The Texts</u> From the twelfth lesson on, along with the exercises (0.25), readings will be used. These readings will be taken from Old-Babylonian texts which are fairly complete in themselves. They will include Laws (Lessons 12 and 16), Letters (Lessons 13-19), and Documents (Lesson 17). The readings in Lessons 20-27 contain texts which sometimes involve dialects and intermediary stages of the language. For these texts, the student should use the glossary given at the end of the book.

Lesson 1

GRAMMAR

1.1 The Semitic Root   The chief peculiarity of the Semitic languages is a phenomenon by which the basic meaning of a word adheres to the root, a permanent order of two, three, or four consonants. To each root there belongs a root vowel (which does not appear in all the forms of the verb). Conjugation of these roots is attained through vocalic and consonantal changes which take place between any two consonants of the radical or which are added after the root or prefixed to it. From the postulated Akkadian root **prus*, with the basic meanings of separate or decide, we can form a whole host of different forms and meanings:

purus, decide

iprus, he decided

(ša) taprusu, (what) you (may have) decided

paris, he is decided

iptaras, he has decided

parāsum, to decide

pārisum, one who decides, deciding

One can distinguish between verbal roots and nominal roots.

1.2 The Akkadian Verbal Root   Most Akkadian verbal roots consist of three consonants and a short vowel between the second and third consonant. The short vowel can be *a*, *i* or *u*:

**ṣbat*, grasp, seize

**šḫiṭ*, fall upon, attack

•knuš, to surrender

•mḫur, receive

1.3 In glossaries and lexicons, Akkadian verbs are listed not by root but by infinitive. The infinitive of the root *•ṣbat* is *ṣabātum*, to grasp, also used as a nominal, the seizure. Like a noun, it can be declined. (Gen. *ana ṣabātim*, for grasping, in order to grasp.) The vowel after the first consonant is *a* (short) and after the second consonant is *ā* (long).

kanāšum, to bow, yield, the surrender

šaḫāṭum, to attack, the attack

maḫārum, to receive, the reception

With the dropping of the *mem* at the end (1.7), the infinitive is read *ṣabātu*, *ana ṣabāti*, etc.

1.4 The Tenses, Preterite and Present   There are four tenses in Akkadian: the Present, Preterite, Perfect (9.1) and Stative (1.5). The Preterite, Perfect, and Present are conjugated with the help of prefixes. The prefix of the third person is *i-* and that of the second person is *ta-* (5.4). The root itself without fundamental changes forms the basis of the Preterite. The Present doubles the middle consonant of the root and adds a short *a* vowel before it.

Root	Preterite	Present
•ṣbat	*iṣbat*, he grasped	*iṣabbat*, he grasps
•knuš	*iknuš*, he yielded	*ikannuš*, he yields
•šḫiṭ	*išḫiṭ*, he attacked	*išaḫḫiṭ*, he attacks
•mḫur	*imḫur*, he received	*imaḫḫar*, he receives

In the Present, the vowel between the doubled middle consonant and the third consonant [often called the theme vowel] is identical to the root-vowel. An exception to this is found in the group of "vowel-change" verbs with the root-vowel u. These take the vowel a in the present.

Prt. imhur

Prs. imahhar

The Present tense serves not only to express present action but future action: imahhar, he receives or he will receive. It is the normal tense in the apodoses of omens (0.28). The Preterite is a past tense form. Still, in conditional sentences after šumma (if), it is used with a present meaning: šumma martum ishur, if the gall bladder is turned... [This is probably to be explained by understanding that Semitic "tenses" did not originally have to do with time of action, but kind of action. Thus, Preterite speaks of completed action in any time (but usually past), while Present speaks of incomplete action (usually in the present or future).] In the vocabularies, the root-vowel will be given along with the infinitive. In the case of verbs of the "vowel-change" class, both vowels will be given:

kanāšum, (u) to yield

mahārum, (a/u) to receive

Verbs for which no root-vowel is given occur only in the Stative.

1.5 The Stative In opposition to the Present and the Preterite which treat of activity, the Stative is used to express states of being. Therefore for the Stative, temporal aspects of the verb are not important. It can have a present, past, or future meaning. For the most part (although not always) it is used passively. So ṣabit, he is captured, was captured, will be captured. But sometimes, he is, was, will be a captor. [In this case, the activity is stressed not as a dynamic but as a *state*.] The Stative has the vowel *a* after the first consonant and *i* (for the most part) after the second consonant.

damiq, he is good from *damāqum*, to be good

sapiḫ, he is destroyed from *sapāḫum*, to destroy

tarik, he is dark from *tarākum*, to be dark

1.6 The Nominal Root The roots of the primary nouns which deal with things, animals, people, or qualities are mainly built up from two or three consonants and short or long vowels:

•bīt (*bītum*), house

•rubā (*rubûm*), prince

•nakr (*nakrum*), unfriendly, enemy

•rabi (*rabûm*), large

Along with the primary nouns, there are those which are derived from verbal roots (1.2). These are called "deverbal nouns."

ṣabtum, the prisoner from *ṣabātum*, to sieze

1.7 Declension of the Singular The noun has three cases: the Nominative (with the ending -*um*), Genitive (-*im*), and Accusative or Objective case (-*am*). [Although nouns in English no longer have case-endings, they correspond syntactically to these three cases.] The Genitive is used after prepositions and in conjunction with the *status constructus* (2.7) to show possession. The *mem* of the case ending (so-called mimation) drops frequently so that the endings are simply -*u*, -*i*, and -*a*:

Nom. *bītum* (or *bītu*), the house, a house

Gen. *ina bītim* (or *bīti*), in the house, in a house

Acc. *bītam* (or *bīta*), the house, a house

If the nominal root ends in a vowel, it is contracted in such a way that the vowel of the case-ending is retained. Two exceptions to this practice are: _a_ plus _i_ goes to _ê_; _ia_ is generally not contracted:

Nom. _rubûm_ (< _*rubā'um_), the prince

Gen. _ana_ _rubêm_ (< _*rubā'im_), to the prince

Acc. _rubâm_ (< _*rubā'am_), the prince

Nom. _rabûm_ (< _*rabi'um_), the great one

Gen. _rabîm_ (< _*rabi'im_), of the great one

Acc. _rabiam_ the great one

The adjective follows the substantive to which it belongs [in both case and position]:

Nom. _šarrum_ _dannum_, the mighty king

Gen. _ana_ _šarrim_ _dannim_, to the mighty king

Acc. _šarram_ _dannam_, the mighty king

The substantive may be either determined or undetermined:

šarrum, the king or a king

1.8 Word Order The verb stands at the end of the sentence; the subject generally stands at the beginning, and the object between the subject and the verb. If the object is especially to be stressed, it can precede the subject.

1.9 Union of Sentences For combining sentences (and clauses) the enclitic particle _-ma_ is used with the meaning of and, or and then.

EXERCISES

P. 1. šum-ma mar-tum is-hu-ur. 2. šumma iz-bu-um ta-ri-ik-ma ṣa-li-im. 3. šumma ta-al-lù da-ki-iš.

A. 4. na-ak-ru-um[1] kussiam i-ṣa-ab-ba-at. 5. ḫa-tum e-li um-ma-nim i-ma-qú-ut.[4] 6. a-wi-lum i-ḫa-al-li-iq. 7. šar-ra-am da-an-na-tum i-ṣa-ab-ba-at. 8. ša-mu-ú-um ra-du-um i-za-nu-un.[4] 9. né-šum[1] ḫarrānam i-ša-ḫi-it. 10. šu-uk-ka-lum er-ba-am i-ma-ḫa-ar. 11. šar-ru-um na-ak-ru-um a-na šar-ri-im i-ka-nu-uš.[1] 12. ap-lu-um ra-bu-ú-um kussiam i-ṣa-ba-at.[1] 13. a-na šar-ri-im da-mi-iq. 14. mi-il-kum sà-pi-iḫ.

[1] 0.26; [2] 0.32; [3] 0.29; [4] 0.23.

šumma, if

martum, bile, gall bladder

saḫārum, (u), to turn

izbum, abortion, miscarriage

tarākum, to be gray, dark [lit. to strike]

-ma (enclitic) and, and then

ṣalāmum, (i), to be black

tallum, diaphragm

dakāšum (a/u), to break out, be swollen

nakrum, the enemy

kussûm, (< *kussium) throne, seat

ṣabātum (a), seize, grasp, to be master of something

ḫātum, panic, fear

eli, on

ummānum, army, host

maqātum (u), to fall

awīlum, man, human being

ḫalāqum (i), to perish, be ruined

šarrum, king

dannatum, calamity

šamûm, rain

rādum, thunderstorm, heavy rain

zanānum (u), to rain

nēšum, lion

ḫarrānum, way, caravan, campaign

šaḫātum (i), attack, leap

šukkalum, minister, vizir

erbum, tribute, income

maḫārum (a/u), to receive, obtain

ana, to, for

ana šarrim, to the king

kanāšum (u), to yield, surrender

aplum, heir

rabûm (< *rabium), great

aplum rabûm, eldest son

damāqum (*i*), to be good, favorable

milkum, plan, counsel

sapāḫum (*a*/*u*), to destroy, to level, scatter

Lesson 2

GRAMMAR

2.1 The Feminine of the Noun Akkadian distinguishes between the two genders, masculine and feminine. To construct the feminine forms (whether nouns dealing with females or the feminine form of the adjective) -t- or -at- is added to the nominal root:

bel-um, master bel-t-um, mistress

nakr-um, hostile, unfriendly nakar-t-um, unfriendly (fem.)

The feminine form of the adjective is also used to express feminine abstract ideas:

dannum, strong, fem. dannatum (adjective) strong or (as substantive) strength

And sometimes abstract ideas take on a concrete meaning, e.g., dannatum, strength, can also mean fortress.

2.2 The Formation of the Feminine with -t- The feminine ending -t- occurs after nominal roots which end in a single consonant. It also is found after nominal roots ending with a vowel; in this latter case the vowel is lengthened:

bēlum, master fem. bēltum, lady, mistress

rabium, great, large fem. rabītum

If the root of an adjective or of a deverbal noun ends in two consonants, an anaptyctic (or "helping") vowel is inserted between the consonants:

nakrum, hostile fem. nakartum

rapšum, broad fem. rapaštum

damqum, good fem. *damiqtum*

ṣeḫrum, small fem. *ṣeḫertum*

ṣabtum, captive fem. *ṣabittum*

2.3 The Formation of the Feminine with -at- The feminine ending takes the form -*at*- after a root which ends in a doubled consonant or after the root of a primitive noun (*kalbum*, dog) if this ends in two different consonants. [Remember that the root of *kalbum* is *kalb*.] If the root has the vowel *e*, the -*at*- is changed to -*et*-:

dannum fem. *dannatum* (also with meaning of calamity or fortress)

ellum, pure fem. *elletum*

šarrum, king fem. *šarratum*, queen

kalbum, dog fem. *kalbatum*, bitch

For the formation of the feminine of a deverbal noun which ends in two consonants, cf. 2.2.

2.4 Consonantal Changes in the Formation of the Feminine The consonants *n* and *d* are assimilated to the feminine ending -*t*-. The ending then becomes -*tt*-. Analogously, ṣ before -*t*- becomes *š*:

lemnum, bad, angry fem. *lemuttum* (also with meaning, evil (n.))

mādum, numerous fem. *māttum*

marṣum, sick fem. *maruštum* (also, sickness)

īṣum, few in number fem. *īštum*

Long vowels are not shortened before doubled consonants:

māttum, not **mattum*; *qāssu*, not *qassu* (3.10).

2.5 Primitive (or "Primary") Feminine Nouns Several substantives without -*t*- are feminine, i.e., they are syntactically construed as feminines. In this group one finds such naturally feminine words as ummum, mother and some designations for parts of the body, e.g., šēpum, foot. Other words which are to be construed as feminine include: mātum, land, ummānum, army or host, ḫarrānum, campaign, ekallum, palace, abnum, stone, and nārum, river. Any adjective used with a feminine substantive is, of course, feminine;

ummānum nakartum, the enemy army

mātum rapaštum, a broad land

2.6 The Feminine of the Verb The predicate of a sentence agrees in gender with the subject. In both the Preterite and the Present, the feminine form of the third person singular is identical with the masculine:

iṣbat, he seized or she seized

iṣabbat, he seizes or she seizes

But in the Stative, the feminine is distinguished from the masculine by the ending -at which is added to the masculine form. (In the process of this addition, the i after the second consonant in the masculine is dropped.)

ṣabit, he is captive

ṣabtat, she is captive

damiq, he is good

damqat, she is good

2.7 The "States" of the Noun A noun which has no genitive dependent on it occurs in the Status Rectus and has a case ending:

ummānum, the army

But if a noun occurs which has a following genitive nominal construction dependent upon it, the first noun which governs the construction is written in a form called the Status Constructus [or "construct state" in most English grammars of Semitic languages]. It has no case-ending and no major accent:

ummān šarrim, the army of the king

The construct state is the same for all three cases:

māri awīlim, the son of the man (Nom., Gen., Acc.)

A noun in the construct state can be followed by two nouns (or more) which are in the genitive and form what is called a "construct chain."

tibût māri awīlim, the revolt of the son of the man

The *Status Absolutus* or "absolute state" is treated in 8.9.

2.8 *The Formation of the Status Constructus* Nouns which end in vowels or which end in a single consonant (such as the *-t-* of the feminine) form the construct state simply by dropping any ending:

wāṣûm (< **wāṣium*), going out	wāsi abullim, one who goes out to the gate
bēlum, master	*bēl ālim*, master of the city
tibûtum, revolution	*tibût erbîm*, an outbreak of locusts

If a nominal root ends in a double consonant, either the doubling is simplified or the "helping vowel" *i* is added:

ekallum, palace	*ekal nakrim*, palace of the enemy
šarrum, king	*šar mātim*, king of the land
libbum, heart	*libbi mātim*, interior of the country
kakkum, weapon	*kak bārtim*, weapon of rebellion
	kakki imitṭim, weapon of the right

If a nominal root ends in two different consonants, an anaptyctic vowel is inserted between the two consonants. This will be a vowel which corresponds to the vowel of the root itself:

alpum, cattle	*alap awīlim*, cattle of the man
nikpum, push	*nikip alpim*, string of oxen

bēltum, mistress — *bēlet bītim*, mistress of the house

lumnum, evil, distress — *lumun libbim*, sadness of heart

Polysyllabic feminines which end in a single consonant plus the -*t*- of the feminine, form the construct state by adding an additional vowel *i*:

napištum, life — *napišti awīlim*, life of men

miqittum, defeat — *miqitti ummānim*, defeat of the enemy

2.9 Irregular Formations of the Construct State — Some monosyllabic nominal roots (with a long vowel) appear in the construct both without endings and in a form which ends in *i*:

ālum, city, *āl* or *āli*

mārum, son, *mār* or *māri*

bītum, house, *bīt* or *bīti*

būšum (*bīšum*), property, *būš* or *būši*

šumum, name, *šum* or *šumi*

The word *mīlum*, fullness, appears as *mīli* in construct with the word *irtum*, breast: *mīli irtim* = courage, success (cf. Paradigm 7 in the Appendix).

EXERCISES

P. 1. šumma i-na bāb ekallim[1] i-na i-mi-tim šēpum[2] ša-ak-na-at. 2. šumma kakki i-mi-tim[2] pa-li-iṣ. 3. šumma mar-tum ṣa-al-ma-at. 4. šumma iš-tu si-pi šu-me-el bāb ekallim še[20]-pu na-ap-la-ás-tam[1] ka-aš-da-at.

A. 5. ti-bu-ut er-bi-im. 6. ni-ki-ip al-pi-im. 7. né-ku-úr-tum da-an-na-tum. 8. ti-bu-ut ma-ri a-wi-lim. 9. ka-ak ba-ar-tim. 10. ka-ak-ki na-ak-ri-im. 11. šar-ru-um ma-ta-am na-ka-ar-ta-am i-ṣa-ab-ba-at. 12. sinništum kussiam i-ṣa-ba-at. 13. ab-nu-um ra-bi-tum i-za-an-nu-um. 14. ekal na-ak-ri-im qá-tum i-ka-ša-ad.

15. um-ma-an šar-ri-im i-na ha-ra-nim sú-mu-um i-ṣa-ab-ba-at.

16. ma-tum ra-pa-aš-tum a-na da-an-na-tim i-pa-ah-hu-ur.

17. ta-an-zi-im-ti ma-a-tim i-lu-um im-hu-ur.

0. 18. šum-ma pa-da-nu-um[1] ki-ma qá-as-tim; mi-li i-ir-tim,[3] um-ma-an šar-ri-im i-iš-tum um-ma-an na-ak-ri-im ma-at-ta-am i-da-ak. 19. šum-ma mar-tum ha-al-qá-at; da-am-qá-at. 20. šumma i-na re-eš ubānim[1] pi-il-lu-ur-tum;[2] na-an-ta-lu-um; mi-qí-it-ti ru-bé-e-em. 21. šumma ṣí-ib-tum[1] a-na 6 pa-aṭ-ra-at; en-né-et bīt a-wi-lim ilum i-pa-ṭa-ar.

22. šumma iz-bu-um ki-ma li-bi-tim; ma-tam da-an-na-tum i-ṣa-ab-ba-at-ma ku-ru-um i-ma-qú-ut.

[1] 0.31; [2] 0.34; [3] 3.13.

ina, in, to, on

bābum, door, gate

ekallum (f.), palace

bāb ekallim, palace gate (part of the liver)

imittum, right, right side

šēpum (f.), foot (special liver-characteristic)

šakānum (a/u), to place, put; settle

kakkum, weapon or liver-characteristic

kakki imittim, weapon of the right side, liver-characteristic

palāsum, (a/u) to pierce, penetrate

ištu, from, since

sippum, side of a door

šumēlum, left, left side

naplastum, lobe of the liver

kašādum (a/u), to reach, arrive at; plunder, attain

tibûtum, outbreak, revolt

erbûm (< erbium), locusts, grasshoppers

tibût erbîm, an attack of locusts

nikpum, a push, to push

alpum, cattle

nekurtum, enmity

dannum (f.) dannatum, strong, difficult

mārum, son

bārtum, rebellion

mātum (f.), land, country

nakrum (f.) nakartum, hostile

sinništum, woman

abnum (f.), stone, hail

qātum (f.), hand

ummānum (f.), army, host

ṣūmum, thirst

rapšum (f.) rapaštum, broad, wide

dannatum, calamity, difficulty, fortress

paḫarum (u), to assemble; to gather (intr.)

tanzimtum, complaint

ilum, god

padānum, path (part of liver)

kīma, as

qaštum, bow

mīlum, fullness

irtum, breast

mīli irtim, courage, success

īṣum (f.) īštum, few, small in number

mādum (f.) mattum, many, numerous

idâk (7.2), he will kill, he will beat

ḫalāqum (Stative), to be lost, to be lacking

rēšum, head, upper part, point

ubānum (f.), finger (also part of liver)

pillurtum, cross

nantallûm, darkness

miqittum, defeat, downfall

rubûm (<*rubā'um), prince

ṣibtum, growth (part of liver)

ana 6, [the 6 represents six little wedges in cuneiform] sixfold

paṭārum (a/u), to split, dissolve

enettum, sin

bītum, house

libittum, brick, tile

kurrum, a measure of grain

Lesson 3

GRAMMAR

3.1 Plural of Masculine Nouns Masculine, nominative substantives take the plural ending *-ū* which contracts with the vocalic root ending to *-û*.

šarrum, king *šarrū*, kings

rubûm (<**rubā'um*), the prince *rubû* (<**rubā'ū*), the princes

Adjectives form their masculine plural in *-ūtum* which contracts with the vocalic root ending to *-ûtum*:

nakrūtum, the hostile ones

rabûtum (<**rabiūtum*), the great ones

ūmū gamrūtum, full days

The noun *šībum*, old, venerable, forms a substantive plural *šībū* with the meaning, the witnesses, and a plural adjective *šībūtum*, the oldest ones, the elders.

3.2 The Plural of Feminine Nouns The ending of the feminine plural, both substantival and adjectival is -*ātum*:

bussurtum, message, news, pl., *bussurātum*

naplastum, lobe, pl., *naplasātum*

In nouns whose root vowel is *e*, -*ātum* becomes -*ētum*:

ellum, pure, f. sg. *elletum* (2.3), f. pl. *ellētum*

tērtum, instruction, pl., *tērētum*

Feminine substantives without -*t*- (2.5) form their plurals with -*ātum*:

ekallum, palace, pl. *ekallātum*

eleppum, ship, pl. *eleppātum*

Some substantives are masculine in the singular and feminine in the plural. They also take the plural ending *-ātum*:

našpākum, granary, pl., *našpākātum*

The plural of *martum*, gall bladder, is *marrātum*. (*martum* is the feminine from *marrum*, bitter.) For the feminine plural formed with roots which end in vowels, cf. *rabi'ātum*, great (*i'a* and *i'ā* do not contract, for the most part).

The plural of nouns like *šalamtum*, corpse, is *šalmātum* (<**šalamātum*).

3.3 Plural Only — There are some nouns which occur only in the plural:

mû (<**mā'ū*), water

kišpū, magic

ṣummirātum, desire, striving

nišū (f.), people, men

pānū, face, front

3.4 Declension of the Plural — Genitive and Accusative endings are the same in the plural. Nouns with Nominative endings of *-ū*, *-ūtu(m)*, *-ātu(m)*, and -ētu(m) take in the Genitive-Accusative the endings *-ī*, *-ūti(m)*, *-āti(m)* and *-ēti(m)*:

Nom. *šarrū*, Gen.-Acc. *šarrī*, the kings

rubū, *rubê* (<**rubā'i*), the princes (1.7)

ekallātu(m), *ekallāti(m)*, the palaces

pānū, *pānī*, face

The *m* of the plural endings, *-ūtum*, *-ūtim*, *-ātum*, etc. is the so-called *mimation* and frequently drops. Cf. paradigms 1-3.

3.5 The Construct State of the Plural   Nouns with the plural endings -ūtum, -ātum, and -ētum lose the -um in the construct state:

šībūt alim, the elders of the city

bussurāt hadêm, messages of joy

Nouns with the plural ending -ū (in Gen.-Acc. -ī) are not changed in the construct state:

pānū martim, the front side of the gall bladder

ina pānī abullim, in the face of the gate, before the gate

3.6 The Plural in the Verb   The endings for the third person plural in the Stative, Preterite and Present are -ū for the masculine and -ā for the feminine. In the Stative, -ū and -ā are added to the form of the third singular, and as a result of this the i which is found after the second consonant in the singular will be elided. [In a succession of three syllables where the first is accented and the first and second are open syllables (consonant plus vowel), the vowel of the second syllable will be elided (dropped), e.g., ṣabtū (<*ṣa/bi/tū).]

	Singular	Plural
St. Masc.	ṣabit, he is taken	ṣabtū, they are taken
fem.	ṣabtat, she is taken	ṣabtā, they are taken
Pret. Masc.	imḫur, he received	imḫurū, they received
fem.	imḫur, she received	imḫurā, they received
Pres. Masc.	imaḫḫar, he receives	imaḫḫarū, they receive
fem.	imaḫḫar, she receives	imaḫḫarā, they receive

ṣabtū, ṣabtā can also have the active meaning: they are captors (1.5).

3.7 Possessive Suffixes   The possessive pronouns, my, your, etc. are generally expressed in Akkadian through suffixes. The most important possessive suffixes are -ya (sometimes i, 3.9) for my, -ka, your, -šu, his, -ša, her. The third plural suffixes are -šunu (masculine) and -šina (feminine), their. -šunu then, can refer only to masculine substantives in the plural, e g., šarrū, the kings, and -šina to feminine plural substantives, ekallātum, the palaces.

3.8 Declension of Suffixed Nouns in the Singular In the Nominative and Accusative singular, the substantive before the suffix generally takes the form of the construct state (2.8):

nakrum, the enemy, const. naker

Nom. or Acc. with suffix: nakeršu, his enemy

In the Genitive however, the suffix follows the Genitive singular ending in -im (1.7), the mimation drops and the -i is lengthened with the shift of accent:

nakrim, of the enemy

nakrīšu, of his enemy

As further examples, ummānum, the army (const. ummān) and alpum, the ox, (const. alap):

Nom.	ummānka, your army	alapšunu, their ox
Gen.	ummānīka, of your army	alpīšunu, of their ox
Acc.	ummānka, your army	alapšunu, their ox

With nominal roots which end in a doubled consonant (app-um. nose), an a vowel is inserted between the root and the suffix in the Nominative and Accusative singular:

appum, nose, const. appi (2.8)

Nom. or Acc. sing. with suffix: appašu, his nose

The Genitive singular with the suffix is appīšu, of his nose. As a further example, muhhum, upper side, (const. muhhī):

Nom. _muḫḫaša_, her upper side

Gen. _ina muḫḫīša_, on her upper side

Acc. _muḫḫaša_, her upper side

Cf. paradigms 5 and 7.

3.9 The Possessive Suffix _-ya_, my The suffix of the first person singular has two different forms. It is _-ya_ after a vowel and _-ī_ after a consonant. The Genitive singular of a substantive can also take the _-ya_ form:

ummāni(m), of the army, _ummānīya_, of my army

šarrīya, of my king

The Nominative and Accusative of the singular:

ummānī, my army

šarrī, my king

The cuneiform writing _um-ma-ni_, therefore, can stand for the Genitive singular without mimation, _ummāni_, of the army (1.7), the Genitive plural _ummānī_, of the armies, and the Nominative or Accusative singular with the possessive suffix of the first person singular, _ummānī_, my army.

3.10 Consonantal Changes Caused by Suffixes The _š_ of the possessive-suffixes, _-šu_, _-ša_, _-šunu_ and _-šina_ becomes _s_ after final dentals (_d_, _t_, _ṭ_) or sibilants (_s_, _ṣ_, _z_, _š_). The dentals and sibilants then assimilate to the _s_ as follows:

qāssu (<*_qāt_ + _šu_), his hand (2.4)

išissa (<*_išid_ + _ša_), its base

rēssunu (<*_rēš_ + _šunu_), their head

But the Genitive singular reads:

qātīšu, of her hand

išdīša, of its base

rēšišunu. of their head

The š of the possessive suffix goes back to an original ś (24.4). For qāssu and išissa, one will also find several forms written, e.g., qa-as-sú, qa-sú, and i-ši-is-sà, along with qa-at-sú and i-ši-id-sà. These forms certainly do not witness to the original pronunciation and are to be read qāssu and išissa.

3.11 Suffixes with the Plural   In the plural forms in -ūtum, -ātum, and -ētum, the possessive suffixes (after the dropping of mimation) are attached to the lengthened case ending:

Nom. ṣummirātūka, your striving, Gen. and Acc. ṣummirātīša, of her striving

The plural forms in ū (Gen. and Acc. in -ī) are not changed before the suffix:

errūšu, his entrails

mārīša, of her sons

mûša, its fluid

Cf. paradigm 6.

3.12 Expression of the Genitive   The dependence of one noun upon another in a genitival relationship is generally expressed in Akkadian through the construct state (2.7). ummān šarrim, the army of the king. But the Genitive can also be joined to a noun (in the Status Rectus) by the use of the determinative pronoun ša, with the meaning, that of... e.g.,

ummānum ša šarrim, the army, that of the king - the army of the king

In such cases the noun governing the Genitive is especially emphasized.

Another way of writing the Genitive (used most frequently in omen-texts) is simply to place both nouns side by side and in the same case. The relationship of the two is made clear by the use of a possessive suffix:

> martum appaša, the gall bladder, its nose - the nose of the gall bladder
>
> rubûm qāssu, the prince, his hand - the hand of the prince

This construction makes it possible to transpose the order of the noun governing the phrase and the noun being governed -- [the possessed and the possessor or Regens and Rectum in the traditional grammatical terminology.]

Finally, both expressions for the Genitive can be combined:

> ubān šarrim ša qātīšu, a finger of the king, that of his hand - a finger of the king's hand

3.13 The Glottal Stop as an Initial Sound   The glottal stop - ' - (0.24) is generally not written with special cuneiform signs at the beginning of a word:

> al-pi-im = alpim (actually, 'alpim), of the ox
>
> e-li = eli ('eli), on

But in some cases, to express a glottal stop before a sign which is vowel + consonant (0.16) an additional vowel sign is written (a, e, i, ú):

> ú-ul = ul ('ul), not
>
> a-al = āl ('al), city
>
> i-ir-tum = irtum ('irtum), breast

For the most part, in transcription, the glottal stop is not written:

> alpum, ul, not 'alpum, 'ul

Vowel signs in writings such as ú-ul and a-al do not serve to express vowel length. (ul is short and the first syllable in ālum is naturally long.)

EXERCISES

P. 1. šum-ma 4 na-ap-la-sà-tum. 2. šum-ma da-ap-pu-um ša da-mi-im appi mar-tim[1] ṣa-bi-it.[2] 3. šumma martum re-ša[1] ki-ma si-le-e-em iq-ti-in. 4. šum-ma mar-tum appa-ša ù i-ši-is-sà ṣa-bi-it. 5. šumma iz-bu-um er-ru-šu i-na mu-uḫ-ḫi-šu ša-ak-nu. 6. šum-ma mar-tum mu-ša a-na ki-di-im ḫa-al-ṣú. 7. šum-ma mar-tum pa-nu-ú-ša a-na šu-me-li-im ša-ak-nu-ú. 8. šumma 2 ṣibātum ki-i-ma pi-ti-il-tim pa-at-la.

A. 9. bu-sú-ra-at ḫa-de-e-em. 10. u$_4$-mu ga-am-ru-tum ša nakrim. 11. um-ma-ni nakram i-da-ak. 12. a-al pa-ti-i-ka na-ak-rum i-ṣa-ba-at. 13. um-ma-an nakrim ṣú-mi-ra-ti-ša ú-ul i-ka-aš-ša-ad. 14. na-aš-pa-ka-tim bu-us-ti-tum i-la-pa-at. 15. bu-ú-ši na-ak-ri-i-ka qá-at-ka i-ka-ša-ad. 16. e-le-pa-tim i-na ka-ri-im na-ak-rum i-ta-ba-al. 17. ru-bu-ú be-el lu-um-ni-šu qá-as-su i-ka-aš-ša-ad. 18. re-qú-sà ki-iš-pu a-wi-lam ṣa-ab-tu. 19. mi-il$_5$-la-tum, šatammū é-kál-la-ti i-ma-al-la-lu-ú. 20. ru-bu-tam i-sà-ap-pa-ḫu. 21. ú-ba-an šarrim ša qá-ti-šu i-ma-ra-aṣ. 22. šarrū na-ak-ru-tum sa-li-ma-am i-ša-ak-ka-nu.

O. 23. šumma kakki i-mi-tim mu-uḫ-ḫa-šu qú-ú-um ṣa-bi-it; mi-qí-it-ti um-ma-ni-ya. 24. šumma i-na re-eš naplastim i-na i-mi-it-tim kakkum ša-ki-in-ma ù re-šu ta-ri-ik; i-na ka-ra-ši-im um-ma-an-ka ^{d}Adad i-ra-ḫi-is. 25. šumma i-na i-mi-ti ubanim ši-lum[3] sa-ki-in; mi-qí-it-ti um-ma-ni-ka.

[1] 0.32; [2] 1.5; [3] 0.34.

dappum, drops, lumps

dāmum, blood

ša, who, which, that of

appum, nose

appi martim, nose of the gall bladder

rēš martim, point, tip of the gall bladder

ṣillûm, needle

qatānum (i), to be thin, small

išdum, basis, foundation

errum, intestine, entrails

muhhum, upper side, apex

mû (<*mā'ū) (Pl.), Gen. Acc.
mê, water

kīdum, exterior

ana kīdim, to the outside

halāṣum (a/u), to press out, squeeze

pānū, face, front side

ana šumēlim, leftwards

pitiltum, a tangle, string

patālum, to wrap, to roll together

bussurtum, message, report

hadûm, joy

ūmum, day

gamrum, finished, completed

idâk, (7.2) he will kill, he will beat

ālum, settlement, city

pāṭum, edge, boundary, outpost

ṣummirātum (Pl.), striving, wish

ul, not

našpakum (Pl., našpakātum), granary

bušṭītum, termite, beetle

lapātum (a/u), touch, attack, gnaw

būšum, property, possession

eleppum, ship

kārum, dock, harbor

tabālum (a), remove, carry away

bēlum, master, owner

lumnum, evil, wrongdoing

bēl lumnim, opponent, enemy

rēqūssa, in the future

kišpu (Pl.), magic

millatum, looting, pillage

šattammum, chamberlain, treasurer

malālum (a), to plunder

rubûtum, sovereignty, princely rank

marāṣum (a), to get sick

salīmum, peace-offer, peace-treaty

qûm, cord

karāšum, encampment, camp

dAdad, Adad, weather-god

rahāṣum (i), to prostrate, cut down

šīlum, cavity, aperture, sympton of the liver

Lesson 4

GRAMMAR

4.1 Nominal Forms of the Verb Nominal forms of the verb can be declined. These include: the Infinitive (1.3), the Verbal Adjective (4.2), and the Participle (4.3). Plural forms can be constructed for the Verbal Adjective and the Participle.

4.2 The Verbal Adjective This form is the Stative (1.2) in a *nominalized* form. I.e., it is derived from verbs like *damāqum*, to be good, and *ṣabātum*, to seize, capture

Stative:	Verbal Adjective:
damiq, he is good	*damqum*, the good one
damqat, she is good	*damiqtum*, the good one (f.)
damqū, they are good	*damqūtum*, the good ones
damqā, they (f.) are good	*damqātum*, the good ones (f.)
ṣabit, he is captured	*ṣabtum*, the prisoner
ṣabtat, she is captured	*ṣabittum*, the prisoner (f.)
ṣabtū, they are captured	*ṣabtūtum*, the prisoners
ṣabtā, they (f.) are captured	*ṣabtātum*, the prisoners (f.)

The Verbal Adjective can be used adjectivally or substantivally:

ṣabtum, the one imprisoned, the prisoner

4.3 The Participle In opposition to the passive Verbal Adjective, the Participle is always active. It takes an *ā* after the first consonant and an *i* after the second:

ṣābitum, the captor; *rākibum*, the rider

As a substantive, the participle can also occur in the construct state:

rākib imērim, the rider of a donkey

4.4 Change of *i* to *e* In a closed syllable ending in *r*, *i* is changed to *e*:

iṣḫer (<**iṣḫir*), he became small

paṭer (<**paṭir*), it is split, cut open

maḫer (<**maḫir*), he is received

Still, the participle *māḫirum* occurs, for the shift from *i* to *e* before *r* occurs only in *closed syllables*.

4.5 Change from *a* to *e* In some verbs whose second or third root consonant is *r* or *ḫ*, an *a* shifts often to *e*. For example: *qerēbum* (<**qarābum*), to be near, has the following forms:

Present: *iqerrib*, he draws near (5.2)

Stative: *qerub* (19.10) *qerbet*, is near

similarly:

ṣeḫērum (<**ṣaḫārum*), to be small

iṣeḫḫer, he becomes small (5.2)

ṣeḫer (4.4) *ṣeḫret*, is small

[Note the operation of "vowel-harmony," whereby an *a* in the neighborhood of an *e* often shifts to *e*: *qerēbum* (<*qerābum* <**qarābum*).] But in *paḫārum*, to be assembled, and *maḫārum*, to receive, the *a* remains:

ipaḫḫur, is being assembled

paḫer, is assembled

4.6 Verbs *Primae Aleph* (Whose first radical is aleph) Certain verbs whose first radical is the glottal stop create special forms. One may distinguish two groups among these verbs: the *a*-class, e.g., *akālum*, to eat, and the *e*-class, e.g., *erēbum*, to enter:

a-class:

Infinitive: *akālum* (*a*/*u*) (<*'akalum*), to eat

Preterite: *īkul* (<*i'kul*), he ate, she ate

Present: *ikkal* (<*i'akkal*), he eats, she eats

Participle: *ākilum* (<*'ākilum*), the one eating

Stative: *akil* (f. *aklat*) (<*'akil*), he is eating

e-class:

Infinitive: *erēbum* (*u*) (<*'erēbum*), to enter

Preterite: *īrub* (<*i'rub*), he entered

Present: *irrub* (<*i'errub*), he goes in

Participle: *ēribum* (<*'ēribum*), the one going in

Stative: *erib* (f. *erbet*) (<*'erib*), he is going in

The following rules then, may be derived from the above: the disappearance of the aleph which closed the syllable causes the lengthening of the preceding vowel (as may be observed in the Preterite).

Initial aleph is not written in the Infinitive, Participle, and Stative.

In the Present, it is expressed by the vowel sign *i*:

i-ik-ka-al or *ik-ka-al* (to be read *ikkal*)

i-ir-ru-ub or *i-ru-ub* (to be read *irrub*)

Cf. the writings *a-al* and *ú-ul* (3.13).

The feminine of the Stative and the various plural forms are formed regularly:

īkulū, they ate

irrubā, they enter

erbet, she is going in

Writings like *i-ka-al* and *i-ru-ub* for *ikkal* and *irrub* are to be explained as is *i-ṣa-ba-at* for *iṣabbat*. Consonantal doubling is not expressed in the writing (0.23). Verbs of the a-class are originally verbs of the *First Aleph* one ('$_1$= ') or the *First Aleph* two ('$_2$= h). For example: *akālum*, to eat, corresponds to the Hebrew *'akal*, but *alākum*, to go, corresponds to the Hebrew *halak*. With verbs of the *e*-class which were originally *First Aleph* three, four and five, ('$_{3-5}$= ḥ, ᶜ, ġ) a shift occurs. For example: *erēbum*, to enter, corresponds to the Arabic *ġaraba*, to rise, to go up. The weakening of the *ġ* to *'* has caused a vowel shift of *a* to *e*. The second vowel of the Infinitive was then changed to "harmonize" with the new vowel.

4.7 *The verb alākum, to go* This verb is irregular; it is the only tri-consonantal verb which has the vowel shift *a/i*. Moreover, it forms the *Preterite* with the doubling of the second consonant: *illik*, he went (*illikū*), they went; Present: *illak*, he goes (*illakū*), they go.

4.8 *Verbs Primae Yod* Verbs whose first radical is *y* as *ešērum* (*yšr*), to be straight, exact, correct, coincide in their formation with the *e*-class or *Primae Aleph* verbs:

Preterite: *īšer*, he became right (flourished)

Present: *iššer*, he flourishes

4.9 *Abstracts in -ūtum* The nominal ending -*ūtum* with which the masculine plural of the adjective is formed, is also used to express abstract nominal ideas which are singular and feminine:

ḫarbūtum, devastation, from *ḫarbum*, wastes, barren places

ašarēdūtum, eminence, from *ašarēdum*, first, front rank

The Accusative of the abstracts in -*ūtum* is combined with *alākum*, to go, in a number of idiomatic expressions:

ašarēdūtam alākum, to assume the first place

ḫarbūtam alākum, to be devastated

waṣūtam alākum, to go away, to die

EXERCISES

P. 1. šumma pa-da-nu šu-me-lam ip-šu-uq ù libbi pu-uš-qí-im pa-te-er. 2. šum-ma mar-tum i-ši-is-sà ṣe-ḫe-er. 3. šum-ma ú-ba-na-tum ši-it-ta mu-ḫa-ši-na qû-ú-um ṣa-bi-it ù ka-ak-ki i-mi-it-ti mar-tam i-mi-id. 4. šumma pa-da-nu iš-tu šu-me-lim i-mi-ti naplastim ik-šu-ud ù šēpum šu-me-lam er-bé-et. 5. šum-ma mar-tum a-na li-ib-bi ekallim i-ti$_{7}$-iq.

A. 6. ma-tum i-še$_{20}$-er. 7. e-bu-úr ma-tim ú-ul i-še-er. 8. i-li-it-ti bu-li-im i-ṣe-ḫe-er. 9. e-ri-ib ekallim zú-qí-qí-pu i-za-qá-at. 10. i-na kakkim mi-qí-it-ti a-li-ik pa-ni um-ma-ni-ya. 11. ālum ma-ru-uš-tam i-im-ma-ar. 12. a-ḫu-um a-na bi-it a-ḫi-im i-ir-ru-ub. 13. né-šum i-na ta-ar-ba-ṣi awīlim i-ik-ka-al. 14. a-wi-lum né-me-lam i-ma-ar. 15. aš-ša-at a-wi-lim wa-ṣú-tam i-la-ak. 16. e-bu-ur ma-tim na-ak-rum i-ka-al. 17. ma-tum ḫa-ar-bu-ta-am i-la-ak. 18. u$_{4}$-mu-um i-ru-up-ma ša-mu-um ú-ul i-za-nu-un. 19. er-bu-um a-na ekallim i-ir-ru-ub. 20. a-wi-lum a-ša-re-du-tam i-la-ak. 21. i-na a-li-im bi-it a-wi-li-im i-ša-tum i-ka-al. 22. ālik ḫarrānim re-eš eqlī-šu i-ka-ša-ad, zi-tam i-kal. 23. sērum i-na ḫarrānim a-na pa-ni um-ma-nim i-še$_{20}$-er.

O. 24. šumma iz-bu-um ki-ma ṣe-ri-im; bu-lum i-ṣe-ḫe-er. 25. šumma šu-me-el ubānim i-na iš-di-i-šu e-ek-me-et; a-ša-re-ed na-ak-ri-i-ka qá-at-ka i-ka-ša-ad. 26. šumma bāb ekallim ta-ri-ik-ma a-na li-bi-šu ši-ta ú-ba-na-tu-ka i-ru-ba; ekallam da-an-na-tum i-ṣa-ba-at. 27. šumma bāb ekallim e-pi-iq; nakrum a-bu-ul-lam i-di-il.

šumēlam, left, to the left

pašāqum (u), to be narrow, to become narrow

libbum, heart, middle, middle part

u, and, and then, and also

pušqum, narrow place

ṣehērum (i), to be small

šitta, two

emēdum (i), to lean against, lie against (with Acc.)

erēbum (u), to enter, to meet

eṭēqum (i) (with ana), to pass over, ford

ešērum, to be straight, exact, in order
Present and Preterite, to flourish

ebūrum, harvest

ilittum, posterity

būlum, cattle, animal

ēribum, the one who enters

zuqiqīpu, scorpion

zaqātum (a/u), to sting

kakkum, weapon, armed conflict

ālikum, the one who goes

ālik pānī ummānim, the one who precedes the army

maruštum, evil

amārum (a/u), to see, experience

ahum, brother

ahum...ahum, the one...the other

tarbaṣum, animal pen

akālum (a/u), to eat, devour, enjoy

nēmelum, advantage, profit

aššatum, wife

waṣûtum, departure

waṣûtam alākum, to depart

harbūtum, devastation

harbūtam alākum, to become a waste

erēpum (u), to be cloudy

ašarēdūtum, of the first rank

ašarēdūtam alākum, to enter the first rank

išātum (f. sg.), fire

eqlum, field

reš eqlim, goal

zittum, portion, share

ṣērum, snake, serpent

ešerum ana pānī, to come to (someone)

ekēmum (i), to take away, arrest; St., to be shriveled

ašarēdum, one of the highest rank

erēbum (with ana libbim), to penetrate

epēqum (i), to grow too big, to grow over

abullum, city gate, gate

edēlum (i), to close

Lesson 5

GRAMMAR

5.1 Classification of the Verb Akkadian verbs can be divided into two major classifications. One can distinguish between *active* verbs which describe activities, e.g., *ṣabātum*, to seize, attack, and *qualitative* verbs which describe states or conditions of being, e.g., *damāqum*, to be good.

Inf. *damāqum*, to be good	*ṣabātum*, to capture
Prt. *idmiq*, he became good	*iṣbat*, he captured
Prs. *idammiq*, he becomes good	*iṣabbat*, he captures
St. *damiq*, he is good	*ṣabit*, he is captured, capturing
Part. ---	*ṣābitum*, the captor
Verbal Adj. *damqum*, good	*ṣabtum*, captured

5.2 Qualitative Verbs The Verbal Adjective can be viewed as the basic form of the Qualitative Verb. It can be translated by an adjective. The Infinitive can be translated into English with the addition of *to be*. Both the Preterite and the Present of the Qualitative Verb have ingressive meanings:

qatnum, thin; *qatānum* (*i*), to be thin; *iqtin*, he became thin *iqattin*, he becomes thin

ṣeḫrum, small; *ṣeḫerum* (*i*), to be small (4.5); *iṣḫer*, he became small; *iṣeḫḫer*, he becomes small

The root vowel of the Qualitative Verb is almost always *i*. A participle cannot be derived from it.

5.3 *Active Verbs* The Infinitive can be viewed as the basic form of the active verb. From it are derived an active Participle and a passive Verbal Adjective:

epēšum, to make

ēpišum, maker, making

epšum, made

One can separate these verbs into four classes according to their root vowel (1.4) which only occurs in the Preterite and Present. The verbs of the "vowel-shift" or *a*/*u*-class, those of the *a*-class, and those of the *i*-class are generally transitive. Verbs of the *u*-class are intransitive and describe movement or processes:

Infinitive:	Preterite:	Present:
kašādum (*a*/*u*)	*ikšud*, he plundered	*ikaššad*, he plunders
ṣabātum (*a*)	*iṣbat*, he seized	*iṣabbat*, he seizes
edēlum (*i*)	*īdil*, he closed	*iddil*, he closes
erēbum (*u*)	*īrub*, he entered	*irrub*, he enters
erēpum (*u*)	*īrup*, it became cloudy	*irrup*, it becomes cloudy

As a general rule, no Verbal Adjective is derived from verbs of the *u*-class.

5.4 *The Second Person in the Preterite and the Present* To form the second person singular, one substitutes the prefix *ta-* for the prefix *i-* in the third singular. The plural for both masculine and feminine is formed by adding the prefix *ta-* and the ending *-ā*:

Preterite:

imḫur, he (she) receives; *tamḫur*, you receive

imḫurū, they receive; *tamḫurā*, you (pl.) receive

imḫurā, they (f.) receive; *tamḫurā*, you (pl.) receive

Present:

iṣabbat, he seizes; *taṣabbat*, you seize

iṣabbatū, they seize; *taṣabbatā*, you (pl.) seize

iṣabbatā, they (f.) seize; *taṣabbatā*, you (pl.) seize

In verbs with the vocalization *e*, as *qerēbum* (4.5), *ta-* shifts to *te-*:

teqerrib, you draw near.

Cf. paradigms 14 and 15. The formation of the second person *feminine* singular is discussed in 19.7.

5.5 The Second Person in Verbs Which are *Primae Aleph* In verbs which are First *Aleph* one peculiarity should be noted. With the dropping away of the *aleph* which had originally closed a syllable, the preceding vowel is then lengthened (4.6). In *e*-class verbs here, *ta-* goes to *te-*:

īkul, he ate	*tākul* <*ta'kul*), you ate
ikkal, he eats	*takkal* (<*ta'akkal*), you eat
īkulū, they ate	*tākulā* (<*ta'kulā*), you ate
īrub, he entered	*tērub* (<*te'rub*), you entered
irrub, he enters	*terrub* (<*te'errub*), you enter
irrubū, they enter	*terrubā* (<*te'errubā*), you enter

Cf. paradigms 22 and 23.

5.6 The Ventive In the Present, Preterite, and to some extent in the Stative, special forms are found with the suffix *-am* or *-nim*. Such forms are chiefly found with verbs of *movement*. In Akkadian, a distinction is made between motions which touch specifically on the moment of *departure* or *arrival* (from the viewpoint of the narrator). In this last case, the verb is expressed in the *Ventive*. So, *illak*, he goes, but illakam, the Ventive form of this verb, he comes. However, sometimes the Ventive is found in verbs which have nothing to do with motion. We simply do not know what difference in meaning there may be in such cases between the form with normal endings and the form with Ventive endings.

5.7 The Formation of the Ventive in Preterite and Present The Ventive is made by adding -am to the forms which lack a suffixed ending (3rd pers. sg. and the 2nd pers. sg. masc.). Forms which already have some suffixed ending (3rd and 2nd pers. pl.) form the Ventive by adding -nim:

iqribam, he (she) drew near

taqribam, you drew near

iqribūnim, they drew near

iqribānim, they (f.) drew near

irrubam, he comes toward me

terrubam, you come toward me

irrubūnim, they come toward me

irrubānim, they (f.) come toward me

Cf. paradigms 14 and 15.

5.8 Accusative Suffixes A pronominal object can be expressed through a suffix attached directly to the verb. Accusative suffixes are used to express the direct object:

izzibū-ši, they are leaving her (for mātam izzibū, they are leaving the country)

The most important Akkadian suffixes are: -ka, you (masc.); šu, him; ši, her; -šunūti, them (masc.); and -šināti, them (f.). The š of the third person suffix together with preceding dentals and sibilants becomes ss (3.10):

iṣabbassu (<iṣabbat + šu), he seizes him

Nominal objects are sometimes expressed pleonastically through the use of a substantive and a pronominal suffix attached to the verb. This construction (which is very common in the omens) emphasizes the object:

ilū mātam izzibūši, the gods leave the land

5.9 Dative Suffixes To express an indirect object, Dative suffixes are used. Such suffixes are attached to the Ventive form of the verb:

išapparakkum (<išappar + am + kum), he is writing to you

The most important suffixes are -kum, to you (m); -šum, to him; -šim, to her. The m of the Ventive suffix is assimilated to the initial consonant of the Dative suffix:

irrubūnikkum (<irrubū + nim + kum), they are coming toward you

(Sometimes the m drops from the suffixes -kum, -šum, -šim):

in-na-aš-ši-a-ku = inaššiakku, he will bring to you

5.10 Negations To negate a main clause ul or ula (written: ú-ul, ú-la) is used. It means not and is placed directly before the predicate:

šamûm ul izannun, rain will not fall

In subordinate clauses or for the negation of individual words lā is used. This particle can be placed between prepositions and a substantive:

ina lā lamādīšu, in his inexperience

EXERCISES

A. 1. ayyu-ú-um-ma[1] a-na mi-it-gu-ur-tim i-ša-pa-ra-ak-kum. 2. bi-ši[2] ma-at nakrim a-na ma-ti-ka i-ir-ru-ba-am. 3. ayya-bu-ú-ka a-na a-bu-ul-li-ka i-ru-bu-nim. 4. nakrum er-ṣe-et-ka i-ri-iš-ka[3]. 5. er-ṣe-et nakrī-ka te-er-ri-iš. 6. a-bu-um ar-bu-tam[4] i-la-a-ak[1], i-lu ma-a-tam i-zi-bu-ú-ši. 7. ru-ba-am i-na bi-ti-šu qá-tum i-ṣa-ba-as-su. 8. Tu-ru-ku-tum a-na šar-ri-im i-qé-er-ri-bu-nim. 9. mi-lum ga-ap-šum i-il-la-kam. 10. mi-lum i-la-ka-am, ša-nu-um šum-šu[5] : za-na-an[6] ša-me-e-em, a-ka-al ša-al-la-tim. 11. u_4-mu-um i-ru-pa-am-ma ša-mu-um i-za-nu-un. 12. ti-bu-um ra-bu-um um-ma-na-am i-ka-aš-ša-da-am. 13. nakram qí-it-ru-bi-iš te-ki-im. 14. a-al na-ak-ri-im i-na pi-il-ši ta-ṣa-ba-at. 15. a-wi-lam i-na la la-ma-di-šu ma-ru-uš-tum i-ma-aq-qú-ta-aš-šum. 16. er-ṣe-et nakrī-ka ta-ta-ab-ba-al.

O. 17. šumma bāb ekallim ir-pi-iš; ayya-bu-ú-ka a-na a-bu-ul-li-im i-ru-bu-ni-ik-kum. 18. šumma ṣibtum e-li ṣibtim ir-ka-ab; e-bu-ur ma-a-at na-ak-ri-i-ka ta-ka-al. 19. šum-ma na-ap-la-ás-tum re-ša ip-ṭú-ur; i-na re-eš eqlim um-ma-na-am i-lu-ša i-zi-bu-ši. 20. šumma kar-šum ki-ma di-ši-im; ma-tam ḫu-ša-ḫu-um da-an-nu-um i-ṣa-ba-as-si.

[1] 0.22 (Remark); [2] 2.9; [3] Pres. (4.6, Remark); [4] 4.9; [5] 0.28 (Remark); [6] 1.3.

ayyumma, somebody

ana, to, for, for the purpose

mitgurtum, agreement

šapārum (a/u), write, send

bīšum, property, possession

ayyābum, enemy

erṣetum, territory, land

erēšum (i), to wish, demand

abum, father

arbūtum, flight

arbūtam alākum, to take flight

ezēbum (i), to abandon, to leave in the lurch

Turrukkūtum, the Turukki, a mountain people

qerēbum, to draw near, to come toward

mīlum, fullness, floodtide

gapšum, huge, powerful, bulky

alākum, to go, Vent., to come

šanûm (< *šanium), second, another

šumum, name

šanum šumšu, another, second meaning of an omen

šallatum, booty, plunder

tībum, attack

rabûm (< *rabium), great

qitrubiš, hand-to-hand combat, affray, scuffle

ina, in, toward, by means of

pilšum, gap, breach

lā, not

lamādum (a), learn, experience

ina lā lamādīšu, without his learning of it

maqātum (u), fall, push

rapāšum (i), to be broad

rakābum (a), to ride

rēšum, head, point

karšum, stomach

dīšum, grass

ḫušaḫḫum, hunger, famine

Lesson 6

GRAMMAR

6.1 Strong and Weak Verbs All verbs treated up until now had a root of three consonants. One can describe these verbs with three consonants as tri-radical or strong verbs. Along with these verbs, there are groups of others which are bi-radical or weak verbs. Their root contains only two consonants.

6.2 Verbs Ultimae Vocalis Two consonant roots with a long vowel after the second consonant are sometimes called ultimae vocalis, "final vowel" or "final weak" or "third weak:"

°mlā, to be full

°lqē (= lq'), to take

°bnī, to produce

°šqū, to be high

The verbs presented in final ē in this lesson like leqûm, to take, tebûm, to be raised up, are originally tri-radical roots with aleph as the last radical (°lq', °tb'). Since their conjugation is quite parallel to verbs which are ultimae vocalis, they are presented here.

6.3 Conjugation of Verbs Which are Ultimae Vocalis This group of weak verbs is very similar in external form to the strong verbs: malûm (°mlā), to be full; leqûm (°lq'), to take; banûm (°bnī), to produce, build; šaqûm (°šqū), to be high.

Preterite	Present	Stative
imla, he became full	imalla, it becomes full	mali, it is full

ilqe, he took ileqqe, he takes leqi, it is taken

ibni, he built ibanni, he produces builds bani, it is built

išqu, it became high išaqqu, it becomes high šaqu, it is high

The prefix appears immediately before the root in the Preterite. In the Present, the second consonant is doubled and an a vowel is inserted before the doubling as the vowel of the Present. In the Stative, the root-vowel is normally lost and replaced by an i. Only in verbs with final ū the vowel u remains. Before or after ḫ, a becomes e (4.5):

iṭeḫḫi, he draws near

ḫepi, it is smashed

The verbs which are final ē (final ') also have an e vocalization:

itebbe, he is lifted up, gets up

The long root vowel is shortened in all forms but remains in the Preterite and the Present when a suffix or the enclitic -ma (and) is added:

ta-ra-aš-ši-i-šu = taraššīšu

nadīma, he is lying down and...

as well as at the end of sentences:

i-ba-aš-ši-i [= ibaššī] (along with i-ba-aš-ši), he is

6.4 Verbs Ultimae Vocalis With Vocalic Endings Endings which begin with a vowel, like those of the third person pl. -ū and -ā (3.6) or the third fem. sg. of the Stative, -at and the Ventive -am are contracted with the root vowel. [In such cases the contraction will be of the same class as the long vowel, or if both are short, of the second vowel.] However, iā (ia) and eā (ea) generally remain uncontracted:

imlû, imliā (imlâ) they become full

iṭeḫḫû, iṭeḫḫia, (iṭeḫḫâ), they draw near

itebbeam, he rises

maliat (malât), it (f.) is full

Cf. paradigm 32.

6.5 The Glottal Stop in Medial Position The glottal stop between i and a and between e and a (6.4) is generally not expressed through special signs in Cuneiform:

ma-li-at = maliat (actually mali'at), it (f.) is full

But the glottal stop, as at the beginning of a word (3.13), can be expressed through the vowel sign a:

li-pi-a-am = lipiam (lipi'am), fat (Accus. case)

i-ṭe-eh hi-a-am = iṭehhiam (iṭehhi'am), he drew near

In the transcription (0.15) the glottal stop (') is generally not given. So the word would read lipiam and not lipi'am.

6.6 Second Person in Verbs Ultimae Vocalis In the second person singular and plural the prefix i- of the third person is replaced by ta-. However, in verbs which have ē (originally ') as their final consonant and in verbs which have ḫ as their first or second consonant, the second person prefix is te-:

ibni, he produced	ileqqe, he takes
tabni, you produced	teleqqe, you take
tabnû, tabnia, you (pl.) produced	teḫpi, you smash

Cf. paradigm 32.

6.7 Nominal Forms of the Verbs Ultimae Vocalis Their formation corresponds to the tri-radical verb (4.1-4.3). In the Participle, the root vowel is replaced by i, and in the Infinitive it is replaced by a; thereupon a contraction takes place:

Participle: *lēqûm* (< **lēqium*), taking

Infinitive: *banûm* (< **banāum*), to produce, build

For the verbal adjective, cf. the Stative (6.3). The adjective *rabûm*, great, has the feminine form *rabītum*; *šaqum*, high, on the other hand, takes the feminine form *šaqūtum*.

6.8 *Independent Possessive Pronouns* In addition to the possessive suffixes (3.7), there are independent possessive pronouns which are especially stressed and which are used mostly for the expression of opposites as *my* and *yours*, *your* and *his*. The most important are:

yûm (f. *yattum*), my, mine

kûm (*kattum*), your, yours

šum (*šattum*), his

nûm (*nuttum*) our, ours

They are treated like adjectives; they follow the word they modify and they can be declined:

mātam lā kattam, a land not yours

mimma lā šâm, something not belonging to him

Cf. paradigm 10. For the plural cf. *qarrādu yā'ūtum*, my heroes.

6.9 *The Indefinite Pronoun, mimma* The indeclinable pronoun *mimma*, something-or-other, everything-which...can be used in combination with a negative and, preceding a noun, is in apposition with it:

mimma nudunnâm, everything (which is) dowry = the whole dowry

mimma la šâm, what does not belong to him

6.10 *Constructions With the Accusative* Verbs like *to be full* sometimes require a prepositional phrase in English. "The liver is full of fat." This is expressed with an accusative in Akkadian:

martum lipiam maliat, the liver (Nom.), fat (Acc.) is full (3rd f. Stat.)

Similarly:

martum dāmam laptat, the gall bladder is smeared with blood

6.11 *Assimilation of Labials*   *b* (and sometimes *p*) is assimilated to a following *m*:

terrumma (<*terub* + *ma*), you enter and...

īzimma (<*īzib* + *ma*), he leaves and...

takimma (<*takip* + *ma*), it is spotted and...

The same phenomenon sometimes occurs in the construct state:

ḫiṣim mātim (<*ḫiṣib mātim*), produce of the country

Also *n* can be assimilated to an *m*:

šakimma for the usual *šakinma*, it is placed and...

EXERCISES

P. 1. šumma iz-bu-um qí-na-as-sú pe-ta-at. 2. šum-ma mar-tum da-ma-am la-ap-ta-at. 3. šum-ma mar-tum li-ib-ba-ša li-pi-a-am ma-li.

A. 4. ka-al-bu i-še$_{20}$-gu-ú. 5. e-ka-lum e-ka-lam i-re-ed-de. 6. te-es$_5$-li-it awīlim ilum iš-me. 7. na-ka-ar-ka i-na bi-ti-i-ka mi-im-ma la ša-a-am i-le-qé. 8. i-na bi-ti na-ak-ri-i-ka mi-im-ma la ka-a-am te-le-qé. 9. ta-ap-pa-am ta-ra-aš-ši-i-ma na-ka-ar-ka ta-da-ak. 10. na-ka-ar-ka ta-ap-pa-am i-ra-aš-ši-i-ma i-da-ak-ka. 11. šar-ru ḫa-am-me-e i-te-eb-bu-ú-nim. 12. ma-ri ^{1}ši-ip-ri-im ša ma-a-tim re-eq-tim a-na šarrim i-ṭe-eḫ-ḫi-a-am.13. mi-lik ma-a-tim i-ša-an-ni. 14. ka-ab-tum ki-ma be-li-šu i-ma-as-ṣi. 15. ḫi-ṣi-im ma-tim a-na é-kál-lim i-ru-ub. 16. ma-at nakrim ta-ṣa-ab-ba-at, a-na i-še$_{20}$-er-ti nakrim te-ru-um-ma ni-qí-am ta-na-qí-i. 17. bu-sú-ra-at lu-um-ni-im a-na bi-ti awīlim i-ṭe-ḫi-a. 18. šarrum er-ṣe-tam la ša-tam ù ma-tam la ša-tam qá-as-sú i-ka-aš-ša-ad.

19. la[2] me-ḫe-er-ka i-te-bé-a-ku-um-ma i-da-ak-ka. 20. qá-ar-ra-du ya-ú-tu-un ù ša nakrim iš-te-ni-iš i-ma-qú-tu.

0. 21. šum-ma mar-tum ma-li-at-ma mu-ša wa-ar-qú; ra-du-um i-la-ak.

22. šum-ma mar-tum i-ši-is-sá le-ti; šu-ṣú-um a-na ma-tim i-te-eb-bé-a-am. 23. šumma kakki i-mi-tim i-na re-eš mar-tim ša-ki-im-ma mar-tam ir-de-e; kakki qú-li-im. 24. šumma martum re-sa ki-ma ku-ub-ši-im; šarrum la-ma-sà-am i-ra-aš-ši. 25. šumma martum da-ma-am dan-na-am ma-li-at; su-un-qum ma-tam i-ṣa-ba-at. 26. šum-ma ṣibtum su-ma-am ṣa-ar-pa-at[1]; wi-li-id bu-lim i-še-er. 27. šumma bāb ekallim ma-aš-ka-an-šu i-zi-im-ma i-na šumēlim ša-ki-in; ma-tam la ka-tam nakrum i-ka-ša-ad. 28. šumma ubānam ka-ak-kum ša-ap-li-iš ra-ki-ib; ka-ak-kum nu-ú-um. 29. šumma ubānam ka-ak-kum e-li-iš ra-ki-ib; ka-ak-ki na-ak-ri-im. 30. šum-ma mar-tum mu-uḫ-ḫa-ša ta-ki-im-ma ṣa-ri-ip; mi-qí-it-ti bārîm. 31. šum-ma na-ap-la-ás-tum e-li-iš iš-qu; i-lu ša ma-tim i-ša-aq-qú-ú.

[1] 2.9; [2] 5.10.

qinnatum, anus

petûm (pt'), to open

lipûm (lipium), fat, fatty tissue

malûm (mlā), St. to be full, Prs. and Prt. to become full

kalbum, dog

šegûm (šg'), to be mad, insane

redûm (rd'), to follow, overtake; accompany, lead

teslītum, entreaty, prayer

šemûm (šm'), to listen, hear

nakarum, enemy

mimma, something-or-other

šûm, his

leqûm (lq'), to take

kûm, yours

tappûm, associate, ally

rašum (ršī), St. to have, Prs. and Prt. to obtain

tadâk, you will kill, strike

idâkka, he will kill you, beat you

ḫammûm (**ḫammā'um*), rebel

tebûm (*tb'*), to be lifted up

šiprum, message, report

māri šiprim, messenger, envoy

rēqum, distant

ṭeḫûm (*ṭḫī*), to come near, to come toward

milkum, plan, counsel

šanûm (*šnī*), to be other, Prs. and Prt., to change

ḫiṣbum, profit, produce, yield

maṣûm (*mṣī*), to be like, Prs. and Prt. to become like

kabtum, f. *kabittum*, difficult, heavy, powerful

išertum, temple, shrine

niqûm, sacrifice

naqûm (*nqī*), to sacrifice

u, and, also

meḫrum, like, similar, corresponding

qarrādum, hero

yûm, mine (from my)

ištēniš, together, in common

warāqum (*i*), to be green, to be yellow

letûm (*lt'*), to split

šūṣûm, an exile

qūlum, lament; silence

kubšum, cap

lamassum, protective divinity

dannum, strong, solid, clotted (with blood)

sunqum, need

sūmum, red spot, bruise

ṣarāpum (*ā/ū*), to color red

wildum, posterity

maškanum, place, location

šapliš, under

nûm, ours

eliš, above

takāpum, to be spotted

šaqûm (*šqū*), to be high, Prs. and Prt. to become high, important

Lesson 7

GRAMMAR

7.1 Verbs Mediae Vocalis   Bi-consonantal roots (6.1) with a long vowel between the two consonants are called Mediae Vocalis, "with a middle vowel," or "middle weak," or "hollow" roots. The root vowel of the hollow verbs can be either i or u. Occasionally one finds hollow verbs with an a root-vowel.

There are Qualitative verbs (5.2), e.g.:

ṭiābum (°ṭīb), to be good, beautiful

miādum (°mīd), to be much, many

kānum (°kūn), to be solid, true

and Active verbs (5.3), e.g.:

šiāmum (°šīm), to decide

dâkum (°dūk), to kill

târum (°tūr), to come back

The conjugation of these verbs is quite different from that of the strong verbs.

7.2 Preterite and Present of the Hollow Verbs   In the Preterite, the prefix simply precedes the root:

3rd pers. sg. itūr, he (she) came back

2nd pers. sg. masc. tatūr, you came back

pl. itūrū, itūrā, they came back

tatūrū, tatūrā, you came back

Similarly with verbs which are middle i:

išīm, he (she) decided

tašīm išīmū, etc.

In the Present one must distinguish between the forms which are without endings (3rd pers. sg. and 2nd pers. sg. masc.--these insert the vowel *a* in the Present after the root vowel) and forms which have endings (3rd and 2nd pers. pl. and the Ventive). In the latter cases, the second consonant of the root is doubled:

išīam, he decides, but *išimmū*, *išimmā*, they decide

itûr (<*itūar*), he turns back, but *iturram*, he comes back

The root vowel is shortened before doubled consonants. One should note also that *ua* almost always contracts to *û*, but that *ia* only occasionally contracts to *â*.

idâk (<*idūak*), he kills

but *iqīap*, he relies on

The remaining forms are similarly constructed:

2nd pers. sg. masc. *tadâk* (<*tadūak*), you kill

3rd pers. pl. fem. *imiddā*, they become numerous

Cf. paradigm 30.

7.3 Stative and Nominal Forms of the Hollow Verbs The Stative takes the vowel *i* whether the root vowel of the verb was *i* or *u*.

kīn, he is firm; *kīnat*, she is firm

pl. *kīnū*, *kīnā*

šīm, is decided

In some Qualitative verbs, the Stative is formed with *ā*:

mād, is many; *sām*, is red; *ṭāb*, is good

Some examples of the verbal adjective:

kīnum, true; fem. *kittum*, (subst.) truth

šīmum, made firm; fem. *šīmtum*, (subst.) destiny

māḍum, māttum, many

sāmum, sāmtum, red

In the infinitive an a is inserted after the shortened stem vowel [resulting often in a contraction].

dâkum (<duākum), to slay

šiāmum, to decide

7.4 The Subjunctive The verb of dependent clauses is written in the subjunctive:

ikšud, he plundered

but: ša...ikšudu, he who (sg.) plundered

The subjunctive ending is -u. It occurs only after verbs without endings (3rd pers. sg. and the 2nd pers. sg. masc.). Forms with endings (3rd and 2nd pers. pl. and the Ventive) construct no special subjunctive forms:

idūkū, they have killed, (who) have killed

illikam, he has arrived, (who) has arrived

The subjunctive ending -u also occurs in the third person singular of the Stative:

ša nakru, who is unfriendly

ša mītu, who is dead

In final weak or ultimae vocalis verbs, this -u is contracted with the root-vowel:

ša ikmû (<*ikmiu), who took prisoner, captured

If a suffix is added to a subjunctive form, the u is lengthened:

ša ikšudūšu, who robbed him

Cf. paradigms 14 and 15.

Occasionally one finds cuneiform writings of the subjunctive with a long vowel (0.22):

ša na-ak-ru-ú (*nakru*), who is hostile, unfriendly

7.5 *Relative Clauses* The role of Akkadian relative clauses can be compared perhaps, to genitival phrases. The relative clause makes the meaning of its substantive more precise (so does the noun which is *governed* in a genitival phrase make more precise the meaning of the noun which *governs*). These relative clauses can be bound to the substantive by the determinative pronoun *ša*:

Kubaba ša sarrūtam iṣbatu, Kubaba, who seized control of the kingdom

But the *ša* is sometimes missing and then the governing substantive is placed in the construct state:

ḫarrān illaku, the way which he will go = the campaign which he will undertake

In both cases, the verb of the relative clause is expressed in the subjunctive.

Dependent clauses introduced by *ašar*, where, are actually relative clauses in the construct state:

ašar illaku, the place to which he goes, whither he goes

7.6 *Dual* Nouns and verbs can also have a *dual*, in addition to a singular and plural. The dual serves to express the number two:

qarrādān šena, two heroes

and parts of the body found in pairs:

inān, the (two) eyes

Some words occur only in the dual:

qablān, the middle part

išdān, the lower part, foundation

The dual can occur with or without the numeral two, *šena* (*šitta*).

7.7 The Dual in Nouns   In the dual, there is no distinction between masculine and feminine. As with the plural (3.4), there are only two cases -- the Nominative in *-ān* and the Genitive-Accusative in *-īn*:

šēpān, *šēpīn*, feet

In the construct state or with the addition of any suffix, the *n* of the dual ending is lost:

īnī awīlim, the eyes of the man (Gen.-Acc.)

qablāša, her (its) center, middle-part

An adjective governing a dual takes *feminine plural* endings (3.2).

šēpāšu warkiātum, her (its) hind legs

The dual is replaced by the feminine plural in the case of a feminine substantive which ends in *-tum*.

marrātum šitta, two gall bladders [sing. *martum*]

The *n* of the dual ending frequently is dropped. Forms like *šēpā* and *šēpī* (two feet) occur.

7.8 The Dual in the Verb   The dual forms of the third person are regularly the same as the third person feminine:

irrubā, they (fem.) go in, or both (masc. or fem.) go in

saknā, they (fem.) are placed or both are placed

EXERCISES

P. 1. šumma iz-bu-um pa-ni imērim še$_{20}$-pa-šu ma-aḫ-ri-a-tum še$_{20}$-ep nēšim še$_{20}$-pa-šu wa-ar-ki-a-tum še$_{20}$-ep imērim. 2. šumma i-na re-eš naplastim zi-ḫu[1] na-di-ma ù sa-a-am. 3. šum-ma mar-tum mu-ša a-na še$_{20}$-na zi-i-zu. 4. šumma ubān ḫa-ši qablītum[2] a-na še$_{20}$-na zi-za-at-ma i-na i-mi-tim ṭe$_4$-ḫi-a-at. 5. šum-ma ṣibtum a-na li-ib-bi-im i-tu-úr. 6. šum-ma ma-ra-tum[3] šitta.

A. 7. um-ma-ni it-ti ilim a-na da-ki-im er-še-et. 8. kakki ši-im-tim ša a-wi-lim. 9. be-el ma-a-tim i-ma-a-at. 10. šar-ru-um i-na a-li-šu li-ib-ba-šu ú-la i-ṭi-a-ab. 11. šarrum ma-as-sú ù wa-ar-di-šu i-qí-a-ap. 12. ekallum i-ri-aq. 13. be-el sa-li-mi-ka i-ma-at-ma a-al-šu ta-la-wi. 14. be-lam i-na šu-ub-ti-šu kakkum i-da-ak-šu. 15. ma-ku-ur a-wi-lim i-ṣú-um a-na ma-di i-ta-ar. 16. na-ra-ma-at šar-ri-im i-mi-id-da. 17. qar-ra-da-an šena i-mu-ut-ta-nim. 18. šar-rum a-na še₂₀-na ma-ri-šu ma-as-sú i-za-az. 19. na-ak-ru-um iš-da-a-šu da-an-na. 20. iš-da nakrim ki-na-a-tum. 21. i-ni a-wi-lim šar-rum i-na-as-sà-aḫ. 22. a-mu-ut ᵈLu ḫu-ši-im[1] ša a-wi-lum i-na bu-ul-ṭì-šu mi-tu. 23. šar-ra-am ša it-ti-i-ka na-ak-ru-ú i-na kakki ta-da-ak-ma a-al-šu na-wi-šu er-ṣe-es-sú qá-at-ka i-ka-aš-ša-ad. 24. a-mu-ut Ša-ar-ka-al-šar-ri ša wa-ar-du-ú-šu i-na ku-nu-uk-ka-ti-šu-nu i-du-ku-ú-šu. 25. a-mu-ut A-pi-ša-li-im ša ᵐNa-ra-am-ᵈSîn ik-šu-du-ú-šu. 26. a-wa-at Ku-ub-a-ba ša ša-ar-ru-ta-am iṣ-ba-tu. 27. a-mu-ut Šul-gi ša Tap-pá-ᵈDa-ra-aḫ ik-mu-ú. 28. um-ma-an-ka a-šar i-la-ku zi-tam i-kal. 29. um-ma-nu ḫarrān i-la-ku₁₃ ú-ul i-tu-ra-am.

O. 30. šum-ma mar-tum qá-ab-la-ša[2] ṣa-ab-ta-a; šar-ra-am šu-ut-re-ši-i-šu i-du-uk-ku-šu. 31. šum-ma mar-tum ap-pa-as-sà ù i-ši-is-sà ki-na-a-ma qá-ab-la-a-ša na-as-ḫa; mi-il-kum sa-pi-iḫ.

[1] O.34; [2] O.33; [3] 3.2.

imērum, donkey

maḫrûm (< *maḫrīum), first

warkûm (< *warkīum), hind (adj.)

ziḫḫum, blister, pimple (symptom of the liver)

nadûm (ndī), to throw down, to put down

sâmum (sīm), to be red, to be brown

šena, two

zâzum (zūz), to divide

ana šena zâzum, to divide into two parts

ubānum, finger (also part of lung or liver)

hašûm, lung

qablûm (<*qablīum), middle, central

ubān hašī qablītum, "middle finger" of the lung

târum (tūr), to turn, to return, to turn around

itti, with, with the consent or agreem[illegible]f

dâ[illegible] kil[illegible]trike, beat

[illegible]

ma[illegible] to [illegible]

ula, not

ṭâbum[illegible]ood, we[illegible]

[illegible] slave

qâp[illegible]ust, to entrust

rāqum (rīq), to [illegible] empty

lawûm (lwī), to include, surround

šubtum, dwelling

makkūrum, treasure, property

mâdum (mīd), St. to be much, Prt. and Prs., to become numerous

ana mādim târum, to become many

narāmtum, beloved

išdān, basis, foundation, dependability

kīnum, solid, true, dependable

īnum, eye

nasāhum (a/u), to tear out, to tear loose

amūtum, liver, liver-omen, portent

dLuhušum, personal name

bulṭum, life, life-span

ittīka, with you

nakārum, to be unfriendly, hostile

nawûm (<nawium), encampment, camp

Šarkalšarri, king of the dynasty of Akkad (2222-2198)

kunukkum (sealed) clay tablet, document

Apišal, a city, probably in northern Mesopotamia

mNarām-dSin, a king of the dynasty of Akkad (2259-2223)

awātum, word, thing, concern

Kubaba, (heroic personality)

šarrūtum, kingdom

Šulgi, King of the 3rd dynasty of Ur (2093-2046)

Tappa-dDarah, personal name

kamûm (kmī), to take prisoner, to bind

ašrum, place, position

ašar, where, whither

qablān, middle part

šūt, the ones (archaic plural of the determinative pronoun)

šūt rēšim, (those of the head) = court figures, eunuchs

kânum (kūn), to be solid, true

Lesson 8

GRAMMAR

8.1 Root Augments   Bi-consonantal roots, with a short vowel between the consonants, can be made parallel in form to tri-radicals by the use of a root-augment, an n or a w.

8.2 Verbs Primae n   With the root-augment two groups of verbs are frequently constructed. The first of these are some verbs which determine direction in some fashion:

nadānum, to hand over

naṭālum, to look at

našûm, to raise up

nadûm, to lay down

The other group has to do with verbs which are onamatapoeic:

nakāsum (*kis), to cut off

natākum (*tuk), to drop

nabāḫum (*buh), to bark

There is no difference in conjugation between bi-radical verbs with the root-augment n and tri-radicals whose first consonant is n. To this last group belong qualitative verbs like:

nawārum (i), to be lighted

nadārum (i), to be furious

8.3 The Conjugation of Verbs Primae n   Verbs which are I n are conjugated just like the tri-radicals, but the n is assimilated to a following consonant, so:

Pres. inaṭṭal, he looks, but Pret. iṭṭul (< *inṭul), he looked
Cf. paradigm 26.

8.4 Verbs Primae n and Ultimae Vocalis Some verbs which are I n are also III vowel:

našûm (nšī), to raise up

nadûm (ndī), to lay down

naqûm (nqī), to sacrifice

Their construction corresponds to the verbs which are III vowel (6.2).

Pres. inašši, he lifts up

Pret. išši (< *inši), he lifted up

8.5 Verbs Primae w With the verbs I w, one must distinguish between the active verbs with root-augment w as:

wabālum, to carry

walādum, to give birth

wašābum, to settle

and the qualitative verbs I w where the w is an original component of the root, e.g., warāqum, to be green, yellow.
These two groups admit of different conjugation.

8.6 Present and Preterite of the Verbs Primae w In the active verbs, the prefixes of the third and second person (normally i- and ta- go to u- and tu-:

uššab, he sits, settles

tuššab, you sit

The Present has the vowel a and the Preterite i (cf. alākum, 4.7).
The first root consonant is doubled in the Present and in the Preterite the prefix is lengthened:

ullad, she bears

ūlid, she bore

The vowel *i* disappears from the Preterite if an ending is added:

ūbil, he broke (a path) but *ublam*, he broke in this direction

ublū, they broke

The qualitative verbs like *warāqum*, to be green, form their Preterite and Present according to the model of the *e*-class of verbs which are I *aleph*:

irriq, he becomes green

īriq, he became green

Cf. paradigm 28.

The long vowel *ū* is shortened in closed syllables. *ūbil*, but *ublam*.

8.7 Nominal Forms of the Verbs *Primae* w Without distinction both of the groups described above construct their nominal forms according to the pattern of the tri-radical:

Part. *wāšibum*, the one dwelling

St. *wariq*, he is green, *warqū*, they are green

8.8 Verbs *Primae* w and *Ultimae Vocalis* Some verbs which are I *w* are also III vowel:

waṣûm (**wṣī*), to go out and *watûm* (**wtā*), to find

Pres. *uṣṣi*, he goes out, *utta*, he finds

Pret. *ūṣi*, he went out

Stat. *waṣi*, is going out = protrudes, hangs out

Part. *wāṣûm* (< **wāṣium*), the one protruding

8.9 Status Absolutus Cardinal numbers, the names of gods, and certain "frozen" expressions have a special form, the absolute state.

It is without ending in the masculine. The feminine ending is -*at*. In form then, it corresponds to the construct state (without a dependent Genitive) or to the third singular of the Stative. The absolute state cannot be declined:

ana ālim išten, into one city

dŠamaš, *Šamaš*, the sun-god, but *šamšum*, the sun

ašar ištēn, in one place

8.10 *Cardinal Numbers* The most important cardinal numbers are:

1. *ištēn* (f. *ištiat*)
2. *šena* (*šitta*)
3. *šalaš* (*šalāšat*)
4. *erbe* (*erbet*)
5. *ḫamiš* (*ḫamšat*)
7. *sebe* (*sebet*)
10. *ešer* (*ešeret*)

Numbers are generally written in Cuneiform with numerals (i.e., wedges). They are rarely written out syllabically.

8.11 *The Syntax of the Cardinal Numbers* Numbers generally stand before the thing enumerated; for special emphasis, they can come after it. Only numbers 1 and 2 agree in gender with the thing enumerated:

ana ālim ištēn, in one city

ubānātum šitta, two fingers

With the numbers 3 to 10, a masculine form is used with a feminine substantive and *vice versa*:

marrātum sebe, seven gall bladders

erbet isūšu, four jawbones

The number 1 is used with the singular. The number 2, if it is masculine, generally appears in the dual, the feminine in the plural: *qarrādān šena*, two heroes; *ubānātum šitta*, two fingers. The numbers from 3 on are generally used with the plural. The numbers can, in certain combinations, also be used as substantives: šar erbettišu, to the four winds.

8.12 Multiple Numbers   The multiples like šenišu, two times, šalāšīšu, three times, erbišu, four times, hamšišu, five times, can be combined with ana or adi:

ana šalāšīšu, three times [lit., unto its three]

adi hamšīšu, five times

8.13 Ordinal Numbers   The ordinal numbers are treated like adjectives: E.g., mahrûm (f. mahrītum), first; šanûm (šanītum) second; šalšum (šaluštum) third; rebûm (rebūtum) fourth; hamšum (hamuštum) fifth.

ina sēlim rebîm, on the fourth rib

Cf. paradigm 12.

8.14 Particles   When the enclitic particle -ma serves to emphasize individual words it is then often best translated by "only."

šumma izbum īnšu ištiat-ma = if the aborted animal its eye is one = if the aborted animal has only one eye

To join sentences, in addition to the particle -ma, and, one may find u (generally written ù), and, moreover, however. One may also find -ma u, and also, and yet.

EXERCISES

P. 1. šum-ma ma-ra-tum šalaš.[1] 2. šum-ma ma-ra-tum hamiš.[1] 3. šumma re-eš bāb ekallim a-na še$_{20}$-ni-šu (a-na ša-la-ši-šu) pa-ṭe-er. 4. šumma sí-pi šu-me-el bāb ekallim a-na er-bi-i-šu pa-ṭe$_4$-er. 5.

šumma iz-bu-um er-be-et i-šú-šu. 6. šumma iz-bu-um i-in-šu[2] iš-ti-a-at-ma. 7. šumma iz-bu-um qá-qá-as-sú ka-ayya-nu-um ša-ki-in-ma ù iš-tu li-ib-bi pi-šu qá-qá-as-sú ša-nu-um wa-ṣi. 8. šumma sinništum ú-li-id-ma i-na ú-sú-uk-ki-šu ša šu-me-lim sú-mu na-di. 9. šumma a-mu-tum ša-ar er-bé-ti-ša še$_{20}$-pe-tim ma-li-a-at.

A. 10. ṣa-ab-tum ú-ṣi-i[3]. 11. šarram ši-bu-ut[4] a-li-šu i-na-sà-ḫu-šu. 12. aš-ša-at šar-ri-im zi-ka-ra-am ul-la-ad. 13. a-wi-lum ḫa-li-iq-ta-šu ú-ta-a[3]. 14. šēp na-aḫ-ra-ri-im, a-na na-aḫ-ra-ri tu-uṣ-ṣi. 15. ma-a-at nakrim bi-il-tam i-na-aš-ši-a-ku[5]. 16. a-mu-ut A-ku-ki ša ma-a-tum bi-il$_5$-tam iš-ši-a-šum. 17. ma-ri ši-ip-ri ma-aḫ-ru-ú-um bu-sú-ra-at ḫa-de-e-em na-ši-kum. 18. a-di-ra-at nakrim i-na li-ib-bi um-ma-ni-ya na-da-a. 19. wa-ši-ib ma-aḫ-ri-i-ka a-wa-ti-ka i-za-ab-bi-il. 20. wa-ṣi a-bu-ul-li-ya na-ak-rum i-da-ak. 21. ma-a-tum ka-lu-ú-ša a-na a-li-im iš-te-en i-pa-ḫu-ur.

O. 22. šumma martum ši-rum appa-ša im-še$_{20}$-ma re-sa ip-lu-uš-ma ú-ṣi; a-mu-ut Šar-ru-ki-in ša ek-le-tam il$_5$-li-ku-ma nu-ru-um ú-ṣi-aš-šu-um. 23. šumma re-eš martim na-we-er; ma-az-za-az ^{d}Ištar. 24. šum-ma mar-tum i-na[6] a-bu-ul-lim na-di-a-at; né-ku-úr-tum da-an-na-tum. 25. šumma martum kakkam ib-ni-ma šu-me-lam it-ṭù-ul; ka-al pa-ni-ka te-le-eq-qé-e. 26. šum-ma ma-ra-a-tum[7] sebe; šar kiššatim. 27. šum-ma šitta ma-ra-tum[7] ma-aṣ-ra-aḫ-ši-na[8] iš-te-en-ma; a-mu-ut sa-li-mi-im. 28. šum-ma i-na ṣe-li-im ša-al-ši-im ša šu-me-lim sú-mu-um na-di; e-ri-iš-ti im-me-ri-im. 29. šumma i-na ṣe-li-im re-bi-im ša šu-me-lim su-mu-um na-di; e-ri-iš-ti ni-qí-im. 30. šumma iz-bu-um ši-in-na-šu wa-ṣa-a; šarrum u$_4$-mu-šu ga-am-ru, i-na kussī-šu ša-nu-um uš-ša-ab.

1 2 3 4 5 6 7 8
3.2; 3.13; 0.22 (Remark), 0.23; 3.1 (Remark); 5.9; 0.31; 3.2; 0.32.

šalaš, šalāšat, three

hamiš, hamšat, five

ana šenīšu, twice

ana šalāšīšu, three times

ana erbīšu, four times

erbe, erbet, four

isum, jaw, jawbone

ištēn, istiat, one

-ma (emphatic particle), only, just

qaqqadum, head

kayyānum, normal

-ma u, and, moreover, but

pûm, mouth

waṣûm (wṣī), to go out, to go up, away

walādum (a/i), to give birth

usukkum, cheek

amūtum, liver, liver-sign, omen

šārum, wind, direction

šār erbettim, to the four directions

ṣabtum, captured, the captive

šībum, old

šībūtum, elders

zikarum, masculine, boy

halqum, haliqtum, lost

haliqtum, lost property

watûm (wtā), to find

nahrārum, help

biltum, tribute

našûm (nšī), to lift up, carry
Ventive: to bring

Akuki, personal name

adirātum (pl.), fear

ina libbi, in the midst of, in

wāšibum, the one sitting

mahar, before

mahrīka, before you

zabālum (i), to deliver, betray

wāṣûm, the one going out

kalum, the totality

mātum kalūša, the whole land

šīrum, tissue flesh

mašûm (mš'), to take away, to hide

palāšum (u), to break through, to penetrate

Šarrukīn, King of the dynasty of Akkad (2340-2284)

ekletum, greyness, darkness

nūrum, light

nawārum (i), to illumine

mazzāzum, place, position

dIštar, Ishtar

abullum, gate (also technical term for liver phenomenon)

banûm (bnī), to make, to produce, build

<u>šumēlam</u>, to the left

<u>naṭālum</u> (<u>a</u>/<u>u</u>), to look, to gaze

<u>kal</u> <u>pānīka</u>, all which lies before you

<u>sebe</u>, <u>sebet</u>, seven

<u>kiššatum</u>, world

<u>masṛahum</u>, beginning of bile-duct

<u>masṛah</u> <u>martim</u>, hepatic duct

<u>ṣēlum</u>, rib

<u>šalšum</u>, f. <u>šaluštum</u>, third

<u>erištum</u>, wish, desire

<u>immerum</u>, sheep, sacrificial sheep

<u>rebûm</u>, <u>rebūtum</u>, fourth

<u>šinnum</u> (f.), tooth

<u>šinnān</u> (dual), teeth

<u>wašābum</u> (<u>a</u>/<u>i</u>), to sit, dwell

Lesson 9

GRAMMAR

9.1 The Perfect Along with the Present and the Preterite, there is another prefix tense, the Perfect. This is used for the expression of past time according to the so-called sequence of tenses. In a conditional sentence (after *šumma*, if), it is often used with qualitative verbs in place of the Preterite:

šumma bāb ekallim irtapiš, if the palace gate has gotten wider

If a conditional sentence with a main verb in the Preterite or Stative has a second verb joined to it through the use of the enclitic *-ma*, this further verb is frequently expressed with the Perfect:

šumma martum isḫurma ubānam iltawe, if the gallbladder is curved and surrounds the finger...

9.2 The Perfect of the Tri-radical Verb The indication of the Perfect is the Infix *-ta-* (in Verbs with *e*-vocalization, it is *-te-*) which is inserted after the first root consonant. The vowel after the second consonant corresponds to the vowel of the Present:

ištakan, he has settled, from *šakānum* (*a*/*u*)

iktanuš, he has subjected, from *kanāšum* (*u*)

iqterib, he has drawn near, from *qerēbum* (*i*)

The second person singular has the prefix *ta-* (*te-*) *taštakan*, *teqterib*, etc. With forms that have endings, the vowel (which was originally found after the second root-consonant) disappears.

3 Ps. Pl. *ištaknū*, *ištaknā*

2 Ps. Pl. taštaknā

3 Ps. Sg. of the Ventive iqterbam

In the verbs I Aleph, with the dropping of the aleph which originally closed the syllable, the prefix vowel is lengthened (4.6):

ītakal (<°i'takal), he has eaten (2 Sg, tātakal, you have eaten)

īterub (<°i'terub), he has entered (2 Sg. tēterub, you have entered)

If the first consonant is ṣ, s, z, d or ṭ, then the t of the Perfect is assimilated:

iṣṣabat (<°iṣtabat), he has seized

iddūk (<°idtūk), he has killed

Cf. paradigms 16, 22, 23.

9.3 The Perfect of Bi-radical Verbs The formation of the Perfect of verbs which are III Vowel corresponds to that of the tri-radical verbs:

iktari, he (it) has become short(ened)

ilteqe, he has taken

In verbs which are II Vowel, the Perfect takes the root-vowel (of the Preterite) and the indication of the Perfect is -t- (and not -ta-).

ištīm, he has decided

iktūn, it has become established, firm

In verbs which are I n, the n is assimilated to t:

ittadin (<°intadin), he has given

In verbs which are I w, the Perfect is constructed from a secondary verb which has t instead of w as the root-augment (tbl instead of wbl):

ittabal, he has carried away

ittaṣi, he has come out (8.8)

In the verb wabālum, the Perfect is also built up by the addition of t to the bi-radical root:

itbal, he has brought, carried

Cf. paradigms 26, 28, 30 and 32.

9.4 *Verbs Ultimae Geminatae* [doubled final radical] Bi-consonantal roots with a short vowel between the two consonants can be made like a tri-consonantal root by the doubling of the second consonant. These are often called *Ultimae Geminatae* or *Mediae Geminatae*, i.e., verbs whose final radical or second radical is "twinned." There are *qualitative* verbs as:

danānum, to be strong

edēdum, to be pointed

raqāqum, to be thin, delicate

and a limited number of active verbs including:

ḫarārum (*i*), to plough

arārum (*u*), to tremble

pašāšum (*a*/*u*), to smear

malālum (*a*), to pillage

zanānum (*u*), to rain

9.5 *Conjugation of Verbs Ultimae Geminatae* It is very similar to that of the tri-radical verb. But the 3rd Ps. Sg. of the Stative is derived from the bi-consonantal form with the use of a long vowel:

dān, he is strong

ēd, it is pointed

The remaining Stative forms (those with endings) are formed according to the pattern of the tri-radicals:

dannat, she is strong

dannā, they (dual) are strong

In the active verbs, the Stative is:

ḫarer, *ḫarrat*, is ploughed

pašiš, *paššat*, is spread, smeared

9.6 Verbs *Mediae Aleph* Tri-radical roots with aleph as the middle radical, like *dâṣum* (*d'ṣ*), oppress; *bêlum* (*b'l*), to rule over; and *rêqum* (*r'q*), to depart, generally lose the aleph and form Present and Preterite analogously to the verbs *Mediae Vocalis* (7.2) either with *a* or with the *e*-vowel.

Present (*a*-class) *idâṣ*, he oppresses (pl. *idaṣṣū*)

Preterite *idāṣ*, *idāṣū*

Present (*e*-class) *irêq*, he departs (pl. *ireqqū*)

Preterite *ibēl*, he ruled over (pl. *ibēlū*)

The aleph of the *a*-class corresponds to $'_1$ or $'_2$, that of the *e*-class corresponds to $'_{3-5}$ (4.6).

Cf. paradigm 25.

9.7 The Verb *elûm* One verb which is I Aleph (*e*-class) and III vowel is *elûm* (*'li*), to ascend. Some of its forms are: the Present, *illi* (Ventive *illam*, he comes up here), the Preterite *īli*, and the Perfect *īteli*. The verbal adjective *elûm* is used chiefly with the meaning, the upper as opposed to *šaplûm*, the lower.

9.8 The Verb *išûm* One verb which is I *y* and III vowel is the defective verb *išûm*, to have. It is found in only one tense which is Preterite *in form*, but Stative in use. It is the so-called prefixed Stative:

īšu, he has

tīšu, you have

īšu, I have

Another verb, *rašûm*, to have or to obtain, serves as an (ingressive) Present and Preterite for *išûm*:

irašši, he will obtain

irši, he obtained

9.9 The Locative-adverbial With adverbs like *šaplānum*, below, and *elēnum*, above (when the mimation drops, these forms are *šaplānu* and *elēnu*), the endings -*u*(*m*) are not identical with the nominative ending but are vestiges of a case which has not otherwise lasted in Old-Babylonian (20.2) and here has locative meaning. The locative ending remains even if the word in the locative is joined as a preposition with a substantive (*elēnum abullim*, above the gate), or with a possessive suffix (*elēnušša* [<**elēnum-ša*] above it), or if a preposition precedes the locative-adverbial (*ana šaplānum*, toward below = downwards).

EXERCISES

P. 1. šumma bāb ekallim pa-ši-iš. 2. šumma ubānum i-na qá-ab-li-i-ša ḫa-ar-ra-at. 3. šum-ma mar-tum ap-pa-ša ki-ma ṣi-il-le-em e-ed[1]. 4. šum-ma mar-tum ki-ma zi-ib-ba-at ḫu-mu-uṣ-ṣí-ri-im da-an-na-at. 5. šumma martum ubānam il_5-wi-ma re-ša i-na bāb ekallim iš-ta-ka-an. 6. šumma bāb ekallim ir-ta-pi-iš. 7. šumma ubānum ir-ta-qí-iq. 8. šum-ma na-ap-la-ás-tum a-na pa-da-nim iq-te-er-ba-am. 9. šum-ma mar-tum it-be-e-ma mu-úḫ-ḫi ú-ba-ni-im iṣ-ṣa-ba-at. 10. šumma bāb ekallim a-na ni-ri-im[2] i-li. 11. šumma bāb ekallim ma-aš-ka-an-šu i-zi-im-ma a-na e-le-nu-um i-te-li-a-am. 12. šum-ma a-mu-tum iq-ru-ur-ma pi-iṭ-ra-am[3] ba-ba-am la i-šu ba-ab ekallim mar-tum ù ú-ba-nu-um la i-ba-aš-ši.

13. šum-ma mar-tum i-ši-is-sà a-na e-le-nu-um appa-ša a-na ša-ap-la-nu-um.

A. 14. i-na kakkim um-ma-nu-um i-ru-ur-ma kakkī-ša i-ta-ba-ak.

15. ša ṣe-ri-im ša li-ib-bi a-li-im i-da-a-aṣ. 16. a-li-ik ḫa-ar-ra-nim ḫa-ar-ra-nu-um a-na ḫa-ar-ra-nim i-na-di-šu, u_4-mu-šu i-re-eq-qú. 17. a-mu-ut [4] dŠul-gi ša A-pa-da-ra-aḫ i-ṇé-ru.

O. 18. šum-ma mar-tum it-be-e-ma it-ta-ší; ru-bu-ú-um i-na da-an-na-tim uṣ-ṣí. 19. šumma iz-bu-um ki-ma nēšim; a-mu-ut mNa-ra-am-dSîn ša ki-ša-tam i-bé-lu-ú[5]. 20. šum-ma mar-tum ik-ta-ri; na-ak-ru-um kussiam i-bé-el. 21. šum-ma mar-tum is-ḫu-ur-ma ú-ba-na-am il-ta-we-e; šar-ru-um ma-ta-am na-ka-ar-ta-am i-ṣa-ab-ba-at. 22. šumma ḫašûm imittam ú šumēlam ṣa-ar-pa-at; i-ša-a-tum i-li-a-am. 23. šumma e-le-nu-um bāb ekallim ši-lum na-di; ṣi-ḫi-iṭ ne-ši-im. 24. šumma i-na bāb ekallim zi-ḫu ṣa-bi-it-ma ù da-a-an; aš-qú-la-al ša-me-e-em.

[1] 3.13; [2] 0.31; [3] 0.34; [4] Personal name with divine determinative; [5] 7.4 (Remark).

pašāšum (a/u), to cover, paint, smear

ḫarārum, to plough, dig, hollow out

edēdum, St., to be pointed

zibbatum, tail

ḫumuṣṣīrum, rat

danānum (i), to be strong, solid

raqāqum (i), to be thin, weak

tebûm (tb'), to be raised up, to raise oneself

nīrum, yoke (also part of liver)

elûm (*'li*), to climb up, to direct oneself upwards

elēnum, above

ana elēnum, upwards

qarārum (*u*), to be wrapped up

piṭrum, cleft, gap

bābum, door, entryway, access

išûm (*yšu*), to have

bašûm (*baši*), to be present

šaplānum, below

ana šaplānum, downwards

arārum (*u*), to tremble

tabākum (*a*/*u*), to throw away, to pour out

ṣērum, desert, steppe

ša ṣērim, that of the desert, desert dweller (also collective)

ša libbi ālim, city dwellers (also collective)

dâṣum (*d'ṣ*), to oppress

ālik ḫarrānim, the traveller, one who goes to the (battle) field

rêqum (*r'q*), to be distant

Appa-Daraḫ, personal name

nêrum (*n'r*), to kill

bêlum (*b'l*), to master, rule

karûm (*krī*), to be short

imittam, left, toward the left

šiḫṭum, leap, attack

ašqulālum, stormcloud, whirlwind

Lesson 10

GRAMMAR

10.1 Verbal Stems The verbal root can be changed (and its meaning modified) through the use of prefixes and infixes and by the doubling of its middle radical. A number of stems then can be constructed from the roots so modified. In each stem there are the imperative (13.1), the four tenses and the nominal forms. All of the forms which have been treated up to now belong to the G-stem [from *Grundstamm*, basic stem], and they take as their base the unmodified verbal root. There are three other chief stems. [The terminology used below may be applied to a wide range of Semitic languages.] These other stems include the D-stem (which has doubling of the middle radical [11.1]). [The D-stem is a *factitive* stem, sometimes with *causative* overtones, sometimes with *intensive* overtones.] Another is the Š-stem which adds the prefix *š* (*a*) to the root (12.1). The third stem is the N-stem, a sort of passive (N, 10.2) in which the prefix *n* (*a*) is placed before the root.

10.2 The N-Stem The indication of the N-stem is the stem-prefix *n* (*a*). The N-stem serves (with active verbs) as a passive to the G-stem:

imaḫḫaṣ, he beats (Pres. G)

immaḫḫaṣ (<**inmaḫḫaṣ*, Pres. N), is beaten

Still, the N-stem is frequently used in a reciprocal sense:

> _immarū_ (Pres. G), they see, _innammarū_ (Pres. N), they see one another, they meet

> _emid_ (St. G), is supported by, _nenmudū_ (Pl. Masc. of St. N), they are supported by one another, they rest on one another

The N-stem of the Stative verbs can have ingressive meaning:

> _ibašši_ (Pres. G), it will be present, _ibbašši_, it will come to be present, it will result

Some verbs occur only in the N-stem:

> _nābutum_ (_'bt_), to flee
>
> _naplusum_, to look at

Cf. paradigms 21, 24, 27, 29, 31 and 33.

10.3 _The Formation of the Present and Preterite on the N-Stem_ The _n_ which is prefixed to the root in the N-stem assimilates to the first consonant. The prefixes of the 3rd and 2nd person are, as in the G-stem, _i-_ (1.4), and _ta-_ (in verbs with _e_-vocalization it is _te-_). (5.4-5.5) The Present is formed with doubling of the middle radical:

> _iššakkan_ (<*_inšakkan_), it will be set
>
> _taššakkan_, you will be set
>
> _iššakkanū_, _iššakkanā_, they will be set
>
> _taššakkanā_, you are set, you will be set

The Preterite is _iššakin_, was set (10.4).

In forms with vocalic endings (3rd and 2nd Pers. pl., Ventive, Subj.), the vowel after the second consonant disappears:

> _iššaknū_, _iššaknā_, they are placed

In verbs which are I Aleph the ' assimilates to an _n_:

> _innammar_ (<*_in'ammar_), it is seen, it will be seen
>
> _innamer_ (<*_in'amer_), it was seen

e-class:

inneddil, is closed, will be closed

innedil, was closed

Ventive and Subjunctive are, as in the G-stem, formed with the suffixes -*am*, -*nim* (5.7) and -*u* (7.4):

innasḫam (*innasiḫ* + *am*), was torn loose

ša iššaknūšum (*iššakin* + *u* + *šum*), on which it was laid

Many consonantal doublings of the type *dd*, *zz* can, in certain forms dissimilate to *nd*, *nz*. So the Pres. N of *edēlum* takes the form *innendil* along with *inneddil*, was closed.

Cf. paradigm 16.

10.4 Root Vowels in the N-Stem Verbs of the vowel-shift class (1.4) as *maḫārum* (*a/u*), receive, (G *immaḫḫar*, *imḫur*), form the Present N with *a*, the Preterite N with *i*.

immaḫḫar, it is received, will be received

immaḫer (4.4), was received

Also verbs of the *a*-class, as *maḫāṣum* (*a*) have *a* in the N Present and *i* in the N Preterite:

immaḫḫaṣ, is beaten

immaḫiṣ, was beaten

On the other hand, verbs of the *i*-class, as *parākum* (*i*), to bolt (G *ipparik*, *iprik*), have *i* in both the Preterite and Present N:

ipparrik, is bolted

ipparik, was bolted

10.5 The Formation of the Perfect of the N-Stem In contrast to the formation of the Perfect in G where the infix -*ta*- is inserted after the first root consonant (9.2), in the Perfect of n, the -ta- appears between the stem-indicator N and the root:

ittaškan (<*intaškan), is made

In verbs I Aleph, the n eventually becomes a part of the root;

ittanmar, was seen

ittenmid, was closed

The Perfect-N always has the same vowel as the N-Present:

ittamhar, has been received

ittaprik, was bolted

10.6 Nominal Forms and the Stative of the N-Stem   In the N-infinitive (which is identical in form with the Verbal Adjective N), and also in the Stative, na- (or ne-) appears before the verbal root. These forms show a u-vowel between the second and third consonant:

naškunum, to be set (Infin. N), set (Verb-Adj. N)

naškun, naškunat, has been set (Stative)

In verbs which are I Aleph, forms develop either through compensatory lengthening, once the aleph drops, or with a secondary nasalization:

nābutum (<*na'butum), to flee

but nanmurum, to be seen, to meet one another

The N-Stative occurs very rarely in active verbs, since the G-Stative already has a passive meaning. But an N-Stative is found in nābutum and in the verbs which have a reciprocal meaning in the N:

nābut, has fled

nenmudū, they have depended on one another

The verbal adjective N nanmurum is the prototype of the nominal formation nanmurtum, a meeting, appearance. The participle is formed with the prefix mu-:

mušš̌aknum (< *munšaknum), that which is placed, being made

munnabtum, the refugee, the exile

Cf. paradigms 21 and 24.

10.7 The N-Stem of the Bi-Radical Verb Like the triradical verbs, the verbs which are III vowel (6.2) form a Present and Perfect in which the theme [or root] vowel appears in the final syllable:

nabšûm (bšī), to come into being, result

Pres. ibbašši, it results

Perf. ittabši, it has resulted

neltûm (lt'), to be split

Pres. illette

naddûm (< *nandûm), to be thrown down

Pres. innaddi

Pl. innaddû, innaddiā (6.4)

The Preterite however is always constructed with i:

illeti, was split

innedi, was thrown

In the verbs which are Medial Vowel (7.2), the Present has the vocalization iddâk (< induak), he is killed.

The verbs which are I n (8.3) and I w (8.6) construct their N-stems as do the tri-radical verbs:

Pres. innaqqar, is destroyed; Preterite innaqer

Pres. iwwallad, is born; Preterite iwwalid

Cf. paradigms 27, 29, 31, 33.

10.8 The Plural in -ānū In some of the masculine substantives a plural in -ānū/-ānī is formed (along with plural in -ū/-ī). These are the so-called *individual plurals* whose function seems to be to stress the individuality of those making up the plurality.

šarrānū, a number of individual kings

šarrū, the kings (a totality)

ālānū (Nom.), *ālānī* (Gen.-Acc.), individual cities

ekkalum, palace, takes a feminine plural in -*ātum* (3.2) and a masculine plural in -*ānū*: *ekallānū*, *ekallānī*, individual palaces.

EXERCISES

P. 1. šumma mar-tum in-na-as-ḫa-am-ma i-na ba-ab ekallim ik-tu-un.

2. šum-ma šitta na-ap-la-sà-tum ṣe-el-lu-ši-na né-en$_6$-mu-du-ú.

A. 3. né-ku-ur-tu-um iš-ša-ak-ka-an. 4. i-ša-tum in-na-ap-pa-aḫ. 5. bu-ṭu-uq-tum ib-ba-at-ta-aq. 6. bi-it a-wi-lim i-sà-pa-aḫ[1]. 7. wa-ṣi a-bu-ul-li-ka it-ti nakrim ú-la in-na-mar. 8. ka-ab-tum in-na-bi-it. 9. šar-ru-um i-na li-bi é-kál-li-šu i-du-ak[1]. 10. āl šarrim i-la-wi[1] iṣ-ṣa-ba-at-ma in-na-qá-ar. 11. a-mu-ut Amar-^{d}Su'en-na ša še-nu-um a-na še-pi-im iš-ša-ak-nu-šum i-na ni-ši-ik še-ni-im i-mu-tu. 12. ku-ru-um i-ḫe-pe-e[1]. 13. a-lu-um a-na še$_{20}$-na il$_5$-le-te. 14. i-na ku-uṣ-ṣi ku-uṣ-ṣum ib-ba-aš-ši, i-na um-me-a-tim um-šum ib-ba-aš-ši. 15. ḫu-ša-ḫu-um ša ša-al-ma-tum[2] in-na-an-du-ú ib-ba-aš-ši-i. 16. zi-nu i-na ša-me-e iš-ša-aq-qá-lu. 17. šar-ra-nu i-na pu-uḫ-ri-im in-na-am-ma-ru. 18. a-la-nu-ka in-na-aq-qá-ru ti-la-nu in-na-ad-du-ú. 19. é-kál-la-ni qá-tum i-ka-ša-ad. 20. na-ak-rum a-na li-ib-bi a-li-i-ka i-te-bé-a-am-ma a-la-ni-i-ka i-ki-im-ma i-ta-ba-al. 21. šar-ru-um šar-ra-am i-na kakki i-da-ak-ma a-la-ni-šu na-wi-šu du-ra-ni-šu er-ṣe-es-sú ù ṭe-eḫ-ḫi-šu qa-as-sú-ú i-ka-aš-ša-ad.

0. 22. šumma iz-bu-um pa-ni barbarim ša-ki-in; mu-ta-nu da-an-nu-tum ib-ba-aš-šu ú a-ḫu-um a-na bi-it a-ḫi-im ú-ul i-ru-ub. 23. šum-ma mar-tum i-na qá-ab-li-ša ta-ar-ka-at; da-mu iš-ša-ak-ka-nu. 24. šum-ma mar-tum appa-ša da-ma-am la-pi-it; šukkalmaḫḫum im-ma-ḫa-aṣ. 25. šumma bāb ekallim li-pi-iš-tam ma-li; a-bu-ul-lum in-né-en-di-il, a-lum ma-ru-uš-tam i-mar. 26. šumma ubānum a-na i-mi-tim ka-mi-a-at; a-wi-lum i-na a-li-i-ka a-na ṣí-bi-it-tim in-na-ad-di. 27. šumma ḫašûm imittam ú šumēlam še$_{20}$-pa-an ša-ak-na; na-an-mu-ur-tum. 28. šumma warkat ḫašîm it-te-en$_{6}$-mi-id; sa-li-mu-um iš-ša-ka-an.

[1] 0.23; [2] 3.3 (Remark).

nasāḫum (a/u), to tear loose; N, to be torn loose

ṣellum = ṣēlum, rib, side

emēdum (i), to put, place, be in contact with; N, to depend on one another, to ally

šakānum (a/u), to set, establish; N, to be established, concluded, to break out (hostilities)

napāḫum (a/u), to blow, ignite; N, to be ignited, to break out (fire)

butuqtum, breach in a dam or dike

batāqum (a/u), to cut through; N, to break through

sapāḫum (a/u), to scatter; N, to be dissolved

amārum (a/u), to see; N, to be seen, appear

nābutum (N: i), N, to flee, run away

dâkum (dūk), to kill; N, to be killed

lawûm (lwī), to lock in, include, surround

ṣabātum (a), to seize; N, to be seized

naqārum (a/u), to destroy; N, to be destroyed

Amar-^{d}Su'enna, Amarsu'ena, King of the III dynasty of Ur (2045-2037)

niškum, bite

šēnum, shoe

ḫepûm (ḫpī), to smash; N, to be smashed

letûm (ltʾ), to split; N, to be split

ana šena neltûm, to be divided in two

kuṣṣum, winter, cold

bašûm (*bšī*), to be; N, to come into being, result

ummeātum, summer

umšum, heat

šalamtum, corpse

nadûm (*ndī*), to throw; N, to be thrown down

zinnum, downpour

šamû, *šamā'u*, heaven, the heavens

šaqālum (*a*/*u*), to weigh; N, to be weighed out, be scarce
to hang; N, to be hanged

puḫrum, gathering

tillum, heap of ruins, Tell

dūrum, wall, fortified settlement

ṭeḫḫûm (<**teḫḫium*), border territory

barbarum, wolf

mūtum, death

dāmu, blood, murder

šukkalmaḫḫum, grand vizier

maḫāṣum (*a*), beat; N, to be beaten

lipištum, pus, discharge

edēlum (*i*), lock; N, to be locked

kamûm (*kmī*), to bind, make fast

ṣibittum, prison

nanmurtum, a meeting

warkatum, back, reverse

Lesson 11

GRAMMAR

11.1 *The D-Stem* The indication of the D-stem (10.1) is the doubling of the second root-consonant. According to its function, the D-stem is generally *factitive*. It describes the bringing about of a state or process described in the G-stem:

> *ḫalāqum*, to disappear, to perish;
>
> *ḫulluqum* (Inf. D), to cause to disappear, to destroy
>
> *kanāšum*, to surrender;
>
> *kunnušum*, to make someone surrender
>
> *ṭiābum*, to be good;
>
> *ṭubbum*, to make good

Moreover, the D can frequently be used in place of the G without any real difference in meaning, especially if there is a plural element in the process or state [or even in the subject].

> *martum muḫḫuša takip*, the upperside of the gallbladder is spotted (Sg. of the Stative G), but
>
> *martum budāša tukkupā*, both sides of the gallbladder are spotted
>
> *paṭer*, it is split
>
> *puṭṭur*, it is split many times

11.2 *The Prefix Tenses of the D-Stem* The prefixes of the D-stem are (in opposition to the G and N-stem) *u-* for the third person singular and plural, and *tu-* for the second person. The root-vowel classes of G- (1.4) and N- (10.4) do not come into play here. The vowel after the doubled middle radical is *a* in the Present and *i* in the Preterite and Perfect; the vowel after the first consonant is a:

Pres. ukannaš, he conquers

tukannaš, you conquer

ukannašū, ukannašā, they conquer

tukannašā, you (pl.) conquer

Pret. ukanniš, he conquered

In the D Perfect, the infix -t- is inserted after the first consonant:

uktanniš, has conquered

In verbs which are I Aleph, u'a and u'e shift to u (4.6):

Pres. ussar (<*u'assar), to enclose, include

Pret. usser (<*u'esser) (4.4), he enclosed

Perf. ūtesser (<u'tesser), has enclosed (with compensatory lengthening of the prefix due to disappearance of the Aleph)

The third person of the Present and the Preterite of I Aleph verbs are consistently written (as Present G) with a vowel sign at the beginning of the word: ú-us-sa-ar, ú-us-se-er or ú-sa-ar (ussar) u-se-er (usser). Cf. paradigm 17.

11.3 The Nominal Forms and the Stative of the D-Stem In the D-infinitive (which is identical in form with the D-verbal-adjective), and in the D-Stative, the vowel is u both after the first consonant and after the second doubled consonant.

Inf. V.-Adj. kunnušum, oppress, oppressed

St. kunnuš, kunnušat, is oppressed

In verbs I Aleph:

ulluṣum, to bring to rejoicing (Inf. D from elēṣum, rejoice)

ulluṣ libbim, joy of the heart

The participle is formed with the prefix mu-:

<u>mukannišum</u>, the oppressor

[Note that elision of the theme vowel does not occur here (in contrast to N part.) since the preceding syllable is here closed and not (as in N) open.]

Cf. paradigms 21 and 24.

11.4 <u>Verbs Which are III Vowel in the D-Stem</u> In the verbs which are vocalic in the third radical the root vowel is replaced (as in the tri-consonantal verbs in the D-stem) by <u>a</u> in the Present, and <u>i</u> in the Preterite and Perfect.

Pres. <u>urabba</u>, he enlarges, makes great

Pret. <u>urabbi</u>

Perf. <u>urtabi</u>

Verbs final <u>e</u> (III') form the Present with <u>e</u>:

<u>uṭebbe</u>, to lower, let down, submerge

Pret. <u>uṭebbi</u>

Perf. <u>uṭṭebbi</u> (cf. 9.2)

With the addition of vocalic endings, contractions take place:

<u>urabbû</u> (<°<u>urabbaū</u>), <u>urabbâ</u> (<°<u>urabbaā</u>), they magnify

The Infinitive is <u>rubbûm</u>, to make great; the Stative <u>rubbu</u>, <u>rubbât</u>, is made great.

Cf. paradigm 3.3.

11.5 <u>Verbs mediae vocalis in the D-Stem</u> The doubling of the second consonant is possible in these verbs only when the verbs have endings. There is no difference here between verbs which are medial <u>ū</u> and those which are medial <u>ī</u>. The vowel of the Present is <u>a</u> and that of the Perfect is <u>i</u>.

Pres. *ukān*, he establishes

ukannū, *ukannā*, they establish

Pret. *ukīn*, *ukinnū*

Perf. *uktīn*, *uktinnū*

The Stative is *kūn*, *kunnat*, Inf. *kunnum*, Part. *mukinnum*

Cf. paradigm 31.

11.6 Verbs *Mediae Aleph* in the D-Stem   Verbs which are *Mediae Aleph* (e.g., *nêšum*, *n'š*, to live, to recover)(9.6) construct the Preterite of the D-stem in a manner corresponding to verbs which are medially vocalic:

unāš, he will bring to life

11.7 The Verbs I *n*, I *w* and Doubled Final Consonant in the D-Stem

In the D-stem, the verbs of these groups follow the model of the tri-consonantal verb:

wašārum, to be loose; *wuššurum*, to set loose; Pres. *uwaššar*

alālum (and *ḫalālum*), to hang, suspend; St. D *(ḫ)ullul*, is hung

Cf. paradigms 27 and 29.

11.8 The Irregular Verbs *izuzzum* and *itūlum*   The root of *izuzzum*, to stand, is **ziz*. It is enlarged through the addition of an *n* prefix.

Pres. (used as a Stative, 11.9) *izzaz* (<**inzaz*), he stands

tazzaz, you stand

Pret. *izziz*, he stood

Perf. *ittaziz*, he has stood

With the addition of vocalic endings, the *z* is doubled:

izzazzū, *izzazzā*, they stand

tazzizzā, you stood

mazzāz tazzazzu, the place (on) which you stand (7.5)

The root of _itūlum_, to lie, is _*tīl_ (with a _long_ vowel in opposition to _ziz_). It is also enlarged with an _n_.

Pret. _ittīl_, he lay down

Perf. _ittatīl_, he has lain down

11.9 _The Prefix Stative_ In some verbs, the Present or Preterite serves the function of the Stative and for that reason a special form for the Stative is not constructed:

išûm, to have (9.8); _īšu_, he has (Preterite in form)

izzuzzum, to stand (11.8); _izzaz_, he stands (Present in form)

and _kullum_ (root <_*kūl_), _ukāl_, is holding, holds (Present; this verb occurs only in the D-stem.)

From _kullum_, in addition to the prefixed Stative, only the Infinitive and the Participle are constructed:

mukillum, holding

mukīl rēš lemuttim, who assists in evil, = name of a demon

11.10 _The Anaphoric Pronoun_ As a personal pronoun, _šū_, he, serves for the third person masculine and _šī_, she, for the third person feminine; for the genitive and accusative, _šuāti_, him, and _šiāti_, her. _Šū_ is actually an _anaphoric_ pronoun and can be used as a substantive or as an attributive. In the latter case, _šū_ can be translated, the one mentioned, the one cited, or that one.

Nom. _mātum šī_, the land mentioned

Gen. _mātim šâti_ (<_*šiāti_), of the land mentioned

Acc. _mātam šâti_ (<_*šiāti_) the land mentioned

The plurals are _šunu_, feminine _šina_, they, the ones mentioned. The genitive-accusative is _šunūti_, _šināti_.

EXERCISES

P. 1. šumma ubān ḫa-ši qablītum i-mi-tam ù šu-me-lam šu-lu-ša pu-ṭù-ra-at. 2. šumma naplastum zi-iḫ-ḫi[1] ú-lu-la-at. 3. šum-ma i-na i-ši-id mar-tim pi-iṭ-ru-um ša-ki-im-ma[2] a-na zu-um-ri-ša ṭù-uḫ-ḫu. 4. šumma kakki i-mi-tim tu-ú-ur. 5. šumma bāb ekallim ka-ayya-nu-um ša-ki-in-ma ša-nu-um ú-ša-pi-il-ma warkat a-mu-tim ša-ki-in. 6. šumma bāb ekallim ka-ayya-nu-um ša-ki-im-ma ša-nu-um ú-ša-qì-ma e-le-nu[3] ša-ki-in. 7. šum-ma mar-tum is-ḫu-ra-am-ma šu-me-la-am iz-za-az. 8. šum-ma i-na a-mu-tim 4 na-ap-la-sà-tum iš-te-ni-iš iz-za-az-za. 9. šumma ubān ḫa-ši qablītum ma-aš-ka-an-ša i-zi-ba-am-ma i-na mu-uḫ-ḫi ubān ḫa-ši ša šu-me-li-im it-ta-zi-iz. 10. šum-ma mar-tum in-na-as-ḫa-am-ma ú-ba-na-am i-de-er-ma ù i-na ma-ayya-li-ša it-ta-ti-il.

A. 11. i-na ma-az-za-az ta-az-za-az-zu i-lum ú-ša-lam-ka. 12. bi-it a-wi-li is-sa-pa-aḫ, ša-nu šum-šu: mu-ki-il re-eš le-mu-ut-tim. 13. naker-ka ma-at-ka ú-ḫa-al-la-aq. 14. awīlum ṣú-mu-ra-at ú-ṣa-ma-ru qá-as-su i-ka-ša-ad. 15. ma-a-ru i-na bu-ul-ṭi a-bi-šu-nu bi-it a-bi-šu-nu ú-sà-ap-pa-ḫu. 16. ma-at na-ak-ri-im tu-sà-na-aq, a-ša-ar iš-te-en[4] tu-pá-ḫa-ar-ši. 17. šar-rum be-el te-re-ti-šu ú-ra-ab-ba. 18. a-gu-ú-um i-te-eb-bé-a-am e-le-pa-tim ú-ṭe-bé. 19. ra-ki-ib i-me-ri nakram ú-ta-ar. 20. a-lam ta-ṣa-ab-ba-at ša-al-la-su tu-wa-aš-ša-ar. 21. ú-lu-uṣ li-bi, aš-ša-at a-wi-lim zi-ka-ra-am ú-la-ad. 22. šēp awīlim idi ilim ú-ul wu-šu-ra-at. 23. ma-tum ši-i in-na-an-di[5]. 24. bi-ša-am ša ma-tim ša-a-ti ma-tum ša-ni-tum i-ta-ab-ba-al.

O. 25. šumma bāb ekallim sú-un-nu-uq; i-na kakkim nakrum um-ma-nam ú-sà-ar, u_4-ma-am re-qá-a-am šattammū ekallam ú-sà-na-qú. 26. šumma iz-bu-um up-pu-uq; a-mu-ut I-bi-^{d}Sîn, ša-aḫ-lu-uq-tum. 27.

šum-ma mar-tum li-pi-a-am ku-us-sà-a-at; ku-ṣú-um i-ba-aš-ši-i. 28. šum-ma mar-tum mu-uḫ-ḫa-ša ta-ki-im-ma ṣa-ri-ip; mi-qi-it-ti bārîm. 29. šum-ma mar-tum bu-da-ša tu-ku-pa-a-ma ṣu-ur-ru-pa; mi-qí-it-ti ra-ša-ši-im. 30. šumma kakki i-mi-it-tim iz-zi-iz; ka-ab-tu-um ša li-ib-bi be-li-šu ú-ṭa-ab-bu-ú ib-ba-aš-ši. 31. šumma iz-bu-um pa-ni nēšim ša-ki-in; šarrum da-an-nu-um ib-ba-aš-ši-ma ma-tam ša-ti ú-na-aš. 32. šum-ma mar-tum ši-ši-ta-am ú-ka-al; a-na be-el im-me-ri-im mu-ur-ṣà-am ú-ka-al.

[1] 6.10; [2] 6.11 (Remark); [3] 9.9; [4] 8.9; [5] 10.3 (Remark).

šulušā, three times

paṭārum (a/u), to split

alālum, to hang (intr.); D, to hang (trans.)

zumrum, body

teḫûm (tḫī), to be near; D, to cause to draw near

târum (tūr), to return; D, to turn back, to beat back (enemies)

warkat, behind

šapālum, to be under, subject; D, to go downwards

šaqûm (šqū), to be high; D, to go upwards

izuzzum, to stand, to step

edērum (i), to embrace, to hug

mayyālum, bed

itūlum, to lie

mazzāzum, place

šalāmum (i), to be well; D, to keep well, to make well

kullum (kūl), to hold, to hold fast

mukillum, the one holding

rēšam kullum, to hold the head, to assist, support

lemnum f., lemuttum, evil

lemuttum, evil (n)

mukīl rēš lemuttim, one who assists evil (name of a demon)

ḫalāqum (i), to perish; D, to destroy

ṣummurātum = ṣummirātum (pl.), wish, longing, desire

ṣummurum, to strive for

sapāḫum (a/u), to scatter; D, to scatter

sanāqum, to be narrow; D, to make narrow, to control

ašar ištēn, in one place = in that place

paḫārum, to assemble; D, to gather (trans.)

tērtum, commission, instruction

bēl tērētim, deputy, delegate

rabûm (rbī), to be great; D, to make great

agûm, flood

ṭebûm (ṭb'), to drop; D, to drop, cause to drop

rākibum, the rider

rākib imēri, the donkey rider, band of donkey riders

wašārum, to be loose; D, to set loose, to lead (booty) away

elēṣum, to be happy, rejoice; D, to make happy

ulluṣum, jubilation

idum, arm, side

idi, at, to the side of

šū, šī, he, she, the one mentioned

esērum, to enclose; D, to enclose

ūmam rēqam, of a distant day, in the future

epēqum (i), to embrace; D, to overgrow, to grow together

Ibbi-^{d}Sîn, Ibbi-Sîn, King of the III Dynasty of Ur (2027-2003)

šaḫluqtum, destruction

kasûm (i), to bind; D, to overgrow

bārûm (*bārium), seer, diviner

ṣarāpum, to color red; D, to color red

būdum, shoulder, side

rašāšum (a functionary)

tiābum, to be good; D, to do good

nêšum (n'š), to be alive; D, to bring to life

šišītum, membrane

bēl immērim, owner of the sacrificial animal

murṣum, sickness

Lesson 12

GRAMMAR

12.1 <u>The Š-Stem</u> The indicator of the Š-stem (10.1) is the root-prefix <u>š(a)</u>. According to its function, the Š-stem is causative. It expresses the bringing about or the causing of a process whose fulfillment is described in the G-stem.

<u>maqātum</u>, to fall; <u>šumqutum</u> (inf. Š), to let fall, to make fall

<u>waṣûm</u>, to come out; <u>šuṣûm</u>, to lead out, to bring out

In the Stative verbs, the Š-stem is <u>factitive</u> like the D-stem.

<u>ešērum</u>, to be in order; <u>šūšurum</u>, to bring into order

12.2 <u>The Prefix Tenses of the Š-Stem</u> The prefixes are (as in the D-stem) <u>u</u>-for the third person and <u>tu</u>-for the second person. <u>Ša</u> is inserted between the prefix and the root. In e-class I Aleph verbs it is <u>še</u> that is inserted. The vowel after the middle root consonant is <u>a</u> in the Present and <u>i</u> in the Preterite and Perfect. The Perfect inserts the infix -<u>t</u>- after the <u>š</u> of the stem-prefix.

Pres. <u>ušamqat</u>, he lets fall

<u>tušamqat</u>, you let fall

<u>ušamqatū</u>, <u>ušamqatā</u>, they let fall

<u>tušamqatā</u>, you (pl.) let fall

Pret. <u>ušamqit</u>, he caused to fall

Perf. <u>uštamqit</u>, he has caused to fall

In verbs which are I Aleph, the aleph is assimilated to the middle consonant:

<u>ušallak</u> (<°<u>uša'lak</u>), he causes to go

<u>ušerreb</u> (<°<u>uše'reb</u>), he causes to enter

In the Preterite and Perfect the disappearance of an aleph which had closed a syllable leads to compensatory lengthening (4.6):

<u>ušālik</u> (<°<u>uša'lik</u>), he caused to enter

<u>uštērib</u> (<°<u>ušte'rib</u>), he has caused to enter

Cf. paradigm 17.

12.3 <u>The Nominal Forms and the Stative of the Š-Stem</u> In forms which are otherwise without prefixes, the root-prefix of the Š-stem is <u>šu</u>. The Š-infinitive (which is identical in form with the verbal-adjective) and the Š Stative, insert the vowel <u>u</u> after the middle root-consonant:

<u>šumqutum</u>, to cause to fall, (inf.), having caused to fall, (verb adj.)

<u>šumqut</u>, <u>šumqutat</u>, has been caused to fall

In verbs I Aleph (and I <u>y</u>, 4.8) with compensatory lengthening:

<u>šūšurum</u>, to bring into order

<u>šūšur</u>, <u>šūšurat</u>, has been brought into order

The participle is formed with <u>mu-</u>:

<u>mušamqitum</u>, the one felling, laying low

Cf. paradigms 21 and 24.

12.4 <u>Verbs Final Vowel in the Š-Stem</u> Verbs which are Final Vowel correspond in the Š-stem to the tri-radical verbs. As in the D-stem (11.4) the root vowel is replaced by <u>a</u> in the Present and by <u>i</u> in the Preterite and Perfect:

Pres. <u>ušamla</u>, he fills

Pret. <u>ušamli</u>, he filled

Perf. u<u>š</u>tamli, has filled

Verbs which are III e (III ʾ) form the Present with e:

ušepte, has opened; Pret. ušepti; Perf. uštepti

With the addition of vocalic endings, contractions take place:

ušamlû (< *ušamliaū), they fill

The Infinitive is šumlûm, to fill, the Stative šumlu, šumlât, is filled. From waṣûm, to go out (8.8), the Present of the Š-stem is formed, ušeṣṣe, he leads out, the Preterite ušēṣi, and the Perfect uštēṣi. (12.7) The verbal adjective is šūṣûm, the one exiled. Cf. paradigm 33.

12.5 Verbs mediae vocalis in the Š-Stem Differing from the tri-radical verb, verbs which are medial vocalic take the root prefix š in the Š-stem (and not ša), (ušamīt > ušmīt)

Pres. ušmāt, he lets die, he causes to die

Pret. ušmīt

Perf. (with insertion of -ta-) uštamīt

In forms with vocalic ending (as in the D-stem), the second consonant is doubled and the preceding vowel is shortened:

ušmattū, they let die, they cause to die

ušmittū, they caused to die

Inf. šumūtum, to have killed

Cf. paradigm 31.

12.6 Verbs Primae n in Š-Stem The formation of the Š-stem of verbs which are I n corresponds to the tri-radical verbs but the n is assimilated in all forms:

Pres. ušaqqar (< *ušanqar), he has (someone) destroy

Pret. _ušagger_ (*_ušanger_)

Perf. _uštagger_

Inf. _šuggurum_

nadûm (_ndī_) forms the Š-stem in a normal fashion (for III vocalic) (12.4):

Pres. _ušadda_, he has (someone) throw

Pret. _ušaddi_

Perf. _uštaddi_

ša libbīša uštaddīši = that of her womb he had caused her to reject = he had caused her abortion

Cf. Paradigm 27.

12.7 _Verbs I w in the Š-Stem_ Verbs I _w_ form their Š-stem from the bi-consonantal root (_bil_). In the Present, there is a doubling of the first consonant. In the Preterite and Perfect, there is a lengthening of the vowel before the first consonant:

Pres. _ušabbal_, he has (someone) carry

Pret. _ušābil_

Perf. _uštābil_

Stat. _šūbul_, is caused to carry

Some verbs I _w_ are treated in the Š-stem as though they were members of the I _y_ group, whose formation is identical with I Aleph verbs of the _e_-class. E.g., from _wašābum_, to settle, is derived the Pres. _Š_ _ušešše b_, he has (someone) take up a position. The Pret. is ušēšib and the Perfect _uštēšib_.

Similarly handled in the Š-stem is _waşûm_, to go out (12.4).

One must be careful not to confuse _šūbulum_ (Š for _wbl_) and the irregularly constructed forms of the Š-stem from _abālum_, to be dry:

Stat. šābul, is dried up

V. Adj. šābulum, dried up

Cf. Paradigm 29.

EXERCISES

P. 1. šumma i-na ma-aṣ-ra-aḫ martim zi-ḫu na-di-ma me-e la ú-še$_{20}$-e-ṣi. 2. šumma a-na bāb ekallim zi-iḫ-ḫu šu-ru-ub-ma qá-aq-qá-ar-šu a-ki-il. 3. šum-ma mar-tum šu-me-el-ša da-ma-am ša-bu-la-am pa-ši-iš.

A. 4. nakrum ma-tam ú-ša-am-qa-at. 5. ma-at nakrī-ka tu-ša-am-qa-at. 6. nakrum ú-še$_{20}$-re-ba-am-ma i-na lib-bi ma-ti-ka ša-la-tam ú-še$_{20}$-eṣ-ṣe-e. 7. ša-al-la-at ta-ša-al-la-lu ú-la tu-še-ṣe. 8. um-ma-an na-ak-ri-im i-te-eb-bé-am-ma ša-al-la-at be-el im-me-ri u-še$_{20}$-eṣ-ṣe. 9. wa-ši-ib ekallim pi-ri-iš-tam ú-še-eṣ-ṣe. 10. ra-bí-a-na i-na a-li-šu ú-še$_{20}$-ṣú-ú-šu.

O. 11. šumma bāb ekallim šu-ú-šu-ur; a-na ḫarrānim šu-ul-mu-ú-um[1].
12. šumma šena bāb ekallim ša-nu-um i-na i-mi-tim ša-ki-in; na-ak-rum ma-tam ú-ša-da. 13. šum-ma pa-da-nu-um ša-ki-in; i-lum ki-bi-is a-wi-lim ú-še-še-er.

READING PASSAGE (from Hammurabi's Code)

1. šum-ma a-wi-lum i-na ḫar-ra-nim wa-ši-ib-ma kaspam ḫurāṣam abnam ù bi-iš qá-ti-šu a-na a-wi-lim id-di-in-ma a-na še$_{20}$-bu-ul-tim ú-ša-bíl-šu, a-wi-lum šu-ú mi-im-ma ša šu-bu-lu a-šar šu-bu-lu la id-di-in-ma it-ba-al; be-el še$_{20}$-bu-ul-tim a-wi-lam šu-a-ti i-na mi-im-ma ša šu-bu-lu-ma la id-di-nu ú-ka-an-šu-ma a-wi-lum šu-ú adi ḫamšī-šu mi-im-ma ša in-na-ad-nu-šum a-na be-el še$_{20}$-bu-ul-tim i-na-ad-di-in.
2. šum-ma aš-ša-at a-wi-lim aš-šum zi-ka-ri-im ša-ni-im mu-sà uš-di-ik; sinništam šu-a-ti i-na ga-ši-ši-im i-ša-ak-ka-nu-ši.

[1] O.22.

3. šum-ma a-wi-lum mārat a-wi-lim im-ḫa-aṣ-ma ša li-ib-bi-ša uš-ta-di-ši; 10 šiqil kaspam[1] a-na ša li-ib-bi-ša i-ša-qal. šum-ma sinniš-tum ši-i im-tu-ut; māras-sú i-du-uk-ku.

waṣûm (wṣī), to go out; Š, to bring out, to lead out, to betray

erēbum (u), to enter; Š, to cause to enter, to penetrate

qaqqarum, ground, earth

akālum (a/u), to eat, to devour

šābulum, dried up

maqātum (u), to fall; Š, to bring to a fall

šalālum (a), to plunder, to take booty

pirištum, secret

rabiānum, leading citizen of a town, mayor

ešērum (i), to be in order; Š, to bring into order

šulmum, (salvation) good health, safety

nadûm (ndī), to throw (away); Š, to cause to be thrown away

kibsum, step, track, walk, gait, path

1 14.12.

Lesson 13

GRAMMAR

13.1 The Imperative of the G-Stem   The imperative corresponds to the root in its simplest form, i.e., to the Preterite without a prefix (1.4), e.g., in *šiāmum*, determine

Pret. *išīm*, he determines

Root **šīm*

2nd Pers. Sg. M. of the imperative: *šīm*, determine!

The second person singular F. has the ending -*ī*:

šīmī, determine!

In the plural there is only one form, used for both genders; it is developed with a long *ā*.

šīmā, determine!

13.2 Formation of G-Imperatives for Tri-Consonantal Verbs   Between the first and the second root consonant a helping vowel is inserted which corresponds to the root-vowel. In verbs which are I Aleph (4.6), this vowel, after the dropping of the aleph, becomes *a* in verbs of the a-class and *e* in verbs of the e-class:

Inf.	Pret.	Root	2nd Sg. Masc. Imperative G
ṣabātum (*a*)	*iṣbat*	**ṣbat*	*ṣabat*, grasp!
kanāšum (*u*)	*iknuš*	**knuš*	*kunuš*, yield!
ṣarāmum (*i*)	*iṣrim*	**ṣrim*	*ṣirim*, strive!
parāsum (*a/u*)	*iprus*	**prus*	*purus*, decide!
apālum (*a/u*)	*īpul*	**'pul*	*apul* (<**'upul*), appease!
alākum (*a/i*)	*illik*	**'lik*	*alik* (<**'ilik*), go!
erēbum (*u*)	*īrub*	**'rub*	*erub* (<**'urub*), enter!

Cf. paradigms 18 and 23.

13.3 The Formation of the Imperative of the Bi-Consonantal Verbs in G

Like the tri-consonantal verbs, the verbs III vocalic (6.2) form their imperative with a helping vowel which corresponds to the root vowel. In verbs which are final *e* (III ʼ) an *e* is inserted:

qabûm	*iqbi*	*°qbī*	*qibi*	speak!
manûm	*imnu*	*°mnū*	*munu*	count!
leqûm	*ilqe*	*°lqʼ*	*leqe*	take!

With verbs that are medially vocalic (7.1) the simplified root forms the imperative. Verbs which are medial aleph (9.6) take the vowel *ā* or *ē* in the imperative:

šiāmum	*išīm*	*°šīm*	*šīm*	determine!
zâzum	*izūz*	*°zūz*	*zūz*	divide!
bêlum	*ibēl*	*°bʼl*	*bēl*	rule!
šâmum	*išām*	*°šʼm*	*šām*	buy!

In roots which are amplified with the root augment *w* (I *w* 8.5), the imperative is formed from the unaugmented root. On the other hand, in roots which are augmented with *n* (I *n* 8.2), a vowel corresponding to the root-vowel is placed before the root and thus forms the imperative:

wabālum (*a*/*i*)	*ūbil*	*°bil*	*bil*	bring!
nadānum (*i*)	*iddin*	*°din*	*idin*	give!
nasāḫum (*u*)	*issuḫ*	*°suḫ*	*usuḫ*	remove!

The imperative of *izuzzum*, to stand (11.8) is *iziz*, step along!

Cf. paradigms 25, 26, 28, 30, 33.

13.4 The G-Imperative with Vocalic Endings

With the addition of

the endings ī and ā (13.1) and the Ventive ending -am, the root vowel disappears from tri-consonantal verbs and from verbs which are I w:

sabat, seize! sabtī, seize! sabtā, take up!

šupram, send here! šuprānim, send here! (pl.)

idnam, give here!

For the remaining groups of verbs:

qibiā, speak!

zūzā, share!

bilam, bring here!

Cf. paradigm 18.

13.5 The Precative As a substitute for the imperative in the third person (he ought to...), the Precative is used. It is formed by substituting li for the prefix i- or u- of the third person of the Preterite:

isbat, he lay hold of; lisbat, let him lay hold of!

lisbatū, lisbatā, may they lay hold of!

ublam, he brought here (8.6); liblam, may he bring here!

uballitū, they maintained life; liballitū, may they maintain life!

Cf. paradigm 19.

13.6 Prohibition A negative command in the second person is expressed with lā, not (5.10), and the Present:

Imp. idin, give!, but the Prohibitive, lā tanaddin, do not give,

lā tanaddinā, you shall not give

lā tazâz, do not share!; lā tazuzzā, you (pl.) shall not share! (7.2)

13.7 The Plural of abum and ahum The nouns abum, father, and ahum, brother, form their plurals with a doubling of the root consonant:

abbū, fathers; Gen.-Acc. *abbī*

aḫḫū, *aḫḫī*, brothers

13.8 *Triptotic Declension of Nouns With Suffixes* The greater portion of nouns have a *diptotic* declension when joined with possessive suffixes (3.7, 13.9); i.e., they admit of only two cases (3.8).

Nom. and Acc. *ummānka*, your army

Gen. *ummānīka*, of your army

Several bi-consonantal nominal roots, e.g., *bīšūm*, property, *ṣābum*, soldier, *mārum*, son, *abum*, father, *aḫum*, brother, and *kalum*, totality, have a *triptotic* declension with the possessive suffixes; they distinguish Nominative (*u*), Genitive (*i*) and Accusative (*a*).

abūka, your father; *abīka*, of your father; *abāka*, your father (acc.)

mātum kalūša = the land, its totality = the whole land

bīšāšina, their property (acc.)

ṣābāka, your army

Cf. paradigm 5.

13.9 *The Possessive Suffixes* The suffix of the first person singular -*ya*, my, changes to *'a* if it is preceded by a nominative plural ending of *ū* or *û*:

rēdû'a (<*rēdiū* + *ya*), my soldiers

To the suffixes which were treated earlier (3.7) may now be added -*kunu*, -*kina*, your, -*ni*, our, and the suffix for the second person singular feminine, -*ki*:

bēlkunu, *bēlkina*, your master

bēlīni, of our master

Cf. paradigm 9.

13.10 Pronominal Suffixes with the Verb   In addition to the Accusative suffixes already mentioned (5.8), there are:

-šunūti, šināti, them

-kunūti, -kināti, you

-ni, me

-niāti, us

and also the Dative suffixes:

-šunūšim, -šināšim, to them

-kunūšim, -kināšim, to you

-nim, to me

-niāšim, to us

The Dative suffixes generally occur with the Ventive (5.9):

(iknukanniāšim) (iknuk + am + niāšim) = he has sealed to us = through a sealed document he has allotted to us

Only the first person singular, -ni of the Accusative suffixes is regularly used with the Ventive:

ulammidanni (ulammid + am + ni), he informed me, he makes me know, he teaches me

ulammidūninni (ulammidū + nim + ni), they informed me

Cf. paradigms 9 and 20.

13.11 The First Person in the G- and N-Stems   The prefix of the first person singular is a-, that of the first person plural is ni-. The first person plural has no ending:

iṣbat, he seized; taṣbat, you seized; aṣbat, I seized

iṣbatū, iṣbatā, they seized; taṣbatā, you seized; niṣbat, we seized

aqabbi, I said; niqabbi, we said; Pret. aqbi; Perf. aqtabi

ammahhaṣ, I was beaten; nimmahiṣ, we were beaten

In the e-class of I Aleph verbs, the first person singular of the Preterite is ērub, I entered; of the Present errub, I enter. In Cuneiform, ērub is not distinguished from erub (13.2). Both are written e-ru-ub. The first person plural in the Preterite is nīrub, we entered, Present nirrub, Perfect nīterub.

The verbs which are final e (III ʾ) form the first person singular with e.

eleqqe, I take; Pret. elqe; Perf. elteqe

Cf. paradigms 14-16, 22, 23.

13.12 The First Person in the D- and Š-Stem and in Verbs Which are I w

In the D- and Š-stem (and in verbs which are I w in the Present and Preterite of the G-stem) the prefixes of the first person singular are u-(as in the third person) and the first person plural nu-:

ukanniš, I yielded or he yielded

nukanniš, we yielded

ušamqat, I cause to fall or he causes to fall

nušamqat, we cause to fall

ubbal, I bring or he brings

nubbal, we bring

Pret. ūbil, nūbil, but (Perf.) (9.3) attabal, nittabal

Cf. paradigms 17 and 28.

13.13 The Infinitive as Object

The accusative of the infinitive can serve as the object of a transitive verb:

mimma nudunnâm...turram niqbi = we have commanded the whole dowry to be given back

13.14 The Temporal Conjunction kīma

The preposition kīma, as,

can also be used as a conjunction with the meaning, as soon as, if, when, to introduce subordinate clauses. The verb of such a clause is in the subjunctive:

kīma unnedukkī tammarū, as soon as you read my letter

13.15 The Universal Relative mala After mala, as much as, so much as..., the verb stands in the subjunctive (as after ša):

eqlum mala ina qātīšunu ibaššû, as much land as is in their hands

13.16 The Old-Babylonian Letter Format The letter begins with the naming of the addressee. The formula ana NN qibīma, to so-and-so, speak! is addressed to the scribe who reads the letter out loud to the addressee. There follows the declaration of the letter-writer: umma NN -ma, thus speaks so-and-so. Formulas of blessing are found in letters to superiors and equals. They are not found in letters of superiors to subordinates. The blessings generally take the form: dŠamaš liballiṭka, may Šamaš preserve you in life! Quotations from a third party are specially emphasized as through the formula: kīam ulammidanni, so does so-and-so inform me. Such a phrase can come before or after the quotation.

EXERCISES

P. 1. šumma bāb ekallim ta-ri-ik-ma ù ši-it-ta ú-ba-na-ti-ya a-na libbim ub-ba-al.

A. 2. ša-al-la-at a-ša-al-la-lu dAdad i-ra-aḫ-ḫi-iṣ. 3. a-ḫu-um a-ḫa-šu i-da-ak. 4. a-pi-il šar-ri-im a-ba-šu i-da-ak-ma kussi a-bi i-be-el. 5. te-eš-mu-um, ṣa-ba-a-ka ša a-na ke-er-ri-im ta-ṭa-ra-du it-ti nakrim in-na-am-ma-ar. 6. ni-šu bi-ša-ši-na a-na ma-ḫi-ri-im ú-še-ṣe-a. 7. re-du-a a-na ekallim i-ir-ru-bu.

wabālum (*a*/*i*), to bear, carry

ana libbim wabālum, to bring in, to fit in

tešmûm, favorable hearing, concession

ṣābum, group of people, troop

kerrum, campaign

ṭarādum (*a*/*u*), to send, dispatch

maḫīrum, value, price

rēdûm (<°*rēdium*), soldier

READING PASSAGE (Old-Babylonian Letters)

1. a-na ^{d}Šamaš-ḫa-ze-er qí-bí-ma; um-ma Ḫa-am-mu-ra-pí-ma: ^{m}Ī-li-i-qí-ša-am nārum rakbûm ki-a-am ú-lam-mi-da-an-ni: um-ma šu-ú-ma: ^{md}Sîn-īriš ù Ap-lum aḫ-ḫi a-bi-ya eqlī ib-ta-aq-ru-ni-in-ni. ki-a-am ú-lam-mi-da-an-ni. - wa-ar-ka-tam pu-ru-ús-ma eqlam ma-la i-na qá-ti-šu-nu i-ba-aš-šu-ú mi-it-ḫa-ri-iš zu-us-sú-nu-ši-im[1].

2. a-na ^{d}Šamaš-ḫa-ze-er ^{md}Sîn-mu-ša-lim ù tap-pé-šu-nu qí-bí-ma! um-ma Ḫa-am-mu-ra-pí-ma: ^{lú}e-di-ku^{meš} ki-a-am ú-lam-mi-du-ni-in-ni: um-ma šu-nu-ma[2]: i-na eqlim ša be-el-ni ik-nu-ka-an-ni-a-ši-im 6 būr qá-qá-ad eqlī-ni ^{d}Šamaš-ḫa-ze-er ù tap-pu-šu i-ki-mu-ni-a-ti-ma pu-ḫa-am a-šar-ša-ni eqlam ú-ka-al-lu-ni-a-ši-im. ki-a-am ú-lam-mi-du-ni-in-ni. a-na mi-nim qá-qá-ad eqlī-šu-nu te-el-qé-a-ma a-šar-ša-ni eqlam ta-ad-di-na-šu-nu-ši-im? ka-ni-kam ša ak-nu-ku-šu-nu-ši-im am-ra-ma a-na pi-i ka-ni-ki-im-ma šu-a-ti eqlam id-na-šu-nu-ši-im. eqlam[3] a-šar-ša-ni la ta-na-ad-di-na-šu-nu-ti.

3. a-na ^{d}Šamaš-ḫa-zèr qí-bí-ma! um-ma Awīl-^{d}Nin-urta-ma: ^{d}Šamaš li-ba-al-li-iṭ-ka! aš-šum eqil ^{md}Šum-ma-ilum ša ^{m}Ra-bi-^{d}Sataran ṣa-ab-tu, eqlam a-na kaspim i-ša-am.....ki-ma un-ne-du-uk-ki ta-am-ma-ru eqlam

ša-a-ti a-na Ra-bi-[d]Sataran-ma i-di-in! a-li-ik, i-na-an-na aš-pu-ra-ak-ku, ṣi-ri-im-ma a-pu-ul-šu!

4. a-na Mu-ḫa-ad-du-um qí-bí-ma! um-ma dayyānū Bābili-ma: [d]Šamaš ù [d]Marduk li-ba-al-li-ṭú-ku-nu-ti! aš-šum di-nim ša [m]Ìl-šu-i-bi-šu mār Warad-[d]Sîn ù [m]Ma-at-ta-tum[4]: a-wa-ti-šu-nu ni-mu-ur: di-nam ki-ma ṣi-im-da-at be-li-ni nu-ša-ḫi-is-sú-nu-ti-ma mi-im-ma nu-du-un-na-a-am ša [m]Ma-at-ta-tum a-na ma-ar-ti-ša id-di-nu-ma a-na bīt Ìl-šu-i-bi-šu ú -še-ri-bu-ši a-na Ma-at-ta-tum tu-ur-ra-am ni-iq-bi; rēdâm it-ti-ša ni-iṭ-ṭar-dam[5], mi-im-ma ba-al-ṭá-am ša i-na-an-na in-na-aṭ-ṭa-lu a-na Ma-at-ta-tum li-id-di-nu.

[1] 5.8; [2] 11.10; [3] accusative of attraction, with respect to the field; [4] 0.20;

[5] *niṭṭardam*, assimilation of *t* to *ṭ* (14.9).

Lesson 14

GRAMMAR

14.1 The -*ta*-Infix as a Stem Modification Alongside its function in the formation of the Perfect tense (9.1), the -*ta*- infix may be used to modify the stem itself. Thus, beside the chief stems (the *G*, *D*, and Š), there is another group of stems: those which are formed through modification of these chief stems by the infix *t*. Thus are formed the *Gt*, *Dt*, and *Št*. Like the chief stems, these too form all the tenses, nominal forms, and the imperative.

14.2 The Gt-Stem The *Gt* is largely used in a reciprocal sense:

> *maḫāṣum*, to beat; *mitḫuṣum*, to fight with one another (*Gt* infin.)
> *akālum*, to eat; *atkulum*, to devour one another
> *ṣabātum*, to seize; *tiṣbutum* (14.8), to touch one another
> *iṭṭul*, he looked at; *ittaṭlū*, they looked at one another

In other verbs, the *Gt* stem has the meaning, to do something in perpetuity. This meaning is particularly common with verbs of motion:

> *alākum*, to go; *atlukum*, to go forever, to depart
> *uṣṣi*, he goes out; *ittaṣṣi* (14.6), he draws forth
> *irrub*, he enters; *īterrub*, he enters once-for-all

14.3 The Formation of the Gt-Stem in the Tri-Radical Verb The infix -*ta*- (in verbs with *e*-vocalization, it is -*te*-) occurs between the first and the second consonant. In forms which are without prefix, it is shortened to -*t*-. The prefix-tenses are formed with the prefixes of the G-stem *i*, *ta*-, *a*-, *ni*-. They take the root-vowel after the second consonant, but this drops out in the Preterite, before vocalic endings.

Pres. *imtaḫḫaṣ*, he fights

Pret. *imtaḫaṣ*, he fought

imtaḫṣū, they fought one another

In verbs which are I Aleph (4.6), the dropping of the aleph which had originally closed the syllable causes the lengthening of the prefix vowel:

Īterrub, *Īterub*, he enters, entered once and for all

The very rare Perfect *Gt* is formed with two *-ta-* infixes, one for the Perfect and the other for the stem. The latter is shortened to *-t-*. Imperative, Infinitive, and Stative *Gt* take the vowel *i* before the infix *-t-*. After the second consonant, the Imperative takes the root-vowel; the Infinitive and the Stative take *u*:

mitḫaṣā, fight one another

mitḫuṣum, to fight with one another

ritkubū, they are riding toward one another

The Preterite *Gt*, and the Perfect *G* (9.2 - 9.3) have the same vocalization in all verbs. For this reason, analysis of forms can be very difficult.

Cf. paradigms 16, 21-24.

14.4 The Gt-Stem of the Bi-Radical Verb Verbs *ultimae vocalis* follow the formation of the *Gt*-stem of the tri-radical verb.

Pres. *irtaddiā*, Pret. *irtadiā*, they follow/followed one another

In verbs which are I *n*, the assimilation of *n* to *t* takes place:

ittakkirā (<°*intakkirā*), they become hostile to one another

ittaṭlū, they looked at one another

For the formation of the Gt stem of the I w verbs which take t as root augment instead of w, compare the Perfect G (9.3) and waṣûm (14.6). Only the Preterite Gt is attested for verbs which are mediae vocalis, iddūkū, they killed one another (14.9).
Cf. paradigms 27, 29, 31, and 33.

14.5 The Gt-Stem of alākum The verb alākum, to go, forms a Present and Preterite Gt with a doubling of the t:

Pres. ittallak, he goes away (Gt)

Pret. ittalak, he went away (Gt)

Perf. ittalak, when appearing as Perfect G, is most often seen in Ventive:

Perf. ittalkam, has arrived

Cf. paradigm 22.

14.6 The Gt of waṣûm The verb waṣûm (*wṣi), to go out toward (8.8) forms the Present Gt ittaṣṣi, he draws away (14.2) and the Preterite Gt ittaṣi (Perfect G ittaṣi, he came toward [9,3]).

14.7 The Gt-Stem from izuzzum The irregular verb izuzzum, to stand (11.8), forms the Present Gt ittazzaz, he enters. It does not form a Preterite Gt.

14.8 Consonantal Changes Verbs whose first root consonant is d, ṭ, s, ṣ, or z are irregular in the unprefixed forms of the Gt (Imperative, Infinitive, Stative). The first consonant and the t of the infix reverse positions so that the forms begin with t (metathesis):

tiṣbutum, to seize one another (for *ṣitbutum)

tidkušat, is swollen (for *ditkušat)

14.9 *Assimilation* The *t* of the infix -*ta*- is assimilated in [prefixed forms of] verbs whose first consonant is *d*, *ṭ*, *s*, *ṣ*, or *z*:

taṣṣabbatā (<**taṣtabbatā*), you seize one another

iddūkū (<**idtūku*), they killed one another

The same phenomenon of assimilation occurs with the infix -*ta*- of the Perfect (9.2, note):

niṭṭardam, we have sent

14.10 *The Imperative D* The Imperative of the D-stem corresponds to the Preterite D (*ukaššid*) without a prefix. But the vowel of the first syllable becomes *u*:

kuššid, banish

gummer, make ready

In verbs which are *ultimae vocalis*:

putti, open (Pret. *upetti*, 11.4)

In verbs *mediae vocalis*:

kīn, fasten, consolidate; *kinnā*, (Pl.)

tēr, give back; *terrā*, (Pl.)

In verbs I *w*:

wuššer, set free (or with the dropping of the *w* it becomes *uššer*)

14.11 *The Conjugation of the Stative in the Singular* Along with the third singular masculine *ṣabit*, he is seized, seizing (1.5), and the third singular feminine *ṣabtat* (1.5), first and second persons of the Stative can also be formed. The endings for the second person singular masculine are -*āt* or -*āti*; for the second person feminine -*āti*; for the first person singular -*āku*. In verbs with *e*-vocalization, these are -ēt, -ēti, and -ēku. These endings are added (as is the third singular feminine -at), to the Stative of the third person singular masculine. In the process, the Stative vowel i (2.6) drops out.

ṣabtāku, I am seized, seizing

ṣehrēti, you are small (4.5)

In subjunctive forms, the vocalization is the same because the subjunctive u only occurs on verbal forms without endings:

āl lawiāt (= ālam ša lawiāt, 7.5), the city which you are surrounding

Cf. paradigm 13.

14.12 Composite Nouns   Units of measure burum, a bur, a surface measure and kurrum, a kur, a measure of grain, are so closely bound with eqlum (field) and še'um (grain) that new words are formed from the combination with declensions all their own:

Nom. būr-eqlum

Gen. būr-eqlim

Akk. būr-eqlam (originally būr-eqlim in all three cases)

Similarly in other units of measure:

10 šiqil kaspam, ten shekels of silver

EXERCISES

P. 1. šumma erištum[1] ù kakkum it-ta-aṭ-lu-ú. 2. šum-ma šitta ṣibātum ir-ta-di-a. 3. šumma martum i-mi-tam ù šu-me-lam ti-id-ku-ša-at. 4. šumma iz-bu-um qá-qá-as-sú a-na ha̮-al-li-šu ka-mi-is-ma it-ti zi-ib-ba-ti-šu ti-iṣ-bu-ut.

A. 5. mi-lu-um i-na na-ri-im it-ta-za-az. 6. ma-tum ši-i su-un-qá-am i-mar, naker-ša e-li-ša it-ta-za-az. 7. a-ha̮-ta-am na-ak-ru-um it-ta-aṭ-ṭa-al. 8. wa-ṣum it-ta-la-ak a-na a-lim i-ru-ub. 9. ú-tu-uk-ku a-na ekallim i-te-er-ru-ub. 10. at-ta ù na-ke-er-ka ta-aṣ-ṣa-ab-ba-ta-a-ma a-ḫu-um a-ḫa-am ú-ša-am-qá-at. 11. a-al wa-aš-ba-a-ti in-na-aq-qá-ar. 12. āl la-wi-at a-na libbi-šu te-ru-ub.

O. 13. šumma bāb ekallim 2-ma ri-it-ku-bu-ú; šukkalum kussí be-li-šu iš-te-né-e. 14. šum-ma mar-tum ip-lu-uš-ma it-ta-ṣí; a-wi-lum it-ta-aṣ-ṣi. 15. šum-ma mar-tum i-ši-id-šà[2] le-ti; ma-ta-an it-ta-ak-ki-ra. 16. šum-ma mar-tum ù ú-ba-nu-um ši-it-nu-na-a; pu-úḫ-ru-um ú-la im-ta-ga-ar. 17. šumma ubān ḫašîm qablītum šu-me-el-ša pa-ṭe$_4$-er; ku-ši-id, la ta-ka-la!

[1] 0.34; [2] 3.10 (Remark).

erištum, wish, demand; also some kind of liver-marking

naṭālum (a/u), to look on; Gt, to look at one another

redûm (rdī), to follow; Gt, to follow one another, to go or to be parallel

dakāšum (a/u), to swell, to break out

ḫallum, the upper thigh

kamāsum (i), to fasten together

ṣabātum (a), to grasp; Gt, to seize one another, to grow together

nārum, river

izuzzum, to stand; Gt, to halt (flood) (with eli) to prevail over

elīša, over it, above it

aḫītum, side

aḫītam, at the side

alākum (a/i), to go; Gt, to depart

utukkum, (friendly) demon, ghost

erēbum (u), to enter; Gt, to enter forever, once-for-all

attā, you

wašābum (a/i), to sit, settle, dwell

ana libbim erēbum, to draw in, to penetrate

rakābum (a), to ride; Gt, to ride against one another

šanûm (šnī), to be other; Gt, to change permanently

waṣûm (wṣī), to go out; Gt, to go away

nakārum (i), to be hostile; Gt, to become mutually hostile

šanānum, to be the same; Gt, to be like one another

to quarrel

mitgurum, to unite oneself

kašādum (a/u), to attain; Dt, to drive out

READING PASSAGE (Old-Babylonian Letters)

1. a-na dŠamaš-ḫa-ze-er mdSîn-mu-ša-lim ù tap-pê-šu-nu qí-bí-ma! um-ma Ḫa-am-mu-ra-pí-ma: a-šar 4 būr eqil a-na Ištar-illas-su na-da-nam e-si-ḫa-ak-ku-nu-ši-im, 5 būr eqlam bīt a-bi-šu gu-um-me-ra-šum-ma id-na-šum.

2. a-na dŠamaš-ḫa-ze-er qí-bí-ma! um-ma Ḫa-am-mu-ra-pí-ma; mīlum a-la-kam i-ip-pé-ša-am, mu-ú ma-a-du; nam-ka-ri ša a-na appārim ša-ak-nu pu-ut-ti-i-ma eqlam ša i-ta-at Larsam me-e mu-ul-li,

3. a-na dŠamaš-ḫa-ze-er qí-bí-ma: um-ma Awīl-dNin-urta-ma: dŠamaš li-ba-al-li-iṭ-ka! 6 būr A-ḫa-mar-ši i-na uruŠi-ri-im-tim, 12 būr dSîn-īriš, 12 būr Bītum-ra-bi, eqlam ki-in-šu-nu-ši-im; la i-ta-ar-ru-ma la i-ma-ḫa-ru-ni-in-ni! pi-qá-at um-ma A-ḫa-mar-ši-ma; 10 būr eqlam ša-ak-na-ku. 6 būr eqlam-ma (8,14) tu-ka-an-šum,

4. a-na dŠamaš-ḫa-ze-er qí-bí-ma: um-ma Awīl-dNin-urta-ma; dŠamaš li-ba-al-li-iṭ-ka! aš-šum eqlim ša mÚ-ta-mi-ša-ra-am nārim ša uruGu-na-tum ša a-na mI-lí-e-mu-qí na-ad-nu, a-wi-lum an-ni-ki-a-am a-na eqlim ša-a-ti ṭú-up-pu. a-nu-um-ma ṭú-up-pi uš-ta-bi-la-ak-kum, še-a-am ù eqlam a-na I-lí-e-mu-qí te-e-er.

5. a-na Awīl-dBa-ú qí-bí-ma: um-ma A-ḫu-um-ma ;... dSîn-A-bu-šu ù ma-ra-ti-šu ú-še-er.

Lesson 15

GRAMMAR

15.1 The Dt Stem   The D stem can be modified by the infix *-ta-* (14.1) and this expresses the passive of the D (11.1):

uwaššar, he sets free

ūtaššar, he is set free

15,2 The Formation of the Dt in the Tri-Radical Verb   The Dt forms are distinguished from the *D* (11.2) only through the insertion of the infix *-ta-* after the first root consonant:

Pres. D. *uḫtabbat*, he is kidnaped; (Pres. D. *uḫabbat*, he snatches

Pret. D. *uḫtabbit*, he was kidnaped (Pret. D. *uḫabbit*)

Perf. Dt. *uḫtatabbit* (Perf. D. *uḫtabbit*)

In the e-class of the verbs I Aleph, the *-ta-* shifts to *-te-*:

ūtesser, he is enclosed (Pres. D. *ussar*)

The Imperative Dt. is *ḫutabbit*, be robbed! (Imper. D. *ḫubbit*, 14.10) Stative, Verb-Adj. and Infinitive are not formed in the Dt. The Preterite Dt has the same vocalization as the Perfect D; (both forms are *uḫtabbit*).

Cf. paradigms 21 and 24.

15.3 The Formation of the Dt-Stem in the Bi-Radical Verb   In verbs which are *ultimae vocalis*, the Dt corresponds to the forms of *uḫtabbat* (15.2):

uqtatta, is brought to an end (*qtī*, to be at an end)

In verbs I *w*, the prefix vowel is lengthened:

Pres. Dt *ūtaššar*, he is set free

Pret. Dt <u>ūtaššer</u>, he was set free

(or Perf. D, he has set free)

Cf. paradigms 29 and 33.

15.4 <u>The Imperative Š</u> The Imperative of the Š resembles the Preterite of the Š (<u>ušamqit</u>, 12.2), but without a prefix and with a <u>u</u> as the vowel of what becomes the first syllable: <u>šumqit</u>, let fall! In verbs I Aleph, <u>šūhiz</u>, let him take! (Pret. Š <u>ušāhiz</u>, 12.2). Similarly in verbs which are I <u>w</u> (12.7): <u>šūšibā</u>, may you (fem. pl.) dwell! The Imperative Š of the verbs <u>ultimae vocalis</u> (III vowel) takes vocalizations like <u>šurši</u>, let him obtain!; <u>šūṣi</u>, may you (masc. sing.) go out! and <u>šūṣiā</u>, may you (fem. pl.) depart! The Imperative Š of verbs <u>mediae vocalis</u> (12.5) takes the form <u>šumīt</u>, let him die!

15.5 <u>The Verb warûm, to lead</u> The Š-stem of the verb <u>warûm</u> (<u>wrū</u>) is, unlike <u>waṣûm</u>, to go out (12.4), formed with an a-vocalization.

Pres. <u>ušarra</u>, he lets (someone) lead

Pret. <u>ušāri</u>

Imper. <u>šūriam</u>, let (someone) lead toward us

Pl. <u>šūriānim</u>

The G-stem of this verb is often replaced through the secondary form <u>tarûm</u> (<u>trū</u>), to fetch:

Pres. <u>itarru</u>, he fetches

Pret. <u>itru</u>, he fetched

Precative <u>litrūnikkum</u>, they should fetch you

15.6 The verb wârum, to go A verb mediae Aleph (9.6) and I w is wârum. In the D-stem, it takes a Present uwâr, he causes to go, he sends and the Preterite, uwēr, he sent, ordered.

15.7 Personal Pronouns There are special personal pronouns for the first and second persons:

attā (fem. attī), you (sing.)

attunu (fem. attina), you (pl.)

anāku (masc. and fem.), I

nīnu (masc. and fem.), we

As a substitute for the personal pronoun in the third person the anaphoric pronoun is used:

šū, the one mentioned, he

šī, she

šunu (fem. šina), they (11.10)

These pronouns give special emphasis to the subject and are mostly used in nominal sentences:

umma attā-ma, you (spoke) as follows

Cf. paradigm 8.

15.8 Subjunctive in Subordinate Clauses In all subordinate clauses introduced by such words as kīma, as soon as, if (13.4), inūma, when, or adi, until, the verb of the clause takes the subjunctive:

adi še'um...uqtattû, until the grain is (made ready) finished

15.9 Main Clauses After šumma The predicate of clauses introduced by šumma, if, does not stand in the subjunctive. Such clauses ought rather to be considered as independent clauses. šumma ought then to be translated as, assumed that, or given that:

šumma martum ishur, given that the gall bladder is turned = if the gall bladder is turned

For the Preterite after šumma cf. 1.4; for the Perfect, 9.1.

15.10 Logical Subordination After verbs of saying there sometimes follows in Akkadian an unconnected main clause which would be a subordinate clause in English:

šupur bēl awātīšu litrūnikkum, write the man his legal opponent let him bring to you = write that the man should bring his legal opponent to you

ṭēmum liššapranniāšim abul dŠamaš lippettīma še'um...līrub

may authority be sent to us that the Šamaš-gate may be opened and that the grain may come in!

15.11 The Infinitive with Prepositions In place of a final dependent clause, the Infinitive with ana can be used:

ana ṣēnim...šubqumim = for the shearing of the sheep = in order to get the sheep sheared

The Infinitive with ina can replace a temporal clause:

ṭuppī anniam ina amārim, in the reading of this my tablet = as soon as you read this my tablet

15.12 Nominal and Verbal Use of the Infinitive The Infinitive is a verbal noun. It can be construed then both as a noun and as a verb. In a nominal construction, the Infinitive can appear in the construct state with the actual subject of the action following in the genitive case:

zanān šamê, the falling of rain

On the other hand, when the object of the verb is being stressed the Infinitive is generally construed as a verb. The object is then placed in the Accusative case and precedes the Infinitive:

ṭuppī *anniam* *ina* *amārim* = in the reading of this my tablet = when you read this my tablet

But if the object stands between the preposition and Infinitive, the object takes the genitive case, apparently dependent on the preposition.

ana *abullim* *naṣārim* (for *abullam* *ana* *naṣārim*) = to the gate to watch = in order to watch the gate

15.13 The Plural of *awīlum* The substantive *awīlum*, man, forms a normal plural in the Nominative *awīlū* (*a-wi-lu-ú*), Genitive-Accusative is *awīlē* (*a-wi-le-e*). Similarly, *ṣuḫārum*, servant, lad, takes a Genitive-Accusative *ṣuḫārē* and a dual *ṣuḫārēn*, both lads.

15.14 The Use of the Perfect The ordinary past tense is the Preterite. If the writer wishes to emphasize that a process is just now completed, the Perfect is used and this frequently in combination with such words as *annuma*, now, just now, and *inanna*, now.

anumma *ṭuppī* *uštābilakkum*, now have I had my tablet brought to you

If the writer wishes to emphasize the temporal sequence of two processes in the Past, the first verb stands in the Preterite and the second in the Perfect:

uwēramma *aṭṭardam*, I have commissioned (them) and sent them

For the use of the Perfect after *šumma*, cf. 9.1.

EXERCISES

A. 1. ma-ra-tum uḫ-ta-ab-ba-ta-ma a-bu-um ar-bu-tam i-la-a-ak[1]. 2. bu-tu-qa-tum ub-ta-ta-qá.

O. 3. šum-ma na-ap-la-ás-tum ki-ma un-qí-im; ma-a-tum ú-te-es-sé-er. 4. šum-ma i-na šu-me-el ú-ba-nim ka-ak-kum is-ḫu-ur; še-pu-um a-na ma-at na-ak-ri-im ú-ta-ša-ar.

[1] 0.22.

VOCABULARY

mārtum, daughter

ḫabātum (a/u), to rob, plunder; Dt to be robbed

batāqum (a/u), to break through; Dt to be broken through

unqum, ring

esērum (i), to enclose; Dt to be enclosed

wašārum, to be at large, free; Dt to be set free

READING PASSAGE (Old-Babylonian Letters)

1. um-ma Warad-^{d}Gu-la-ma: ^{d}Gu-la, ^{d}Da-mu ù ^{d}Ur-ma-šum a-bi li-ba-al-li-ṭú; i-na ma-za-zi-im ša ta-az-za-zu lu-ta-ab-bé-er!...

2. a-na...ù...[1] qí-bí-ma! um-ma Sa-am-su-di-ta-na-ma: ša ta-aš-pu-ra-nim: um-ma at-tu-nu-ma: še-um ša i-na er-ṣe-et Sippar-ya-aḫ-ru-rum ib-ba-šu-ú, i-na pa-ni ummān nakrim i-na ki-di a-na na-de-e ú-ul na-ṭú. be-el-ni li-iq-bi, ṭé-mu-um li-iš-ša-ap-ra-an-ni-a-ši-im abul ^{d}Šamaš li-ip-pé-ti-ma še-um šu-ú a-na li-ib-bi a-lim li-ru-ub. ša ta-aš-pu-ra-nim. ki-ma še-um me-re-eš a-lim i-na e-ṣe-di uq-ta-ta-at-tu-ú, abul ^{d}Šamaš pé-ti-a-ma a-di še-um me-re-eš a-lim uq-ta-at-tu-ú, dayyānī šu-ši-ba-a-ma a-na abullim na-ṣa-ri-im la i-ig-gu-ú.

3. a-na ^{d}Šamaš-ḫa-ze-er qí-bí-ma! um-ma Ḫa-am-mu-ra-pí-ma: a-nu-um-ma a-wi-le-e eb-bu-tim a-na ṣēnī ša li-tim šaplītim šu-ub-qú-mi-im ú-we-e-ra-am-ma aṭ-ṭar-dam-ma ṭup-pi an-ni-a-am i-na a-ma-ri-im a-na Larsam a-li-ik! it-ti awīlē ša a-na buqūmim e-si-ḫu i-zi-iz-ma[2] buqūmam šu-ub-qí-im.

4. a-na ^{d}Sîn-i-din-nam qí-bí-ma! um-ma Ḫa-am-mu-ra-pí-ma: ra-bi-a-an ^{uru}Me-de-e-em^{ki} aš-šum ḫi-bi-il-ti-šu ú-lam-mi-da-an-ni. a-nu-um-ma ra-bi-a-an ^{uru}Me-de-e-em^{ki} šu-a-ti a-na ṣe-ri-ka aṭ-ṭar-dam; wa-ar-ka-as-su pu-ru-ús! šu-pur be-el a-wa-ti-šu li-it-ru-ni-ik-kum-ma di-nam ki-ma ṣi-im-da-tim šu-ḫi-is-su-nu-ti!

5. a-na Li-pi-it-^{d}Ištar ù Awīl-^{d}Ba-ú qí-bí-ma! um-ma A-ḫu-um-ma: a-nu-

um-ma i-me-ra-am ša ^{m}Sà-si-ya i-iq-bu-ku-nu-ši-im šu-ri-a-ni-im!

6. a-na Na-bi-^{d}Gu-la ù Bal-mu-nam-ḫé qí-bí-ma! um-ma ^{d}Sîn-a-ya-ba-aš-ma: ^{d}Šamaš li-ba-al-li-iṭ-ku-nu-ti! ^{I}Ig-mil-^{d}Sîn ù Ba-aq-qum rē'um ka-ni-ki it-ba-lu-ni-ku-nu-ši-im[3]. a-na pi-i ka-ni-ki še-am i-na še bilat I-din-ya-tum šu-ṣi-a! šum-ma še-um i-na še bilat I-din-ya-tum la i-ba-aš-ši, i-na še bilat ^{d}Marduk-la-ma-sa-šu šukkalim šu-ṣi-a!

[1] Addressees of the letter not preserved in the text; [2] 13.3 (Remark); [3] 9.3 (Remark).

Lesson 16

GRAMMAR

16.1 The *Št* Stem   The *Š*-stem, further modified by a -*ta*- infix (14.1), becomes the *Št*-stem and serves in some verbs as a causative for the *Gt*-stem (14.2):

> *mitḫurum*, to be like another; *šutamḫurum* (Inf. *Št*), to make oneself like another
>
> *tiṣbutum*, to seize one another; *šutaṣbutum*, to have (them) seize one another

Some verbs have special meanings in the *Št*:

> *šutēšurum*, to bring into order, to have justice done (from *ešērum*, to be in order)
>
> *šutašnûm*, to make double (*šanûm*, to be double)
>
> *šutebrûm*, to be apparent (*barûm*, to see, look at)

Some verbs occur only in the *Št*-stem:

> *šuteṣbûm* (°*ṣb'*), to conduct in order
>
> *šutā'ûm* (°*wḫī*), to be superfluous, inactive

The *Št* treated here is sometimes described in grammars and dictionaries as the *lexical* *Št*-stem or *Št*². This is in opposition to the very uncommon passive *Št* or *Št*¹. In form, these two *Št* stems are distinguished only in the formation of the Present: *Št*¹: *uštapras* and *Št*²: *uštaparras*, 16.2.

16.2 The Formation of the *Št* in the Tri-Consonantal Verb   The *Št* forms are distinguished from the corresponding forms of the Š only by the infix -*t*(*a*)- which is inserted after the root-prefix *š*(*a*). In the

Present, the middle consonant is doubled:

Pres. Št uštaṣabbat, he has them seize one another

(Pres. Š ušaṣbat, he has [him] seize [somebody])

Pret. Št uštaṣbit (same form as Perf. Š; Pret. Š ušaṣbit)

Perf. Št uštataṣbit (Perf. uštaṣbit)

Imper. šutaṣbit (Imper. Š šuṣbit, 15.4)

Infin. šutaṣbutum

Stat. šutaṣbut

In the e-class of verbs which are I Aleph (and I y, 4.8), the -ta- shifts to -te-: šutēšer, keep in order!

Cf. paradigms 21 and 24.

16.3 Formation of the Št in Bi-Consonantal Verbs   In verbs which are III Vowel:

the Present corresponds to uštaṣabbat (16.2); uštašanna (šnī), he makes double

Pret. uštebri, became transparent (brī)

St. šutašnu (fem. šutašnât), is doubled

Cf. paradigm 33.

16.4 Verbs Mediae Aleph with Consonantal Aleph   Most verbs which are mediae Aleph follow the conjugation of verbs which are mediae vocalis (9.6). There are some in which the Aleph does not drop out and these verbs correspond to the tri-consonantal verbs:

na'ādum (i), to pay attention, to give a sign

Pres. ina''id

Pret. i''id (<*in'id)

Imp. i'id (cf. idin, 13.3)

All verbs mediae aleph, including those which normally follow the mediae vocalis pattern, form the participle with a consonantal aleph:

šā'imum, buyer (šâmum)

bā'irum, fisherman (bârum), to catch

Similarly, the Stative is formed with aleph:

na'id, to inform; fem. na'dat

The doubling of the aleph in forms like ina''id is given in the transcription (0.15) out of fidelity to the morphology involved (doubling of middle consonant in the Present). Still, one should not conclude that the reduplication of the aleph is phonetically real. The same is true for the doubled y in dayyānum, kayyānum, etc.

16.5 The Verb šutā'ûm, to be Superfluous, Free   The root w'i occurs only in the Št stem:

Pres. ušta''a, he is idle

Pret. uštā'i, he was idle

Prohibitive: lā tušta''āši be not idle (about this)

16.6 The Verb idûm (yd'), to Know   Only the Preterite of this verb occurs; it is used as a Stative (Prefix -- Stative, 11.9):

īde, he knows

tīde, you know

īde, I know

The participle is mūdûm, the one who knows.

16.7 Assimilation of n   n can be assimilated before pronominal suffixes and -ma:

idiššum (<idin + šum), give to him

inaddišši (<inaddin + ši), he/she gives it (fem.)

šakimma (<šakin + ma) along with šakinma, is settled and...

16.8 Apocopated Pronominal Suffixes If the pronominal suffixes -šu, him and -ši, her, it (5.8) appear after a verbal form which ends in a vowel, they are often shortened to š.

lā tanaddiš (<tanaddi + šu/ši), do not hurl it! (13.6)

16.9 Personal Names Akkadian personal names are either nouns (Aplum, Lipit-^{d}Ištar) or sentences (^{d}Sîn-īriš, Aḫam-arši). They can be written with or without the determinative m (0.20). Names are unchangeable; they take the same form for all cases: mār Aḫum, son of Aḫum (but mar aḫim, son of the brother).

16.10 Names as "Labels" Affectionate names are derived from nouns and participles which indicate relationships, or from the names of animals:

Aplum, the heir

Aḫum, brother

Baqqum, gnat

Sāsīya, my moth

Muḫaddûm, he who causes joy (D part. from ḫadûm)

This type of appellation can also be formed from nouns which are combined with the name of a god or an indication of a god:

Awīl-^{d}Ninurta, man of Ninurta

Warad-^{d}Sîn, slave of Sîn

Lipit-^{d}Ištar, work of Ištar

Nabi-^{d}Gula, called by Gula

Nūr-ᵈKabta, light of Kabta

Apil-ilim, heir of the god

16.11 Sentence-Names Most of the sentence-names are composed of a Subject (the name of a god or a similar designation, as ilum, god, or bītum, temple), and a Predicate (generally the Preterite or Stative.) Other names are composed of an object and a verbal form (generally the first person singular).

A. A Divine Name and the Preterite

ᵈSîn-īriš, Sîn has requested

ᵈSîn-idinnam (<iddin + am), Sîn has given me

Ilī-iqīšam, my god has presented (a son) to me

Ilšu-ibbīšu, his god has called him

Imgur-ᵈSîn, Sîn has granted the wish

Igmil-ᵈSîn, Sîn has been favorable

Iddin-yattum, my (divinity) has given

B. A Divine Name and the Stative

ᵈŠamaš-ḫāzer, Šamaš is helper

ᵈŠamaš-emūqī, Šamaš is my strength

Ilī-emūqī, my god is my strength

ᵈSîn-illassu, Sîn is his family

ᵈMarduk-lamassašu, Marduk is his protective divinity

ᵈSîn-mušallim, Sîn keeps him well (D St. Part. from šalāmum)

Rabi-ᵈSataran, great is Sataran

Bītum-rabi, great is the temple

C. A Divine Name and the Precative

ᵈŠamaš-liwwir, may Šamaš give streams of light (nawārum)

D. Object and Preterite

Aḫam-arši, I have obtained a brother

Ūta-mīšaram, I have found the right (wtā, 8.8)

E. Special Names

dSîn-ay abaš Sîn, may I not be shamed! (Vetitive particle ai and abāš from bâšum)

Šumma-ilum, if a god (will help me)

16.12 Non-Akkadian Names Many names which occur in Akkadian texts are not Akkadian, but Canaanite (Ḫammurabi, Samsuditana), or Sumerian (Balmunamḫe, Ur-dUtu, Luga, Iškur-gal-bi).

EXERCISES

P. 1. šumma i-na i-mi-it-ti bāb ekallim pi-il-šum[1] ip-lu-uš-ma ù e-le-nu-um uš-te-eb-ri. 2. šumma e-le-nu pa-da-an i-mi-tim šu-ub-tum šu-ta-aš-na-a-at.

O. 3. šumma a-mu-tum ši-li sà-aḫ-ra-at-ma ù šu-te-eb-ru; a-mu-ut Šar-rum-ki-in ša ek-le-tam i-iḫ-bu-tu-ma nu-ra-am i-mu-ru. 4. šum-ma mar-tum na-aḫ-sà-at; na-a'-da-at. 5. šumma ubān ḫa-ši qablītum re-sa ša-ti-iq; a-na šar-ri-im na-i-id.

VOCABULARY

pilšum, ditch, hole

šutebrûm (brī), to be transparent

šanûm (šnī), to be other, to be second; Št., to double

saḫārum (u), to surround, to turn around

Šarrum-kīn, Šarrum-kīn, king of the dynasty of Akkad (2340-2284)

ḫabātum (a/u), to wander through; to penetrate; to plunder

nahāsum (i), to yield, fall back

na'ādum, St. G, to inform

šatāqum, to crush

READING PASSAGE FROM THE CODE OF HAMMURABI

1. šum-ma a-wi-lum a-na bīt e-mi-im bi-ib-lam ú-ša-bi-il ter-ḫa-tam id-di-in-ma a-bi mārtim: mārtī ú-ul a-na-ad-di-ik-kum! iq-ta-bi; mi-im-ma ma-la ib-ba-ab-lu-šum uš-ta-ša-an-na-ma ú-ta-ar.

2. šum-ma a-wi-lum nadītam i-ḫu-uz-ma mārī la ú-šar-ši-šu-ma a-na ^{mí}šu-gi$_4$-tim a-ḫa-zi-im pa-ni-šu iš-ta-ka-an; a-wi-lum šu-ú ^{mí}šu-gi$_4$-tam i-iḫ-ḫa-az a-na bītī-šu ú-še-er-re-eb-ši ^{mí}šu-gi$_4$-tum ši-i it-ti nadītim ú-ul uš-ta-ma-aḫ-ḫa-ar.

3. šum-ma a-wi-lum nadītam i-ḫu-uz-ma amtam a-na mu-ti-ša id-di-in-ma mārī it-ta-la-ad, wa-ar-ka-nu-um amtum ši-i it-ti be-el-ti-ša uš-ta-tam-ḫe-er; aš-šum mārī ul-du be-le-sà a-na kaspim ú-ul i-na-ad-di-iš-ši, ab-bu-ut-tam i-ša-ak-ka-an-ši-ma it-ti amātim i-ma-an-nu-ši.

4. šum-ma itinnum bītam a-na a-wi-lim i-pu-uš-ma ši-pé-er-šu la uš-te-eṣ-bi-ma igārum iq-tu-up; itinnum šu-ú i-na kasap ra-ma-ni-šu igāram šu-a-ti ú-dan-na-am.

OLD BABYLONIAN LETTERS

5. a-na ^{d}Šamaš-ḫa-ze-er qí-bí-ma! um-ma ^{d}Sîn-i-din-nam-ma: ^{d}Šamaš ù ^{d}Marduk li-ba-al-li-ṭú-ka! aš-šum eqil kurummat Iškur-gal-bi ^{m}Ur-^{d}Utuaḫū-šu it-ta-al-ka-ak-kum[2]; ṭe-em-šu ma-aḫ-ri-ka li-iš-ku-un-ma šu-te-še-er-šu!

6. a-na Nu-ur-^{d}Kab-ta qí-bí-ma! um-ma ^{d}Šamaš-li-wi-ir-ma: ^{d}Šamaš ù

[1] 0.35; [2] 14.5.

^{d}Nin-si$_4$-an-na a-na da-ri-a-tim li-ba-al-li-ṭú-ú-ka! ki-ma immerī ti-šu-ú[3] eš-me-ma 1/3 ma-na kaspim ša-a'i-im-ma ka-li-a-ku. a-nu-um-ma ṭup-pi ^{m}I-ba-šar-rum ṣu-ḫa-ar a-wi-lim ša immerī ḫa-aš-ḫu uš-ta-bi-la-ak-kum. ...immerī i-di-iš-šum ù ṣu-ḫa-ru ša il-li-ka-ak-kum it-ti a-la-ak-tim šu-ta-aṣ-bi-ta-aš-šu.

7. a-na Lù-ga-a qí-bí-ma! um-ma ^{d}Šamaš-ga-ar-ri-ma: ^{d}Šamaš li-ba-al-li-iṭ-ka! aš-šum ^{m}Ba-ba-a[4] a-ḫa-ti-ya a-wa-ti-ša ṭa-mu-ur. a-mi-ni di-in-ša la ta-di-in? a-na bi-ti a-bi-i-ka ú-da-mi-iq ù at-ta ti-de-e[5]. am-mi-ni tu-uš-ta-'i-i-ši? aš-tap-ra-ak-kum[6], di-in-ša i-ša-ri-iš di-in-ma la tu-uš-ta-'a$_4$-a-ši! a-na ḫa-ba-lim la ta-na-di-iš! ù ṭe-e-em-ša ga-am-ra-am me-ḫe-er un-ne-du-uk-ki-ya šu-bi-lam!

3 9.8 4 0.20 5 16.6 6 15.14.

Lesson 17

GRAMMAR

17.1 Iterative Stems   For each of the four main stems (G, N, D, and Š), another stem can be formed with the further modification of an infix *-tan-*; thus are formed the Gtn, Ntn, Dtn, and Štn. They have iterative or habitual functions. They describe then, the constant repetition of a process (sometimes expressed in the translation by the expression *again and again*) or they characterize an activity as customary (to be in the habit of doing something).

išarriq, he steals; *ištanarriq* (Pres. Gtn), he is accustomed to steal

innappaḫ, is ignited; *ittananpaḫ*, is ignited again and again

17.2 The Gtn Stem   To form an iterative or habitual variation of the G stem, the infix *-tan-* (*-ten-* in verbs with e-vocalization) is inserted after the first root consonant. The *n* of the infix remains only in the Present (by reason of the vowel). In all other forms, it is assimilated to the second root-consonant.

17.3 The Prefix Tenses of the Gtn Stem   Present and Preterite Gtn are formed with the prefixes *i-*, *ta-*, *a-*, and *ni-*. The verbs of the vowel-change class have *a* after the second consonant; the remaining verbs have the root vowel:

Pres. *iptanallaḫ*, he lives in constant fear

Pret. *iptallaḫ* (< **ip-tan-laḫ*), he lived in constant fear

ištanarriqū, they steal again and again

imtanaqqut, he falls again and again

In verbs which are I Aleph, the prefix is lengthened, since the aleph drops (4.6):

Ītanakkal (<**i'-tan-akkal*), he eats again and again

Īterriš (<**i'-ten-riš*), he worked the field again and again

The prefix *a-* of the first person singular shifts to *e* in I Aleph *e*-class verbs: (13.11)

ētennerriš (<**a'-ten-erriš*), I arrange again and again

The Preterite Gtn looks the same as the Present Gt (both forms are *iptallaḫ* or *ištarriq*). Because the double consonant which results from assimilation is not always expressed in the script, similar confusion is possible between the Perfect G and the Preterite Gt (both forms are *iptalaḫ*, *ištariq*).

The Perfect Gtn (*iptatallaḫ*) does not occur in Old-Babylonian. Cf. Paradigms 17, 21, and 24.

17.4 The Unprefixed Forms of the Gtn Stem   Imperative, Infinitive, and Stative Gtn, insert the vowel *i* between the first consonant and the infix -*tan*-. After the second consonant, the Imperative takes the vowel of the Preterite Gtn; the Infinitive and Stative take *u*:

šitarriq (<**ši-tan-riq*), steal again and again!

šitarruqum, to be accustomed to steal

šitarruq, he is/was stealing again and again

In *a*-class vowels of verbs which are I Aleph, the inserted vowel *i* shifts to *a* after the dropping of the preceding aleph. (Cf. Imper. G, 13.2.)

atappulum (<**'i-tan-pulum*), to satisfy again and again (substantive, solicitude)

Cf. Paradigms 21 and 24.

17.5 The Gtn of the Bi-Consonantal Verb Verbs which are III vowel form the Gtn-stem in a manner corresponding to the tri-consonantal verb:

Pres. *ištananni*, is constantly changing

iptenette, he opens again and again

Pret. *ištanni* and *iptette* (<°*ip-ten-te*)

Imp. *bitanni*, bring forth again and again

Verbs which are II vowel (7.1) form the Present:

ittanâr (Pl. *ittanurrū*), he returns again and again

Imperative and Infinitive in verbs II *ī* are formed through the assimilation of the *n* to the semi-vocalic *ī* (*y*) of the root:

ḫitayyaṭ (<°*ḫīṭ*), test again and again!

Inf. *ḫitayyuṭum*

In verbs which are I *n* (8.2), the root-augment *n* assimilates to *-tan-*:

ittanaddin (<°*in-tan-addin*), he is accustomed to give

In verbs which are I *w* the Gtn-stem, as the Perfect G (9.3) and the Gt (14.4) is formed from secondary verbs with a root-augment of *t* instead of *w*:

ittanarrad, he climbs down again and again

Cf. Paradigms 27, 29, 31 and 33.

17.6 The Gtn Stem of *alākum* The verb *alākum*, to go, (4.7) forms its Gtn stem, as the Gt stem, (14.5) with a doubling of *t*:

Pres. *ittanallak*, he goes again and again

Pret. *ittallak*

17.7 The Imperative N In the Imperative of the N stem, (10.2) there occurs the syllable *na-* before the root, as in the Infinitive and Stative N. The vowel after the second consonant is *i*, as in the

Preterite:

naplis, look!

In verbs which are I Aleph, the Imperative is formed either with the dropping of the aleph and compensatory lengthening:

nābit, flee! (10.2)

or with *secondary nasalization* (10.6):

ittīya nanmer, meet with me! (10.2)

17.8 *The Particle kīma, that* When depending on verbs of saying and perceiving, the particle *kīma* (13.14) is used with the meaning *that*:

kīma eleppāt bā'irī ittanarradā iqbūnim, they told me that the fishing boats go down again and again

17.9 *Questions* There are questions with and without interrogative words. Some interrogative words are, e.g., *ammīnim*, why, and *mannum*, who?

mannum beri, who is hungry?

In questions which lack an interrogative word, sometimes the word which is the point of the question may be specially lengthened:

bariākū (*ba-ri-a-ku-û*), shall I actually be hungry?

EXERCISE

A. 1. um-ma-nu-um i-na ta-ḫa-zi-im im-ta-na-aq-qú-ut. 2. šar-ru-um ša-na-i-šu ip-ta-na-al-la-aḫ. 3. mi-il-la-tum, ša-ta-mu ekallam iš-ta-na-ri-qú. 4. ṭe₄-e-em ma-a-tim iš-ta-na-an-ni. 5. ša li-ša-ni-ya i-na ma-a-tim it-ta-na-al-la-ak. 6. wa-ši-ib mà-aḫ-ri-ka-a[1] ka-ar-ṣí-ka i-ta-na-ka-al.

[1] 0.22 (Remark).

VOCABULARY

tāḫāzum, battle

maqātum, to fall; Gtn, to fall again and again

šanā'ûm, another, opponent

palāḫum (a), to fear; Gtn, to be constantly afraid

šarāqum, to steal; Gtn, to rob again and again

šanûm (šnī), to be other; Gtn, to change oneself repeatedly

lišānum, tongue

ša lišānim, that of the tongue = secret agent

alākum (a/i), to go; Gtn, to go again and again, to wander

karṣū (pl.), calumny

karṣī akālum, to calumniate; Gtn, to calumniate repeatedly

READING PASSAGE: OLD-BABYLONIAN LETTERS

1. a-na ^{d}Šamaš-ḫa-ze-er ù ^{d}Marduk-na-ṣe-er qí-bí-ma! um-ma Ḫa-am-mu-ra-pí-ma: eqlam ša a-na Kur-gal-á-maḫ-a-ni ka-an-ku-šum ^{md}Sîn-im-gur-an-ni mār...[2] MU 2^{kam}[3] i-te-er-ri-iš-ma še-šu il-te-eq-qé, ù ša-at-tam eqlam šu-a-ti i-ri-iš-ma še-šu il-te-qé...

2. a-na ^{d}Sîn-ša-mu-úḫ ù A-hu-ši-na qí-bí-ma! um-ma ^{d}Marduk-ka-ši-id-ma: a-nu-um-ma ^{m}I-ba-aš-ši-ilum ù Li-pí-it-Ištar ṣú-ḫa-re-e-en[4] a-na šu-ḫa-ti-in-ni^{sar} ša ma-aḫ-ri-ku-nu e-pu-šu le-qé-e-em aṭ-ṭar-dam. a-di šu-ḫa-ti-in-ni^{sar} šu-nu in-na-ap-pa-lu, ḫi-ta-ya-ṭa-šu-nu-ti-ma i-na si-ma-ni-šu li-in-na-ap-lu-ma a-na Bābilim li-ib-lu-ni-iš-šu-nu-ti.

3. a-na Ì-lí-im-gur-ra-an-ni qí-bí-ma! um-ma Ni-ši-i-ni-šu: belí ù be-el-ti aš-šu-mi-ya li-ba-al-li-ṭu-ka! am-mi-nim ba-ri-a-ku-ma di-a-ti-i la ta-ša-al? i-na bi-ti-ka ma-an-nu-um bé-ri? a-na-ku-ú ba-ri-a-ku-ú?

[1] 0.22; [2] Personal name is missing; [3] The reading of the word-sign MU (šattum, year) cannot be clearly determined in this context; MU 2^{kam}=two years long; [4] 15.13.

šipātī ša ṭup-pí-ya[1] a-na ṣi-ba-at kaspim at-ta-na-di-in. ú-lu kaspam ú-lu ḫurāṣam ú-lu šipātī ša 1/2 manêm šu-bi-lam!

4. a-na ᵈSîn-i-din-nam kār Sipparim ù dayyānī Sipparim qí-bí-ma! um-ma Sa-am-su-i-lu-na-ma: ki-ma a-na ugarim ra-bi-i-im ù ugarim Ša-am-ka-nim eleppāt bā'irī it-ta-na-ar-ra-da-ma nūnī i-ba-ar-ru iq-bu-nim...

5. a-na A-ḫu-ni qí-bí-ma! um-ma Be-la-nu-um-ma: ᵈŠamaš ù ᵈMarduk li-ba-al-li-ṭú-ka!...eleppātū iš-tu ge-er-ri-im is-ni-qá-ni-im. am-mi-ni-im karānam ṭà-ba-am la ta-ša-ma-am-ma la tu-ša-bi-lam? karānam ṭà-ba-am šu-bi-lam ù at-ta a-na ūm 10ᵏᵃᵐal-ka-am-ma it-ti-ya na-an-mé-er!

6. a-na A-ḫu-ki-nu-um qí-bí-ma! um-ma Awīl-ᵈAmurrim-ma: iš-tu u_4-mi-im ša a-na ḫa-ra-ni-im tu-ṣú-ú wa-ar-ki-ka-a-ma ᵐIm-gur-ᵈSîn il-li-ka-am-ma um-ma šu-ú-ma: 1/3 ma-na kaspam e-li-šu i-šu-ú[1]. aš-ša-at-ka ù ma-ra-at-ka it-te-pe-e[2]. ...aš-ša-at-ka ù ma-ra-at-ka i-na ṣí-bi-ti-im i-na ḫi-ta-šu-li-im i-mu-tu[3] aš-ša-at-ka ù ma-ra-at-ka šu-ṣí-i! a-pu-tum.

AN OLD-BABYLONIAN LEGAL DOCUMENT

7. ᵐIpiq-An-nu-ni-tum mār A-pil-ì-lí-šu itti A-ḫu-ni-ya um-mi-a-ni-šu ᵐIm-gur-ᵈSîn mār A-ḫu-um-wa-qar i-na Ya-ab-li-yaᵏⁱ it-ru-šu. a-ta-ap-pu-ul ᵐA-pil-ì-lí-šu a-bi-šu ù Ta-ad-di-in-Nu-nu um-mi-šu i-na qá-ti-i ᵐIm-gur-ᵈSîn[4].

1 0.22; 2 np'; 3 Pres.; 4 To be completed as ..."is now."

Lesson 18

GRAMMAR

18.1 *The Ntn-Stem* In the iterative-habitual (17.1) of the N stem, (10.2), the infix -*tan*- (-*ten*-) occurs between the stem-indicator *n* and the root. The *n* of the infix remains only in the Present; in the remaining forms, it drops out.

18.2 *The Prefix Tenses* Present and Preterite Ntn are formed with the prefixes *i*-, *ta*-, *a*-, and *ni*. The *n* which forms the stem is assimilated to the *t* of the infix -*tan*-.

Pres. *ittanamḫaṣ* (<° *i-n-tan-amḫaṣ*), is beaten again and again

Pret. *ittamḫaṣ* (<° *i-n-tan-mḫaṣ*), was beaten again and again

The Present Ntn then is formed *without* the characteristic doubling of the middle radical which takes place in the Present of all other stems. The vowel after the second consonant is (as in the Gtn 17.3) *a* in the vowel-change class of verbs and the theme-vowel in the other verbs.

Pres. *ittanapqid*, is entrusted again and again

Pret. *ittapqid*

18.3 *The Forms Without Prefixes* In the Imperative, Infinitive, and Stative Ntn, an *i* precedes the infix -*tan*-. The initial *n* which one would have expected as a stem constituent drops out.

Imp. *itaplas* (<° *nitaplas*), look again and again!

The vowel after the second consonant corresponds in the Imperative to that of the Preterite Ntn (18.2); Infinitive and Stative have *u*:

Inf. *itaplusum*

St. *itaplus*

Cf. Paradigm 21.

18.4 *The Ntn-Stem of the Bi-Consonantal Verb* In the verbs I *n* (8.2), the *n* of the root-augment is not assimilated in the Present Ntn:

ittananpaḫ (<**i-n-tan-anpaḫ*), is ignited again and again

The Stative Ntn from *nadûm* is:

itaddu (<**nitandu*), *itaddât* is put down again and again

Cf. Paradigms 27 and 33.

18.5 *The Dtn Stem* In the very rare iterative-habitual form of the D stem (11.1), the infix -*tan*- occurs between the first radical and the doubled second radical of the root. The prefixes correspond to those of the *D* and the *Dt* (*u*-, *tu*-, *u*-, and *nu*-). The *n* of the infix -*tan*- remains only in the Present:

uktanattam, he is accustomed to conceal

In the other forms, the *n* drops out before the doubled middle consonant:

Pret. *uktattim* (<**uk-tan-ttim*)

Imp. *kutattim*

Inf. *kutattumum*

All Dtn forms (with the exception of the Present) are identical in appearance with the corresponding forms of the Dt (15.1):

uḫtabbit, he was robbed (Pret. Dt) or he robbed again and again (Pret. Dtn)

18.6 *The Štn Stem* Similarly rare is the iterative-habitual form of the Š stem (12.1). The infix -*tan*- is inserted between the š element (which forms the stem) and the root itself. The prefixes are (as in the

Š and the Št) u-, tu-, u-, and nu-. Again, the n of the infix does not drop in the Present:

ustanamqat, he lets (it) fall again and again

But in the remaining forms it does drop:

Pret. uštamqit (*u-š-tan-mqit)

Imp. šutamqit

Infin. šutamqutum

The Imperative Štn from arāhum, to be in a hurry, is šutarrih, push on constantly in haste!

The Pres. Štn from waṣûm (8.8) takes the form uštenesse, he lets (things) out again and again = he is in the habit of betraying secrets. With the exception of the Present, all Štn forms are identical with those of the Št (16.1):

šutaṣbutum, to let (them) seize one another (Inf. Št., 16.1) or to let (them) seize one another again and again (Inf. Štn).

18.7 Verbs III Aleph The majority of the verbs which are III aleph e.g., leqûm (lq'), to take, are conjugated according to the pattern of verbs which are III vowel (Verbs final ē, 6.2). But in some verbs, the aleph does not drop out. These verbs are treated like tri-consonantal verbs:

mašā'um (a/u), to take away

Pres. imašša'

Pret. imšu'

The verb buzzu'um, to do wrong, occurs only in the D and the Dtn stem:

Pres. ubazza'

Pret. ubazzi'

Perf. D (and Pret. Dtn) ubtazzi'

18.8 The Voluntative As a sort of wishing-form for the first person singular (I would like to..., I wish to...) the so-called Voluntative is used. It is formed by replacing the prefix of the first person singular a- (e-) or u- with the particle lu-:

ašpur, I wrote; lušpur, I would like to write

ublam, I brought here; lublam, I wish to bring here

udammiq, I did well; ludammiq, I wish to do well

The wishing-form of the third person is the Precative (13.5, 18.9).

18.9 The Stative Precative The desire for a state of being is expressed through the Stative Precative. In this construction, the Stative is used, preceded by the asseverative particle lū which is not joined to the Stative:

lū šalim, may he stay in good health!

lū balṭāta, may you be living = may you live long!

18.10 Asseverative-Form In order to give special emphasis to an expression, the asseverative particle lū may be placed before the verb form. Again in this case, the particle is not joined to the verb:

īde, I know, he knows; lū īde, I certainly know, he certainly knows

lū ubtazzi', he has truly done wrong again and again

18.11 Paranomastic Infinitive Construction To strengthen a given expression, a verbal form can be connected with the Infinitive of the same verb. The particle -ma (8.14) is placed after the Infinitive:

ana awīlim ana qabêm-ma ul aqbi, I certainly did not speak to the man

18.12 Declension of Personal Pronouns Accusative and Dative forms of the personal pronouns attā, you; anāku, I, etc. (15.7) are formed as follows:

<u>kâta</u> (masc.), <u>kâti</u> (fem.), you (Accusative)

<u>kâšim</u> (masc. and fem.), to you (Dative)

<u>yâti</u>, me; <u>yâšim</u>, to me

These forms can be used as substitutes for the enclitic personal pronouns or they can be used to strengthen them (5.8, 5.9, 13.10), and they are always strongly stressed:

<u>yâti ammīnim inazzaranni</u>, why was it <u>me</u> whom he chided?

Cf. Paradigm 8.

18.13 <u>Infinitive with Prepositions</u> Infinitives with prepositions may occasionally be used to express subjunctive subordinate clauses. The Infinitive in these cases can also take an object:

<u>aššum...itaplusim</u>, with regard to looking again and again = that you may look on constantly

<u>ištu suluppī apālim</u>, after paying with (6.10) dates = after repayment to you of the dates

<u>EXERCISE</u>

P. 1. šum-ma mar-tum na-as-ḫa-at-ma it-ta-na-aq-ra-ar.

A. 2. sinništum a-wa-at pu-uḫ-ri-im uš-te-né-ṣe.

O. 3. šum-ma mar-tum bu-da-ša da-ma-am bu-ul-la-am pa-aš-ša; di-pa-ar né-ku-úr-tim, i-ša-tu-um i-na ma-tim it-ta-na-an-pa-aḫ. 4. šumma i-na bāb ekallim ši-lum ip-lu-uš-ma uš-te-eb-ri; wa-ši-ib ma-ḫa-ar šarrim pi-ri-iš-ti šarrim a-na ma-at nakrim uš-te-né-ṣe. 5. šum-ma mar-tum ṣí-iḫ-ḫu-um i-ta-ad-du; šar-ru-um um-ma-an-šu te-ši-tam i-le-et-te. 6. šum-ma šu-me-el ú-ba-nim pu-ṣa-am i-ta-da-at; ti-bu-ut er-bi-im.

VOCABULARY

qarārum (u), to be rolled up, wrapped up, Ntn, to be rolled up many times

waṣûm, to come out; Štn, to divulge (secrets) repeatedly

bullûm, destroyed, disintegrated

dipāru, torch

napāḫum, (a/u), to ignite; Ntn, to be ignited repeatedly

tēšītum, confusion

nadûm, (ndī), to throw down;St. Ntn to be set in many places, to be studded with, to lay down

puṣṣûm, white spot

READINGS: OLD-BABYLONIAN LETTERS

1. a-na a-bi-ya qí-bí-ma! um-ma Zi-im-ri-e-ra-aḫ-ma: ^{d}Šamaš ù ^{d}Marduk da-ri-iš u_4-mi a-bi li-ba-al-li-ṭú! ^{m}I-bi-^{d}Nin-šubur ṣú-ḫa-ri[1] a-ḫi[2] ^{m}Nu-úr-ì-lí-šu ^{md}Na-bi-um-at-pa-lam im-qú-ut-ma[3] ub-ta-az-zi-i'-šu ù ya-a-ši-im ma-ag-ri-a-tim ša a-na e-ṣé-nim la na-ṭa-a id-bu-ub. ṣú-ḫa-ri-ma lu ub-ta-az-zi-i'! ya-a-ti am-mi-nim i-na-az-za-ra-an-ni? a-na a-wi-lim a-na qá-bé-e-em-ma ú-ul aq-bi. um-ma a-na-ku-ma[4]: a-na a-bi-ya lu-uš-pur-ma ṭe_4-em a-wa-tim li-iš-pur-am-ma a-na a-wi-lim lu-uq-bi! ...i-zi-iz! wa-ar-ka-at a-wa-tim šu-a-ti pu-ru-ús-ma ṭe_4-ma-am šu-up-ra-am-ma, lu-ú i-de-e.

2. a-na Nu-úr-^{d}Šamaš ^{m}A-wi-il-^{d}Adad ^{md}Sîn-pí-laḫ ^{m}Ṣíl-lí-^{d}Adad ù wakil 10 ṣābim qí-bí-ma! um-ma ^{d}Šamaš-na-ṣer-ma: da-mi-iq e-pe-šum an-nu-um?

[1] Acc. Ibbi-Ninšubur, my servant; [2] Construct from aḫum, brother (2.9);
[3] Here maqatum, transitive, to cast down; [4] so I think.

nukaribbū našpāk suluppī ip-te-né-tu-ú-ma suluppī il-te-né-qú-ú ù at-tu-nu a-wa-tim tu-uk-ta-na-ta-ma-ma a-na ṣe-ri-ya ú-ul ta-ša-pa-ra-nim. an-nu-um-ma ṭup-pí uš-ta-bi-la-ku-nu-ši; iš-tu suluppī a-pa-li-im a-wi-le-e a-na ṣe-ri-ya šu-ri-a-nim[5]...

3. a-na Be-el-šu-nu qí-bí-ma! um-ma Qúr-di-Ištar-ma: dŠamaš li-ba-al-li-iṭ-ka! lu ša-al-ma-a-ta lu ba-al-ṭa-a-ta! ...ga-me-er eqlī-ka e-ṣi-id-ma še-am šu-li-a-am-ma i-na mu-uḫ-ḫi-šu šu-ta-ar-ri-iḫ! i-nu-ma ta-la-ka-am, qí-iš-ta-ka ta-ma-ar ...

4. iš-tu ituSimānim aš-šum ṣe-eḫ-ḫe-ru-ti-ya i-ta-ap-lu-si-im ú-na-a'-'i-id-ka. ūm 4kam a-di i-na-an-na ṭe4-em ši-ip-ra-tim ma-la i-pu-šu ù eqil šamaššammim ša i-pu-šu ú-ul ta-aš-pu-ra-am. ...i-na-an-na Na-bi-dSîn a-na ma-aḫ-ri-ka aṭ-ṭar-dam, it-ti-šu a-na eqlim ri-id-ma[6] eqil ši-ip-ra-tim ma-la i-pu-šu ù eqil šamaššammim ša i-pu-šu i-ta-ap-la-ás-ma i-na ṭup-pí-ka pa-nam šu-úr-ši-a-am-ma šu-up-ra-am!

[5] 15.5; [6] Imp. from waradum (13.3).

Lesson 19

GRAMMAR

19.1 *Four-radical Verbs* Along with the verbal roots with two or three consonants, a few roots occur in Akkadian which have *four* consonants. E.g., *blkt*, to ford, to cross over, and *prqd*, to lie on one's back. Moreover, there are some tri-consonantal roots with a long vowel after the third consonant (IV Vowel), e.g., *qlpū*, to propel downstream, *ḫlṣī*, to slip, slide. Since these groups correspond to one another in formation and conjugation, they are grouped together as quadri-radical verbs and treated together. All verbs in both of these groups have *l* or *r* as their second radical.
Cf. Paradigm 34.

19.2 *Stem-formation of the Quadri-radical verbs* The quadriliteral verbs form two main stems. In one of them, an *n* is placed before the root. In form then it corresponds to the N-stem of the tri-radical verbs, but it has no passive meaning. The other stem is formed with the prefixing of a *š* before the root. This stem corresponds in form *and in meaning* to the causative š-stem of the tri-radical verbs. In both of these main stems, an *iterative* can be formed by the insertion of a -*tan*- infix.

19.3 *Prefix tenses of the N stem* The quadriliteral verbs do not admit of root-vowel classes. They consistently have *a* in the Present and *i* in the Preterite. The *n* placed before the root (after the Prefixes *i-*, *ta-*, *a-*, or *ni-*) is assimilated to the first consonant:

> Pres. (with doulbed *third* consonant) *ibbalakkat* (<**inbalakkat*) he leans on, *tabbalakkat*, you lean on... etc.
>
> Pret. *ibbalkit*, he leaned on, Pl. *ibbalkitū*, they leaned on
>
> Perf. (with *a* like the Present) *ittabalkat*

The verbs IV Vowel shorten the originally long final vowel:

> *ipparakku*, ceases
>
> *ipparku*, ceased
>
> *iḫḫeleṣṣi*, slides

19.4 The Stative and the Nominal Forms of the N Stem After the third consonant, the Infinitive and the Stative take the vowel *u*. The Participle is formed with the prefix *mu-* and takes *i* after the third consonant:

> Infinitive *nabalkutum*, to cross, ford, transgress
>
> Stative, *naparqud*, *naparqudat* lies on (his) back
>
> Part. *mubbalkitum*, leaning on, depending on

In verbs which are Final Vowel:

> Inf. *naparkûm*, to cease, *nepelkûm*. to be extended
> Stative, *nepelku*, is extended
> Part. *muḫḫelṣûm* (<*munḫelṣium) sliding
>
> thence is derived *muḫḫelṣītum*, a slippery place

19.5 The Š Stem of The Quadriliteral Verbs (N Stem Class) The prefixes *u-*, *tu-* or *nu-* are placed before the Š which precedes the root:

Pres. (with the doubling of the third consonant)
ušbalakkat, brings to revolt

Pret. *ušbalkit*, brought to revolt

In verbs which are IV Vowel:

ušqeleppe, he has (it) driven downstream

ušqelpi, he had (it) driven downstream

Cf. Paradigm 34.

19.6 *The Š group of quadriliteral Verbs* Another group of verbs is to be considered as quadriliteral. Their first consonant is always š. To this group belong *šuqallulum* (*šqll*) to hang, and *šukênum*, to prostrate oneself.
From *šuqallum* a Present is formed, *išqallal*, hangs. This is used also as a Stative (Prefix Stative, 11.9)
The Participle *muškēnum*, who prostrates himself, is derived from *šukênum*. This was a designation for a group of men who lived in direct dependence on the king.

19.7 *The Second Person Feminine Singular* In the Present, Preterite, and Perfect, the second person singular feminine is distinguished from the masculine (5.4) by the ending *-ī*:

tallik (masc.), *tallikī* (fem.) you go

The Ventive ending after the second person singular feminine *-m* and the long *ī* vowel is shortened before it (*-im*):

tallikim, you came

The Second Person Singular of the Imperative is similarly formed:

idin (masc.) *idnī* (fem.), give!

Ventive: *idnam*, *idnim*, give [it] here

šūbilam, *šūbilim*, have (it) brought here!

19.8 The Rt-stem Very rare are occurrences of the R (Reduplication) stems; this includes Rt and Rtn. These are similar to the D, Dt, and Dtn but are formed with reduplication of the middle syllable, rather than consonantal doubling. The difference is most clearly seen by studying the examples. The Rt stem is the most common in occurrence:

Pres. Rt uptararras (Pres. Dt uptarras, 15.2)

Pret. Rt uptararris (Pret. Dt uptarris)

Imper. Rt putararris (Imper. Dt putarris)

The verb danānum, to be strong, occurs in the Rt and has there the meaning to make a trial of strength with one another, and, to prove superior.

Pres. uddanannan, he proves himself superior

2nd Pers. Pl. tuddanannanā, you test your strength

19.9 The Cohortative The Cohortative serves as the wishing-form of the first person plural. It is formed with the particle i, which occurs before the first person plural of the Preterite:

i nillik, let's go! i nidbub, we wish to speak

19.10 The Vocalisation of the G Stative In the third person singular of the G stative, the helping vowel before the third consonant is generally i:

ṣabit, he is attacked, damiq, he is good (1.5)

In verbs which describe states of being (5.2) an a or a u can occur:

rapaš, it is thiçk, wide

šabus, he is angry

qerub, he is near

šamuḫ, he is magnificent (Cf. the personal name ᵈSîn-šamuḫ)

The remaining forms of the G Stative are formed without an anaptytic vowel:

rapšat, it (fem.) is broad.

19.11 The Vocalisation of the G Imperative The helping vowel in the G Imperative (inserted between the first and second radical) almost always corresponds to the theme-vowel (13.2):

ṣabat, seize! (*ṣbat)

But in some verbs of the a-class, the helping vowel is i. E.g., lamādum, to learn, experience:

Imper. G limad, experience!, Fem. limdī, Pl. limdā

19.12 Verbs Which are Aleph and Final Vowels The verbs re'ûm (r'ī), to shepherd, pasture and le'ûm, to be able, form their present with consonantal aleph (16.4):

ire''i, he leads to pasture

ele''i, I am capable of

The aleph is dropped (9.6) in the Preterite:

irē, he shepherded

ilē, he was capable of

The Participle is rē'ûm (rē'ium), shepherd.

One must distinguish between le'ûm, to be able, and la'ûm (l'ū), to be dirty. The latter takes the Stative D lu''u, Fem. lu''ât, soiled.

EXERCISES

P. 1. šumma ubān ḫa-ši qablītum i-na ma-aš-ka-ni-ša na-ba-al-ku-ta-at. 2. šumma ina šu-me-el martim pi-iṭ-rum né-pe-èl-ku. 3. šum-ma ṣibtum it-ta-ba-al-ka-at. 4. šumma i-na bāb ekallim zi-ḫu lu-u' - 'u$_5$-ma ù iš-qá-la-al.

A. 5. îl-šu e-li a-wi-li-im ša-bu-us. 6. ma-tum ša re-e-i-ša ib-ba-al-ki-tu re-e-i-ša e-li-ša iz-za-az. 7. i-na mu-úḫ-ḫe-el-ṣi-tim šēp awīlim i-ḫe-le-ṣi. 8. a-lum ib-ba-la-ka-at-ma be-el-šu i-da-ak. 9. naker-ka ud-da-na-an-na-na-ak-kum.

O. 10. šumma ka-as-ka-sú i-mi-tam ù šu-me-lam ka-pi-iṣ; at-ta u naker-ka tu-ud-da-na-an-na-na. 11. šumma ka-as-ka-sú i-mi-tam ka-pi-iṣ; a-na nakrī-ka tu-da-na-an-na-an. 12. šumma kišād ḫašîm[1] na-ba-al-ku-ut; ṭe$_4$-e-em ma-a-tim iš-ta-na-an-ni. 13. šumma kakki i-mi-tim i-na re-eš mar-tim ša-ki-in-ma ib-ba-al-ki-it-ma ma-áṣ-ra-aḫ mar-tim iṭ-ṭù-ul šar-rum ma-li-ki ú-ul i-ra-aš-ši. 14. šumma ḫašûm na-pa-ar-qú-da-at; ma-as-sú ib-ba-la-ka-su. 15. šumma bāb ekallim né-pe-el-ku-ú; ḫu-ša-aḫ-ḫu-um ib-ba-aš-ši-i. 16. šumma i-na bāb ekallim qú-ú-um ra-pa-aš; mi-li i-ir-tim.

[1] 0.33.

VOCABULARY

nabulkutum (blkt) to turn around; to revolt

nepelkûm (plkī) to be wide

lu''u (St.D) is soiled

šuqallulum (šqll) to hang

šabāsum, to be angry

rē'ûm, shepherd

muḫḫelṣītum, smoothness

neḫelṣûm, (ḫlṣi) to slide

danānum, to be strong, Rt, to prove oneself superior

kaskasum, breastbone

<u>kapāṣum</u>, (i) to bend, buckle

<u>kišādum</u>, neck

<u>mālikum</u>, adviser

<u>naparqudum</u> (<u>prqd</u>), to be on one's back

READING PASSAGE (Old-Babylonian Letters)

1. ^{m}Tam-la-tum tamkārum mār Qí-iš-^{d}Nu-nu eleppam ša Ib-ba-tum malāḫim i-gu-ur-ma a-na Bābili uš-qé-el-pi; ...^{m}Ib-ba-tum šu-a-ti a-na ma-aḫ-ri-ka aṭ-ṭar-dam, ki-ma ra-bu-ti-ka eleppam šu-a-ti pu-uṭ-ṭe$_{4}$-er. pí-qí-is-sú-um-ma a-na Sipparim li-ša-aq-qí-a-aš-ši.

2. a-na um-mi-ya qí-bí-ma! um-ma A-wi-il-...[1]ma-ru-ki-ma: ^{d}Šamaš ù ^{d}...[1] li-ba-al-li-ṭú-ki! ... il-ku-um is-ra-an-ni-ma na-pa-ar-ka-am ú-ul e-li-i, ú at-ti ma-ti-ma ki-ma um-ma-tim ú-ul ta-aš-pu-ri-im-ma li-ib-bi ú-ul tu-ba-li-ṭi. a-nu-um-ma Ma-an-na-ši aš-ta-ap-ra-ki-im. 2 qa šamnim šu-bi-lim. mu-ur-ṣú-um iṣ-ba-ta-ni-ma i-na na-pi-iš-tim an-na-di[2].

3. a-na Ma-ti-be-lu-um qí-bí-ma! um-ma Ni-id-na-at-^{d}Sîn-ma: ^{d}Šamaš li-ba-al-li-iṭ-ka! a-nu-um-ma un-ne-du-uk-ki uš-ta-bi-la-ak-kum. un-ne-du-uk-ki i-na a-ma-ri-i-ka 1 kùr er-bi-i, 300 ka-ma-ri ... i-na e-le-ep-pí-im ṣe-na-am-ma ú at-ta al-ka-am! ṣí-bi-a-tu-u-ka lu-ú ma-da, al-ka-am-ma ṭe-e-mi li-ma-a-ad! ap-pu-tum!

4. a-na Ib-ni-^{d}Sîn mār ^{d}Marduk-na-ṣe-er qí-bí-ma! um-ma Am-mi-ṣà-du-qá-ma: bu-qú-mu i-na bīt a-ki-tim iš-ša-ak-ka-an. ki-ma ṭup-pí an-ni-a-am ta-am-ma-ru, pa-ni ṣēnī ša te-re-'u$_{5}$-ú ṣa-ab-tam ù ka-ni-ka-a-at ṣēnī ša a-na ṣi-i-tim tu-še-ṣú-ú le-qé-a-am-ma a-na Bābili al-kam! la tu-la-ap-pa-tam, i-na ^{itu}Addārim ūm 1^{kam} a-na Bābili sí-in-qá-am!

5. a-na Ipiq-Ištar qí-bi-ma! um-ma ^{d}En-líl-lú-šaga$_5$-ma: ^{d}En-líl li-ba-al-li-iṭ-ka! ki-ma ti-du-ú e-bu-ru-um qé-ru-ub. la tu-uš-ta-a[3], it-ti Na-ḫi-iš-ša-al-mu-um al-kam-ma te$_4$-em bi-ti i ni-id-bu-ub.

[1]The name is not completely preserved.

[2]Literally: I shall be cast out of life--I am near to death.

[3]tuštâ = tušta''a (16.5)

Lesson 20

GRAMMAR

20.1 The Language of Old-Babylonian Poetry   The language of hymns and epics (0.9) is somewhat different from the normal Old-Babylonian as used in letters, legal documents, and other prose of the period (e.g., omens). It is characterised through a rather rich use of older forms and expressions which are not used in prose or are used there only infrequently. The most important peculiarities of the poetic language are the continued use of two cases which otherwise are quite rare--the locative-adverbial (20.2) and the terminative-adverbial (20.3). Also the poetry uses an irregular construct state form (20.4). The rhythmic structure of poetry, with rising and falling stress, demands far greater freedom in word-order and some apocopation of final vowels in pronominal suffixes (20.6) and some artificial lengthening (20.19).

20.2 The Locative-Adverbial   The original locative case in -*u*(*m*) occurs in prose only in adverbs (9.9) like *šaplānum*, below. In poetry, it is very common in combination with the possessive suffix; the -*m* of mimation is assimilated to the suffix:

rešušša (*rēšum* + *ša*) on her head

siqrušša, by her command

The construct state of a locative before a genitive takes the ending -*u*:

qabaltu ṣēri, in the midst of the plain

20.3 The Terminative-Adverbial   The original terminative in -*iš* occurs in prose only as the adverbial ending -*iš* added to adjectives:

isariš, in just fashion (from the adj. išarum, just)

mithāriš, in equal portions (from mithārum, corresponding to one another.)

In poetry, these adverbial endings are especially frequent:

danniš, very much, powerfully

šarhiš, magnificently, splendidly

ištīniš, together (from ištīnum, one)

As a directional case with nouns, the terminative is used only in poetry, either with a dependent genitive:

ipšiš pīšunu, for the doing of their mouth = for their judgment, utterance

or simply with the possessive suffix:

qātišša, into her hand

simtišša, in her form

muttiššunu, before them (muttum, front)

Also the interrogative adverb ēš (ayyiš, whither) contains the terminative-ending -iš.

20.4 The Construct State in -u In poetry, in place of the construct state without an ending, a construct state in -u is frequently found; this is perhaps for rhythmic purposes:

ṣābitu qātīka (for ṣābit qātīka), what your hand grasps

The construct state of kalum, totality, is found in prose as kal or kala; in poetry it is frequently kalu:

kalu marṣātim, all problems, distress

The construct state ending of the plural forms in -ātum/-ātim (3.5), occurs in poetry, for the most part, as -ātu:

ana šīmātu awīlūtim (for ana šīmāt...) according to the skills of mankind

20.5 The Anaptyctic Vowel a in Nouns with Suffixes In prose, the possessive suffixes are attached to the construct state of a given noun (3.8). In poetry, an anaptyctic vowel is often used instead.

migrašunu (for migeršunu), their favorite

Cf. ištāša, with her, (20.10).

20.6 Apocopated Pronominal Suffixes The disappearance of vowels from pronominal suffixes occurs only rarely in prose (16.8). But in some poetic writings, it is very common. Especially the possessive suffixes -ša and -šunu (3.7) change often to -š and -šun.

nazzāzuš, (nazzāzu-ša) her position

libbīšun, of their heart

maḫrīšun, before them

The accusative suffix -šunūti (13.10) can be shortened to -šunūt:

ittanaqqīšunūt, he sacrifices to them constantly (accusative is used here for the dative).

20.7 Anaphoric pronoun ši is (in poetry) šat.

20.8 The Dative of the Personal Pronouns The Dative-forms of anāku, attā, attī, šu, etc. (15.7) are:

yâšim, to me

kâšim, (masc. and fem.) to you

šuāšim (šâšim in poetry also šâšum) to him

šiāšim, to her

niāšim, to us

These forms which are consistently used with ana, serve frequently to show special emphasis:

sabītum ana šâšum izzakaram ana [d]Giš, the wine-drawer spoke to him, to Gilgameš.

20.9 The Prepositions ana and ina The short forms of the prepositions *ana*, to, and *ina*, in on, are *an* and *in*. They occur frequently in poetry in combination with certain nouns and the resulting double-consonants are not always written:

a-ni-ri-i-ši-ú (*annīrīšiu*<*ana nīrīšu*) under his yoke

i-ge-e-gu-un-ni-im (*iggegunnim*<*ina gegunnim*), in the high temple

i-ni-li (*inilī*<*ina ilī*)among the gods

20.10 *The Preposition išti* The preposition *išti* (also *itti*), with, can be combined with suffixes:

ištīšu, with him

ittīya, with me

In poetry, the vowel *a* (20.5) can serve to join the preposition and the suffix:

ištāša, with her

The preposition *ištu*, from, out of, is not to be confused with the preposition *išti* (*itti*), with. *ištu* is not combined with pronominal suffixes.

20.11 *The Prefix of the Third Person of the Feminine* In prose, the third person feminine is identical with the third person masculine:

iṣbat, he/she seized

In poetry, however, sometimes forms with the prefix *ta-* (*te-*, *tu-*) are used for the third person feminine:

tattadin, she gave

tetēriš, she demanded

tušaknišam, she has subdued

20.12 *The Stative of bašûm and izuzzum* There are some verbs which ordinarily form a prefix Stative (11.9) but in poetry they may take normal Stative forms with the same meaning:

baši, he is present (for *ibašši*)

nazuz (pl. *nazuzzū*), he has stepped up, stands (for *izzaz*, *izzazzū*)

20.13 *The verb nâdum* Not to be confused with *na'ādum* (*n'd*), to pay heed, (16.4) is *nâdum*, to praise. It forms a G stem like *dâṣum* (9.6), but forms a D stem with consonantal aleph. The Precative Dt: *litta''id*, may he be praised!

20.14 *The Vetitive* The Vetitive particle *ay*, not, can combine with the first person singular of the Preterite:

ayāmur (*ay* + *āmur*), I shall not see

20.15 *The Potential* To indicate the Potential, the enclitic particle -*man* is employed:

ibrī-man itabbeam, my companion could get up, recover

20.16 *The Negative lā* In poetry, *lā* (5.10) can be used in place of *ul* for the negation of a main clause:

balāṭam...*lā tutta*, you will not find life

20.17 *Comparison* In order to express a comparative, one makes use of the preposition *eli*, over, above:

elšunu ḫaptat, over that one is she powerful = she is more powerful than that one

The Superlative can be paraphrased with the aid of the construct state:

rabīt Igigī = the great one of the Igigu = the greatest of the Igigu

20.18 *The Stative in a Noun* The Absolute State of a Noun corresponds in form to the Stative of the Verb (8.9). Every noun in the Absolute State can therefore be construed as a verb and conjugated:

bēl, he is Lord

bēlēta, you are Lord (14.11)

Similarly with adjectives:

šarḫat, she is magnificent

īnāšā bitrāmā, her eyes are colored

20.19 *Broken Vowels* Writings like *i-bi-us-sé-e* for *ibissê* serve to express a certain coloration of vowels--a sound somewhat between *i* and *u* (perhaps similar to the German ü). In poetry, broken vowels, e.g., *-ši-ú* (for *-šu*) or *na-zu-iz-zu-ú* (for *nazuzzū*) may serve to reproduce a *dissimilation* conditioned by the rhythm of poetry.

READING PASSAGE FROM THE OLD BABYLONIAN VERSION OF THE GILGAMESH EPIC

II 2. En-ki-dùg[1] ša a-ra-am-mu-ma da-an-ni-iš

3. it-ti-ya it-ta-al-la-ku ka-lu mar-ṣa-a-tim

4. il-li-ik-ma a-na ši-ma-tu a-wi-lu-tim

5. ur-ri ù mu-ši e-li-šu ab-ki

6. ú-ul ad-di-iš-šu[2] a-na qé-bé-ri-im

7. ib-ri-ma-an i-ta-ab-bé-a-am a-na ri-ig-mi-ya

8. se-bé-et u_4-mi-im ù se-bé mu-ši-a-tim

9. a-di tu-ul-tum im-qú-tam i-na ap-pí-šu

10. iš-tu wa-ar-ki-šu ú-ul ú-ta ba-la-ṭám

11. at-ta-na-ag-gi-iš ki-ma ḫa-bi-lim qá-ba-al-tu ṣe-ri

12. i-na-an-na sa-bi-tum a-ta-mar pa-ni-ki

13. mu-tam ša a-ta-na-ad-da-ru a-ya-a-mu-ur

[1]Enkidu, the hero, friend of Gilgamesh

[2]16.7

14. sa-bi-tum a-na ša-a-šum iz-za-kar-am a-na ^{d}Giš

III 1. ^{d}Giš[1] e-eš ta-da-a-al

2. ba-la-ṭám ša ta-sa-aḫ-ḫa-ru la tu-ut-ta

3. i-nu-ma ilū ìb-nu-ú a-wi-lu-tam

4. mu-tam iš-ku-nu a-na a-wi-lu-tim

5. ba-la-ṭám i-na qá-ti-šu-nu iṣ-ṣa-ab-tu

6. at-ta ^{d}Giš lu ma-li ka-ra-aš-ka

7. ur-ri ù mu-ši ḫi-ta-ad-dú at-ta

8. u_4-mi-ša-am šu-ku-un ḫi-du-tam

9. ur-ri ù mu-ši su-ur ù me-le-el_5

10. lu ub-bu-bu ṣú-ba-tu-ka

11. qá-qá-ad-ka lu me-se me-e lu ra-am-ka-ta

12. ṣú-ub-bi ṣe-eḫ-ra-am ṣa-bi-tu qá-ti-ka

13. mar-ḫi-tum li-iḫ-ta-ad-da-a-am i-na su-ni-ka

FROM AN OLD-BABYLONIAN HYMN TO IŠTAR

1. il-ta-am zu-um-ra-a ra-šu-ub-ti i-la-tim

2. li-it-ta-i-id be-le-et ni-ši ra-bi-it I-gi-gi[2]

3. Ištar zu-um-ra ra-šu-ub-ti i-la-tim li-it-ta-i-id

4. be-le-et i-ši-i[3] ra-bi-it I-gi-gi

5. ša-at me-le-ṣi-im ru-à-ma-am la-ab-ša-at

6. za-a'-na-at in-bi mi-qí-a-am ù ku-uz-ba-am

7. Ištar me-le-ṣi-im ru-à-ma-am la-ab-ša-at

[1] writing for Gilgameš

[2] The Igigū, a group of gods

[3] *išši*

8. za-a'-na-at in-bi mi-qí-a-am ù ku-uz-ba-am

9. ša-ap-ti-in du-uš-šu-pa-at ba-la-ṭú-um pí-i-ša

10. si-im-ti-iš-ša i-ḫa-an-ni-i-ma ṣi-ḫa-tum

11. šar-ḫa-at i-ri-mu ra-mu-ú re-šu-uš-ša

12. ba-ni-à-a ši-im-ta-à-ša bi-it-ra-a-ma i-na-ša ši-it-a-ra

13. il$_5$-tu-um iš-ta-à-ša i-ba-aš-ši mi-il-ku-um

14. ši-ma-at mi-im-ma-mi qa-ti-iš-ša ta-am-ḫa-at

15. na-ap-la-su-uš-ša ba-ni bu-a-ru-ú

16. ba-aš-tum ma-aš-ra-ḫu la-ma-as-su-um še-e-du-um

25. ša-a-at i-ni-li a-ta-ar na-az-za-zu-uš

26. ka-ab-ta-at a-ma-as-sà el-šu-nu ḫa-ap-ta-at-ma

27. Ištar i-ni-li a-ta-ar na-az-za-zu-uš

28. ka-ab-ta-at a-ma-as-sà el-šu-nu ḫa-ap-ta-at-ma

37. ra-mu-ú-ma iš-ti-ni-iš[1] pa-ra-ak-ka-am

38. i-ge-e-gu-un-ni-im[2] šu-ba-at ri-ša-tim

39. mu-ut-ti-iš-šu-un i-lu-ú na-zu-iz-zu-ú

40. ip-ši-iš pí-šu-nu ba-ši-à-a[3] uz-na-šu-un

41. šar-ru-um mi-ig-ra-šu-un na-ra-am li-ib-bi-šu-un

42. šar-ḫi-iš it-na-aq-qí-šu-nu-ut[4] ni-qí-a-šu el-la-am

43. Am-mi-di-ta-na el-la-am ni-qí-i qá-ti-i-šu

44. ma-aḫ-ri-šu-un ú-še-eb-bi li-i ù as-li na-am-ra-i-i[5]

45. iš-ti Anim ḫa-wi-ri-i-ša te-te-er-ša-aš-šu-um

46. da-ri-a-am ba-la-ṭa-am ar-ka-am

47. ma-da-a-tim ša-na-at ba-la-à-ṭi-im a-na Am-mi-di-ta-na

48. tu-ša-at-li-im Ištar ta-at-ta-di-in

49. si-iq-ru-uš-ša tu-ša-ak-ni-ša-aš-šu-um

50. ki-ib-ra-at er-bé-e-em a-na še-pí-i-šu

51. ù na-ap-ḫa-ar ka-li-šu-nu da-ad-mi

52. ta-aṣ-ṣa-mi-su-nu-ti a-ni-ri-i-ši-ú

57. Ištar a-na Am-mi-di-ta-na šar-ri ra-i-mi-i-ki

58. ar-ka-am da-ri-a-am ba-la-ṭa-am šu-ur-ki

59. li-ib-lu-uṭ

[1]Cf. Z.45

[2]20.9

[3]0.22

[4]This is probably a shortened form of <u>ittanaqqi</u> (shortened for purposes of rhythm)

[5]0.22

Lesson 21

GRAMMAR

21.1 *Middle-Babylonian* The language of the Middle Babylonian letters (0.7) is distinguished from Old-Babylonian chiefly through the dropping of *mimation* (21.2), vowel changes under the influence of certain consonants (21.4--21.5), and some special formations of pronouns (21.7--21.9). There are also syntactic differences, notably a different use of the Perfect (21.14) and the formation of temporal clauses with *kī* (21.15).

21.2 *Mimation* The final ending -*m* of the case-ending (1.7), of the Ventive (5.7), of the Dative personal pronouns (5.9), and of pronominal suffixes, has already largely disappeared in Old-Babylonian. In Middle-Babylonian, mimation remains only where it is supported by a suffix or the enclitic -*ma*:

lilqūnikkumma < *lilqūni* (*m*) + *ku* (*m*) + *ma*
They shall take (it) for you and ...

21.3 *Dropping and change of the Half-vowel w* At the beginning of a word, the *w* drops:

ardu (<*wardum*) servant, slave
ašābu (<*wašābum*), to settle, sit
Part. *āšibu* (<*wāšibum*) the dweller

Between vowels, *w* shifts to *m*:

amīlu (< awīlum), man, human being

umaššer (< uwaššer) he gave up, he renounced

Analogously to the Present umaššar and Preterite umaššer, all those parts of the verb wuššurum which in Old-Babylonian are formed with w, are formed in Middle-Babylonian with an m. The Infinitive of the latter then is not *uššuru but muššuru, to give up, to renounce. (Imp. muššer, let go!)

21.4 Labials and Dentals Before Dentals, m shifts to n:

ḫantiš (< ḫamṭiš), swiftly

The sequence mt shifts to nd:

undeššer (< *umtaššer, Old-Babylonian ūtaššer) he has given up, released

21.5 š before Dentals and Sibilants Before the Dentals (d, t, ṭ) and also frequently before z, s, ṣ, š in Middle-Babylonian shifts to l. In this shift, it does not matter if the š is a root-consonant or an element in the formation of a stem (the š of the Š stem):

kulda (< kušdam), come true!

ulziz (< ušziz, 21.13) he caused to stand, put forward

altaprakku (< aštaprakkum) I have sent to you

ultu (for Old-Babylonian ištu) from, since

21.6 Shift from a to e An a in a closed syllable can (in Middle-Babylonian) become an e if the following syllable contains an i or an e:

undeššer (<*umtaššer) he has given up

ušeddi (<*ušandi) I have ignored

21.7 The Personal Pronouns The Nominative of the personal pronouns (15.7) and the anaphoric pronoun (11.10) correspond to the Old-Babylonian:

anāku, attā, šū, etc.

The Dative (18.12) for the first person is (ana) yâši (Old-Babylonian yâšim), to me, the second person (ana) (kâša) (Old-Babylonian kâšim), to you. The Gen.-Acc. singular of the anaphoric pronoun (which is also used attributively) is šâtu (Old-Babylonian, šuāti):

amīla šâtu, that man

In the Plural, the Dative šâšunu (Old-Babylonian šunūti) is also used as the Accusative.

amīlī šâšunu, those people

21.8 The Possessive Pronouns In place of the stressed independent possessive pronouns yûm etc. (6.8), in Middle-Babylonian attu- is used with the Possessive suffix:

(šibšu) attūšu his (lease)

harrāna attū'a my caravan (21.9)

21.9 The Possessive suffixes Generally these correspond to those of Old-Babylonian. But the first person singular, my, with the nouns ahu and abu is not -ī in the Nominative (3.9) but -īya:

ahīya, (Old-Babylonian ahī) my brother

abīya, my father but: *bēlī*, my Lord

If -*ya* precedes a plural form ending in -*ū* or if it precedes an *attu*- (21.8) it will, as in Old-Babylonian, shift to '*a*:

tamkarū'a, my merchants *ḫarrāna attū'a*, my caravans

21.10 Demonstrative and Interrogative Pronouns The feminine for *annû*, this, is *annītu* and it is frequently used as a substantive:

annīta niqtabi, we have said this

An interrogative adjective is *mīnû*, what? In the Accusative this is *mīnâ*, with regard to what?

21.11 The Conjugation of the Stative in the Plural The Stative singular has the endings -*āku*, -*āt*, -*āti* (14.11). The endings of the Stative in the plural are (for Old and Middle Babylonian) -*ānū* for the first person and -*ātunu*, -*ātina* for the second person.

ṭābānū, we are good

ṭābātina, you (fem.) are good

[*e*-verbs form these endings with -*ē*- instead of -*ā*-.]
Cf. Paradigm 13

21.12 Verbs II Aleph The Verbs which are II Aleph (9.6) are frequently formed in Middle Babylonian with a consonantal aleph:

ša'ālum (along with *šâlum*), to ask

Pres. *iša''al* (*išâl*) he asks

Pret. *iš'al* (*išāl*) he asked

Imp. *ša'al* (*šāl*), ask!

The Gtn stem is always formed with consonantal aleph:

Pres. *ištana''al*, he asks again and again

Imp. *šita''al*, ask again and again

Cf. Paradgim 25

21.13 The Š-Stem of *izuzzum* The irregular verb *izuzzum*, to stand, (11.8) forms in Old-Babylonian the Pres. Š *ušzaz* (Plural *ušzazzū*), he causes to stand, he sets up. The Preterite is *ušziz* (*ušzizzū*). The Imperative is *šuziz*. In Middle-Babylonian, these forms are:

Pres. *ulzaz* and

Pret. *ulziz* (21.5).

21.14 The Use of Tenses The Perfect is in Middle-Babylonian (otherwise than in Old-Babylonian, 15.14) the general tense for expressing the past in declaratory sentences:

ana šīmātī ittaklū, they are hindered in their decision

eqlātī undeššer, he has given up the fields

The Preterite, on the other hand, is used chiefly in negations and in questions:

anāku ul umaššer I have not given up [the fields]

mīnâ ḫiṭa aḫṭi ana belīya, in what regard have I sinned against my Lord?

The Preterite is also used in dependent clauses:

amīlū ša ardīya idūkū, the people who have killed my servants

21.15 Temporal Clauses   The particle *kī*, when, as soon as, (Old-Babylonian *kīma*, 13.14) is very common in Middle-Babylonian. It immediately precedes the verb of the temporal clause:

kī with the Preterite, when, after:

> *šepīšu kī unakkisu itūšu iktalāšu*, after he cut [the enemy's] feet off, he kept him prisoner.
>
> ^{m}*Ḫuzālum kī elqâ ītamarši*, when I had *Ḫuzālum* brought to me, he examined her

kī with the perfect, as soon as,

> *ana pānīka kī altaprakku šita''alšu*, as soon as I have written to you, inquire of him again and again

Several *kī* clauses can stand one after the other but without a conjunction expressed.

> *ṭēm murṣīka kī iš'alūši riksa kī esiḫu urakkasūši*, after he had inquired about the report of her illness (and) after I had obtained material for bandages they bound her.

Similarly used as a temporal particle is *ultu* (Old-Babylonian, *ištu*), with the meaning, since, after:

> *ultu Aḫu-ṭābu ana muḫḫi aḫīya itīqu*, after Aḫuṭābu had gone over to my brother

21.16 The Middle Babylonian Letter-Formula   The Addressee can (as in Old-Babylonian) be addressed by the formula:

> *ana* NN *qibīma*, to NN speak!

The sender of the letter is indicated thus:

<u>umma</u> NN-<u>ma</u>, so (speaks) NN (13.16).

Often the name of the addressee is repeated in the formula:

<u>ummā</u> (<u>um</u>-<u>ma</u>-<u>a</u>) <u>ana</u> NN-<u>ma</u>, thus (he speaks) to ...

<u>ummā</u> stands before a quotation as does <u>akanna</u>, so.

The following little polite flourish is frequently used:

<u>anā dinān bēlīya lullik</u> = In place of my Lord I would like to go = I would like to sacrifice myself for my Lord

READING PASSAGE MIDDLE BABYLONIAN LETTERS

1. a-na ^{m}Amīl- ^{d}Marduk qí-bi-ma! um-ma šarrum-ma; um-ma-a a-na Amīl- ^{d}Marduk-ma: mār ^{m}Šadî-aḫḫū-ú-a it-ti-i-ka a-na Bābili le-qa-am-ma kul-da!

2. a-na ^{md}Amurru-ka-ra-bi-iš-me qí-bí-ma! um-ma ^{d}En-líl-damiq-ma:šib-šu$_{14}$ ša šamaššammi ša ^{d}En-líl-mu-bal-liṭ at-tu-ú-šu ú ša šu-ta-pi-šu muš-še-er-ma šu-ú liš-bu-uš,at-ta la ta-šab-bu-uš.

3. arad-ka ...[1]: a-na di-na-an be-lí-ya lul-lik! um-ma-a a-na be-lí-ya-ma: eqlētū ša be-lí id-di-na, -- ^{m}U-bar-ru a-na be-lí-ya iq-bu-ú, um-ma-a: eqlētī un-de-še$_{20}$ -er, a-na-ku ul ú-maš-še$_{20}$ -er, ^{m}U-bar-ru a-na er-re-ši id-din. ...

4. a-na ^{m}Amīlī-ya qí-bí-ma! um-ma ^{m}Ka-tar-saḫ aḫū-ka-ma: a-na ka-a-ša lu šul-mu! ilānū a-ši-bu ina ^{uru}Kār- ^{d}Beli nap-ša-ti-ka li-iṣ-ṣu-rù! um-ma-a a-na ^{m}Amīlī-ya-ma: ṭup-pa ša šarru ú-še-bi-lak-ku, aš-šum eqli ša ^{uru}Ka-du-ku-ú, ki-i pi-i ṭup-pi ša šarru ú-še-bi-lak-ku ḫa-an-ṭiš šu-pu-ur-ma arad-ka ^{m}Ku-ub-bu-la la i-kal-lu-ú-ma lit-ta-al-ka!

5. arad-ka ^{m}Im-gu-rù: a-na di-na-an be-lí-ya lu-ul-li-ik! a-na bīt be-lí-ya šu-ul-mu! ^{f}Qá-qá-da-ni-tu$_4$ šēp-ša ik-ka-al[2] -ši, -- ^{m}Ḫu-za-lu$_4$ ki el-qá-a i-ta-mar-ši. ṭe-em mur-ṣi-ša ki iš-a-lu-ši ri-ik-sa ki e-si-ḫu u-ra-ak-ka-su-ši. ...

6. a-na be-lí-ya qí-bí-ma! um-ma ^{d}Nin-urta-a-ša-re-ed arad-ka-ma: a-na di-na-an be-lí-ya lu-ul-lik! mi-na-a ḫi-ṭa aḫ-ṭi a-na be-lí-ya? ... ya-a-ši be-li te-e-ma a-ka-an-na il-ta-ak-na-an-ni: um-ma-a: uṭ-ṭe-ta ù šīpātī šu-un-ni-ma mu-ḫu-ur-šu! a-na mu-uḫ-ḫi an-ni-ti āla qí-pa-ku-ma ú-še-di-i? ta-mé-er-ta qí-pa-ku-ma ú-še-ṣi-i? -- u-du-ú-a a-na be-lí-ya ya-a-nu ù be-lí i-de.

7. a-na Na-ap-ḫu-u'-ru-ri-ja šàr ^{kur}Mi-iṣ-ri-i aḫī-ya qí-bí-ma! um-ma Bur-ra-bu-ri-ja-aš šàr ^{kur}Ka-ra-du-ni-ya-aš aḫū-ka-ma: a-na ja-a-ši šu-ul-mu. a-na ka-ša mātī-ka bītī-ka aššātī-ka mārī-ka rabûtī-ka sisī-ka narkabātī-ka da-an-ni-iš lu šu-ul-mu!

a-na-ku ù aḫū-ya it-ti a-ḫa-mi-iš ṭa-bu-ta ni-id-da-bu-ub, ù an-ni-ta ni-iq-ta-bi, um-ma-a: ki-i ab-bu-ni it-ti a-ḫa-mi-iš ṭa-a-bu,ni-i-nu lu ṭa-ba-nu![3] i-na-an-na tamkārū-a ša it-ti Aḫu-ṭa-a-bu te-bu-ú i-na ^{kur}Ki-na-aḫ-ḫi a-na ši-ma-a-ti it-ta-ak-lu-ú. ul-tu Aḫu-ṭa-a-bu a-na mu-uḫ-ḫi aḫī-ya i-ti-qu, i-na ^{uru}Ḫi-in-na-tu-ni ša ^{kur}Ki-na-aḫ-ḫi ^{m}Šu-um-ad-da mār ^{m}Ba-lum-me-e, ^{m}Šu-ta-at-na mār ^{m}Ša-ra-a-tu$_4$ ša ^{uru}Ak-ka amīlē-šu-nu ki iš-pu-ru tamkārī-ya id-du-ku ù kasap-šu-nu it-tab-lu. ...[4] a-na pa-ni-ka ki-i al-ta-ap-ra-ak-ku ši-ta-'a-al-šu-ma li-iq-ba-ak-ku! ^{kur}Ki-na-aḫ-ḫi māt-ka ù šarrū-ša ardū-ka. i-na mati-ka ḫu-um-mu-ṣa-ku. su-ni-iq-šu-nu-ti-ma kaspa ša it-ba-lu šu-ul-li-im! ù amīlī ša ardī-ya i-du-ku du-uk-šu-nu-ti-ma da-mi-šu-nu te-e-er! ù šum-ma amīlū an-nu-ti ul ta-ad-du-uk,i-tu-ur-ru-ma lu-ú ḫarrāna at-tu-ú-a ù lu mārī ši-ib-ri-ka i-du-ku-ú-ma i-na bi-ri-ni mār ši-ip-ri ip-pa-ar-ra-as. ù šum-ma i-na-ak-ki-ru-ka[5]; 1 amīla at-tu-ú-a mŠu-um-ad-da šēpī-šu ki-i ú-na-ak-ki-su, i-tu-šu ik-ta-la-šu. ù amīla ša-na-a mŠu-ta-at-na Ak-ka-ayyu-ú i-na tal-lì ki-i ul-zi-zu-šu, a-na pa-ni-šu iz-za-az. amīlē ša-šu-nu li-il-qú-ni-ik-ku-um-ma a-mu-ur-ma amīla ša-tu ša-al-ma lu ti-i-de. ...

[1]The personal name is not preserved.

[2]In Middle-Babylonian of I Aleph verbs, the vowel sign is not written; Old-Babylonian is i-(ik-_ ka-al (4.6)

[3]18.9

[4]The personal name cannot be read with certainty

[5]Complete as, "thus know ...

Lesson 22

GRAMMAR

22.1 *Neo-Babylonian* The language of the neo-Babylonian letters (0.7) shows a further development from Middle-Babylonian (21.1). There are manifested in it almost all the peculiarities of Middle-Babylonian. In addition to those, Neo-Babylonian manifests even more shifting of consonants in certain combinations (22.3), the gradual disappearance of case endings in declension (22.9), some new pronominal formations (22.4 - 22.6), many new prepositional and adverbial expressions (22.14 - 22.15). The incipient influence of Aramaic is shown (apart from the blurring of case distinctions) by the taking over of the preposition *la* (22.13) and in some changes in word-order (22.17).

22.2 *Late-Babylonian* Even more strongly under Aramaic influence is the language of the late-Babylonian letters (0.7). In some of these letters, the case endings drop completely. The first personal pronoun in the plural is *anēni*, we, (22.4) instead of *nīnu*.

22.3 *Phonetic-changes* With double-consonants, there occurs a frequent *secondary nasalisation* (10.3, note):

dd>nd (frequently written *md*): *inamdin*, he gives

zz>*nz*: *manzāz pānīya*, my delegate

ṣṣ>*nṣ* (frequently written *mṣ*): *ninamṣar*, we guard.

m shifts to *n* when it precedes *š*:

attalkanšu (∠attalkam + šu) I went to him

mt becomes nd

indalū (∠imtalū), they became full

Assimilation of a d to an n takes place in some forms of the verb nadānu, to give:

inna (∠idna) give me!

ittanna (∠ittadna) he has given.

22.4 Peculiarities of the Personal Pronouns and the Pronominal suffixes From ana yâši (21.7) there results the Neo-Babylonian ayyâši, to me.

Along with nīnu, we, another form anēni is developed under influence of the Aramaic anahnā, we.

The suffix of the first person singular (3.9) is -ā (instead of -ī):

puluḫtā (for puluḫtī), my respect = respect for me

aḫū'ā (for aḫi) my brother

abū'ā (for abī) my father

The ending -ya remains unchanged:

bēlīya of my Lord

The dative pronominal suffix of the second person singular masculine (5.9) is -ka.

aqbākka (for aqbākkum) I have imparted a command to you

22.5 Demonstrative Pronouns For annûm, this, Neo-Babylonian uses mostly agû, agātu (fem). It can also have an adverbial usage libbū agā'i, with the meaning: in such fashion. That, in Neo-Babylonian, is ullû, ullītu.

22.6 Universal Pronouns The substantive interrogative pronoun mannu, who?, (neuter mīnu, what?) can also be used in Neo- and late-Babylonian as a universal relative pronoun, whoever:

mannu...ušuzzu, whoever...has arrived

22.7 The indeterminate Pronoun mamma Mamma, someone or other, (non-declinable):

ina libbi ša mamma lā taklāka, in no one did I place my trust (22.10)

22.8 The Enumerative Pronoun In place of kalum, totality, Neo-Babylonian uses the post-positive adjective gabbu, each, every:

mātāti gabbi, all lands

it can also be used substantively:

gabbi ītamrū, they have seen everything

22.9 Case-endings Even in Neo-Babylonian texts the case endings are no longer carefully distinguished. The Accusative ending -a is replaced by -u.

nidittu...inamdin a gift... he gives

Sometimes in Neo-Babylonian the case endings drop completely; this is more frequent in late-Babylonian:

ina muḫḫi mis̥er ullû (for miṣri ullî) with regard

lū šulum (for šulmu) ana abīni, health be to our father!

utur (for utra) ikkal, he enjoys the surplus

The Genitive ending, under the influence of Assyrian, (27.8) is frequently -e for -i.

ina umēšu, in its days = later, in due time

22.10 Vocalic Endings on Verbal forms In verbs which are III Vowel. Neo-Babylonian no longer distinguishes carefully between the vocalic endings -i and -u.

nuṣṣu (for nuṣṣi) we went out

In the first person singular of the Stative the ending -āku (14.11) shortens to -āka or to -āk:

taklāka, I trust

marṣāk, I am sick

Long vowels when they are the final vowels of verbal forms in Neo-Babylonian are sometimes written with aleph:

ḫi-ra-a' for ḫirā, dig!

Another peculiarity (probably only orthographic) are spellings like:

iṣ-bat-ú for iṣbatū, they seized

ta-aṣ-bat-a' for taṣbatā

tu-ša-id-an-ni for tuša''idanni, you have informed me

22.11 The Verb izuzzu/ušuzzu The Preterite of izuzzu, to stand, (11.8) occurs as izziz even in Neo-Babylonian; the remaining forms are frequently built from a parallel form ušuzzu.

Perf. *ittašiz*, he stood

Stat. (20.12) *ušuz* (Plural *ušuzzū*) has entered

22.12 *The Cohortative* In Neo-Babylonian, the first person plural of the Preterite (*without the particle i*) serves as the cohortative (19.9):

nilti we wish to drink

lā nilli, we do not wish to ascend

In Middle and Neo-Babylonian, we drank, would be *niltati* (21.14).

22.13 *Prepositions* Instead of *ana*, to, and *ištu*, from, in Neo- and Late-Babylonian the Aramaic preposition *la* is frequently used:

la qātī šarri lā nilli, from the hands of the king we do not wish to go up = we do not wish to be separated from the king

One must be careful not to confuse the preposition *la* with the negative *lā*. The latter also occurs in the combination *ša lā*:

ša lā pīya, what [is] not of my mouth = without my command

The preposition *ana* serves occasionally to emphasize the accusative:

ana šarri bēlīya likrubu, the king, my Lord he it is whom they would like to bless

22.14 *Prepositional Expressions* Through combinations of prepositions and nouns, there result new prepositional expressions. The original meaning of the noun in these expressions virtually disappears: *muḫḫu*, scalp ana muhhi, by reason of, for

ina muhhi, with regard to

pānu, front

ina pāni, before

ana pāni = lapāni (22.13) opposite, before

pānātu, front

ana pānāt, before, by reason of

libbu, heart

ina libbi, in, between, among

tarsu, the other side, on the other hand

ana tarsi, upwards, up from, against

These expressions can also be joined to suffixes;

ana tarsīšu, against him

22.15 Adverbs For the determination of time are used:

enna (for Old-Babylonian inanna), now

adû, how, henceforth

for place:

akanna, here

ana akanna, toward this place

ana libbi, to that place

of manner:

ma'dä, very much

libbū, corresponding to, accordingly

libbū agā'i, in such fashion (22.5)

22.16 Subordinate Particles   In place of šumma, if, Neo-Babylonian uses kī with the Stative in the Subjunctive:

kī pānīka maḫru, when it is taken up before you = when it is agreeable to you

A further peculiarity of Neo-Babylonian is the use of the relative pronoun ša with the meaning: that:

šarru īde ša lū ma'da marṣāk, the king knows that I am very sick

ašša (ana ša) thereupon, on the strength of that...

ašša libbu ša aqbakku tetepšuma tattanna, corresponding to the instructions I gave you, thus did you perform and contribute

22.17 Word-order   In Neo- and Late-Babylonian there sometimes occurs (under the influence of Aramaic) a change in the normal word-order (1.8):

tammar rīmūtka, you will see your reward

READING PASSAGE - NEO-BABYLONIAN LETTERS

1. a-na šarri be-lí-ya arad-ka šandabakku: ^{d}En-líl ^{d}Nin-urta u ^{d}Nusku a-na šarri be-lí-ya lik-ru-bu! šarru i-de šá lu ma-a'-da mar-ṣa-ak. la mar-ṣa-ak a-na šul-mi šarri at-tal-kan-šú. a-du-ú ^{md}Bel-ú-sa-tu aḫu-ú-a ù 10 mārī banûti šá Nippuri a-na šul-mi šarri be-lí-ya al-tap-ra. šarru i-de[1] mātāti gab-bi a-na muḫḫi māt Aššur i-ze-er-ú-na-ši. šēpā-a-ni ina mātāti gab-bi ul it-ri-da[2]. a-šar ni-il-laka ni-id-da-ka, um-ma: mi-nam-ma šēpī māt Aššur ta-aṣ-bat-a'? a-du-ú abulī-ya nu-up-taḫ-ḫi a-na pit-ḫi ul nu-uṣ-ṣu. -- maṣṣarta šá šarri ni-nam-sar. šukkallū ù rabûti šá a-na a-kan-na šarru

iš-puru gab-bi i-tam-ru-ú. a-na šarri liq-bu-ú[2], šarru a-na qātī mam-ma la ú-maš-šer-an-na-a-ši. mê e-ni ya-a-nu, i-na ṣu-um-me-e la ni-ma-ta. šarru abū-ka mê šá [id]Ba-ni-ti it-tan-na-na-a-ši, um-ma: ši-li-iḫ-ti šá [id]Banī-ti a-na Nippuri ḫi-ra-a'! ...en-na šarru a-na [m]Ū-bar [lu]šá-ku šá Bābili liš-pu-ram-ma ši-li-iḫ-ti sá [id]Bani-ti lid-din-an-na-ši-ma mê it-ti-šú-nu ni-il-ti; i-na ṣu-um-me-e la qātī šarri la ni-il-li ù mātāti gab-bi la i-qab-bu-ú: um-ma: Nippurayyī šá šēpī ša māt Aššur iṣ-bat-ú ina ṣu-um-me-e a-na ṣi-re-e in-da-lu-ú.

2. a-mat šarri a-na [md]Bēl-ibni: šù-mu ayya-ši. lìb-ba-ka lu ṭāb-ka! ina muḫḫi mi-ṣer ul-lu-ú šá Gúr-a-sim-mu šá tu-šá-id-an-ni: ul lib-bu-ú a-ga-i ṭè-e-mu áš-kun-ka um-ma: áš-šá lib-bu-ú šá aq-bak-ka te-tep-šu-ma ta-at-tan-na? mi-nu-ú[3] lu-ú uṣurātī-ka? en-na mi-nam-ma šá la pi-yá a-na lìb-bi tu-ri-id? at-ta ša [lu]man-za-az pānī-ya at-ta ù pu-luḫ-ta-a ti-du-u, lib-bu-ú a-ga-a-'i te-te-pu-uš! u šá la i-du-u ak-ka-a'i-i ip-pu-uš? ...šá [md]Sîn-di-ni-ēpuš ip-pu-šu a-mur-ma mim-ma šá a-na tar-ṣi-šu a-na e-pe-ši ṭa-a-bu e-pu-uš-ma u ina u_4-me-šú tam-mar re-mut-ka.

LATE-BABYLONIAN LETTERS

3. ṭup-pi [md]Sîn-uballiṭ a-na [md]Nabû-šumī-iškun abī-šú: [d]Sîn u [d]Nin-gal šul-mu u balaṭ napšāti šá abī-yá liq-bu-ú! ki-i áš-mu-u [giš]mis-ma-kan-na šurinna it-ti [giš]ḫu-sa-bi-šú-nu ta-am-ḫu-ru. i-na pa-ni abī-yá i-ba-áš-ši. abu-ú-a lu-še-bi-la-

áš-šú, šīm-šú abu-u-a liš-pu-ra-am-ma kasap-šú a-na abī-ya lu-še-bi-la. u ki-i pa-ni-ka maḫ-ru ilten lē'u bab-ba-nu-ú lu-pu-uš-ma šá pa-ni-ka i-na lìb-bi i-ban-nu-ú a-na abī-yá lu-še-bi-la. ina lìb-bi šá mam-ma la ták-la-ka u at-ta lēt-ka la-pa-ni-ja ta-ad-du-u. a-na muḫḫi e-pe-šu šá lē'-āni ar-te-iq[4]. i-na pa-ni-ka la i-šad-da-ad. ul kaspa ul mim-ma e-ri-iš-ka ^{giš}ḫu-ṣa-bi e-te-ri-iš-ka. ...

4. ṭuppi ^{m}Mar-duk ù ^{md}In-nin-šumī-uṣur a-na ^{d}Marduk-šākin-šumī abī-šú-nu: lu-ú šu-lum a-na abī-ni! ^{d}Bēltu šá Uruk u ^{d}Na-na-a šu-lum u balāṭa šá abī-ni liq-ba-a$_4$! i-na pa-na-at nu-kur-tu$_4$ šá Uruk a-kan-na a-né-ni. ...man-nu ina lìb-bi isqī-šú u kirī-šú u-šu-uz-zu ni-di-it-tu$_4$ a-na šarri i-nam-din u ú-tur ik-kal. en-na amta šá bēlī-ya u mārā-šú[5] ana bēlī-ya al-ta-par. ...

[1] 15.10

[2] For <u>itradā</u>, "our feet do not budge into other lands = nowhere are we permitted to set our feet".

[3] Cf. 17.9

[4] <u>artīq</u>

[5] Intended for <u>mārā-ša</u>.

Lesson 23

GRAMMAR

23.1 Young-Babylonian   This somewhat awkward English phrase [for Jungbabylonisch] is a technical term used to describe the language of the literature written in the period of Neo- and Late-Babylonian times. The letters (22.1 - 22.2) of the same period were written in a language quite different from that of the more creative literary efforts. The language of this creative literature called Young-Babylonian, is a rather artificial language. It sought to imitate Old-Babylonian and especially Old-Babylonian poetry (20.1). But the Young-Babylonian literature was also considerably influenced by the contemporary colloquial language of the Neo- and Late-Babylonian. The degree of that influence varies from text to text. A part of the Assyrian royal inscriptions is written in Young-Babylonian. But their language is also influenced by Assyrian (23.9, 23.11).

23.2 Mimation   Mimation has almost completely disappeared in Middle-Babylonian (21.2). It rarely appears in Young-Babylonian:

napištī qīšam, bestow life on me!

mārat ^{d}Anim, daughter of Anu

23.3 Case Endings   Only in a handful of Young-Babylonian

texts are the case-endings distinguished in a manner corresponding to the rules of Old-Babylonian (1.7). Under the influence of Neo-Babylonian (22.9) the Accusative ending -a is largely replaced by -u.

ul iṣṣinū qutrinnu, they do not smell the smoke

bītu irrub, she enters the house

Sometimes the case-endings drop:

ul iššakkan naptan, the meal is not served

In the Plural, the ending -ī can show up in any case:

kišpi ṣubbutū'inni, magical spells have seized me (23.7)

For -ī and ū (especially in the construct state) the Assyrian Plural ending -ē may occur:

qerâtēšunu, their storehouses

ana mākalē ilāni rabûti, for the food of the great gods

In the dual (7.7) the n of the ending -ā(n)or -ī(n) drops regularly and the ending -ā can occur even in the Accusative

luštakkana tulâ, I shall offer my [two] breasts [to the mouths of your children]

23.4 Construct State of the Feminine   Polysyllabic feminine forms like napištum, life, form the construct state with the addition of an -i (2.8):

napišti awīlim, the life of men

In poetry, another form of the construct state of these feminines can also be formed by the insertion of an a between the last consonantal radical and the t:

napšat būlīšu, the life [upkeep] of his cattle

tuklat nišīšu, the trust of his people

23.5 The Terminative--Adverbial as Comparative A peculiarity of Young-Babylonian is the frequent use of the Terminative (20.3) to express comparison:

ditalliš, as ashes, arbutiš, as a desert

alānī šuātunu appul qaqqariš amnu, I burned these cities down and made them [flat as] the earth

In Young-Babylonian poetry, the terminative also occurs in combination with a dependent genitive (20.3):

ušumgal kališ parakkī, alone ruling on all thrones

23.6 Personal Pronouns The Nominative of the Personal Pronoun and of the anaphoric pronoun corresponds to those of Old- and Middle-Babylonian (21.7):

anāku, I

attā, attī, you

šū, šī, he, she

The Accusative plural of the anaphoric pronoun, (which is also used attributively), is šuātunu, šuātina:

alānī šuātunu appul, those cities are the ones I burned down

23.7 Pronominal Suffixes The suffix of the first person singular -i (-ya) is used in Young-Babylonian about as it is in Old-Babylonian (3.9):

ummānī, my army

ina libbīya, in my heart (for Neo-Babylonian, 22.4).

But after plural forms that end in vowels, the suffix takes the form -a:

ruḫē'a, my sorcery, witchcraft

Apocopation of pronominal suffixes (20.6) also occurs in Young-Babylonian.

tāmertuš, its plain

Sometimes -šu, his, and -ša, her, are not distinguished:

šēpāšu and qātāša, his/her hands and feet [occur with reference to the same subject]

In place of the pronominal suffix -ninni (the Accusative suffix of the first person singular in the ventive with a verb that ends in -ū or -ā, 13.10), Young-Babylonian uses -inni:

kišpī ṣubbutū'inni, Magical spells have seized me

23.8 The Indeterminate Demonstrative Pronoun From a doubling of the demonstrative pronoun annû, this, there results the form annanna, annannītu, so and so:

annanna apil annanna, NN, the son of NN

23.9 Verbs II Aleph In the Present, and Stative G of Verbs II Aleph (21.12) an a frequently shifts to e:

ila''ib or ile''ib, she weakens

la'ib or le'ib, is made weak

mâdum (mīd), to be much, is replaced by the root m'd in Neo- and Young-Babylonian:

ma'ādu, to be much

St. ma'id

Fem. ma'dat, is much

Verb.-Adj. ma'du, ma'attu, much

For lu''u, to soil, cf. 19.12

23.10 Vocalic endings of Verbal Forms In verbs which are Final Vowel, Young-Babylonian (under the influence of Neo-Babylonian in this matter 22.10), does not carefully distinguish the endings -i (-ī) and -u(-ū):

bītu uṣṣu (for uṣṣi), she enters the house

ammaki bītu terrubu (for terrubī, note the last few lines of this paragraph) in place of the fact that you (sing. fem.) enter the house = instead of your entering the house

Occasionally vocalic endings appear on verbal forms where, according to normal usage, one would not expect them (superfluous vowels):

bītu irrubu (for irrub) she enters the house

In normal usage, the second person feminine (19.7) takes the ending -ī even in the Subjunctive (7.4).

ša terrubī, you who go in

ammaki...talammanī, instead of your dealing badly

23.11 Assyrian Verbal forms In Young-Babylonian texts which are written in Assyria numerous Assyrian characteristics are to be found. Chief among these are some Assyrian verbal forms (25.4):

aqṭerib (Babylonian = eqtereb), I drew near (26.5)

attumuš (attamuš), I open, start out

upatti (upetti), I opened

23.12 Prepositional Expressions balum, without, can be combined with pronominal suffixes:

baluššu, without him

In Young-Babylonian it occurs in combination with ina:

ina balīki, without you (Fem.)

23.13 Subordinate Particles To introduce subordinate clauses of time and place, the word ēma, wherever, whenever is used:

ēma uṣammaru, whenever I wish

Adversative clauses are introduced by ammaki, instead of. [The particle governs a finite verb, best translated by a participle in English.]

ammaki bītu terrubu bītu tuṣṣî, instead of entering the house, leave it!

READING PASSAGE - OATHS

1. An oath-formula to Marduk

1. šiptu: ga-aš-ru šu-pú-ú e-ṭél Eridu
2. rubû ti-iz-qá-ru bu-kúr ^{d}Nu-dim-mud
3. ^{d}Marduk šal-ba-bu mu-riš É-én-gur-ra
4. bēl É-sag-íl tukulti Bābili ra-im É-zi-da
5. mu-šal-lim napišti a-šá-red É-maḫ-ti-la mu-deš-šú-u balāṭa
6. ṣu-lul ma-a-ti ga-mil ni-ši rap-šá-a-ṭi

7. ušumgal ka-liš parakki

8. šum-ka ka-liš ina pī nišī ṭa-a-ab

9. ^{d}Marduk bēlu rabû i-lu re-mé-nu-ú

10. ina qí-bi-ti-ka ṣer-ti lu-ub-luṭ lu-uš-lim-ma

11. lu-uš-tam-mar ilūt-ka

12. e-ma ú-ṣa-am-ma-ru lu-uk-šu-ud

13. šu-uš-kin kit-tu ina pī-ya$_5$

14. šub-ši amāt damiqti i-na libbī-ya$_5$

15. ti-i-ru u na-an-za-zu liq-bu-u damiqtī

16. ilī li-iz-ziz ina imnī-ya$_5$

17. ištarī li-iz-ziz ina šumēlī-ya$_5$

18. ilu mu-šal-li-mu ina idī-ya$_5$ lu-u ka-ayya-an

19. šur-kám-ma qá-ba-a še-ma-a u ma-ga-ra

20. a-mat a-qab-bu-ú ki-ma a-qab-bu-ú lu-u ma-ag-rat

21. ^{d}Marduk bēlu rabû napištī qí-šam

22. ba-laṭ napišti-ya$_5$ qí-bi

23. ma-ḫar-ka nam-riš a-tál-lu-ka lu-uš-bi

24. ^{d}En-líl liḫ-du-ka ^{d}É-a li-riš-ka

25. ilānū ša kiš-šá-ti lik-ru-bu-ka

26. ilānū rabûtu lìb-ba-ka li-ṭib-bu

2. Salt Imprecation

1. šiptu: at-ti ṭābtu šá ina áš-ri elli ib-ba-nu-ú

2. ana ma-ka-le-e ilāni rabûti i-šim-ki ^{d}En-líl

3. ina ba-li-ki ul iš-šak-kan nap-tan ina É-kur

4. ina ba-li-ki ilu šarru bēlu u rubû ul iṣ-ṣi-nu qut-rin-nu

5. ana-ku annanna apil annanna šá kiš-pi ṣu-ub-bu-tu-in-ni
6. up-šá-še-e le-e'-bu-in-ni
7. puṭ-ri kiš-pi-ya ṭābtu pu-uš-ši-ri ru-ḫe-e-a
8. up-šá-še-e muḫ-ri-in-ni-ma kīma ili ba-ni-ya
9. lul-tam-mar-ki

3. Imprecation of the Goddess <u>Lamaštu</u>

1. šiptu: ez-ze-et šam-rat i-lat na-mur-rat ši-i bar-bar-rat mārat ^{d}A-nu
2. sēpā-šú an-zu-ú qātā-šá lu-'a-tu pān nēši da-pi-nu pānū-šú
3. iš-tu a-pi i-lam-ma uš-šu-rat pe-ret-su bu-ut-tu-qa di-da-a-šú
4. kib-su alpi il-lak kib-su immeri i-red-de i-na šīri u dāmi qātā-šú šak-nu
5. a-pa-niš ir-ru-bu ṣe-ra-niš i-ḫal-lu-up
6. bi-i-tú ir-ru-ub bi-i-tú uṣ-ṣu
7. bí-la-ni mārī-ki-na lu-še-niq u mārātī-ki-na lu-ut-tar-ra
8. a-na pi-i mārātī-ki-na lu-uš-tak-ka-na tu-la-a
9. iš-me-ši-ma ^{d}Ea abū-šú am-ma-ki mārat ^{d}Anim nam-tar-ra-tú[1] amēlūtu tala-ma-ni-ma
10. am-ma-ki ina šīri u dāmi qātā-ki šak-nu
11. am-ma-ki bītu ter-ru-bu bītu tu-ṣi-i
12. mu-uḫ-ri šá tamkāri qa-an-na-šú u ṣi-di-su
13. mu-uḫ-ri šá nappāḫi si-me-ri si-mat qātī-ki u šēpī-ki

14. mu-uḫ-ri šá kutimmi in-ṣa-ab-tú si-mat uznī-ki

15. mu-uḫ-ri šá purkulli sāmtu si-mat kišādī-ki

16. mu-uḫ-ri šá naggāri mulṭu pilakku u du-di-it-ti-ki

17. ú-tam-mi-ki ^{d}Anu abū-ka An-tum ummu-ka ú-tam-mi-ki
^{d}Ea ba-nu-ú šumī-ka

II. FROM THE ASSYRIAN ROYAL INSCRIPTIONS

4. From the Eighth Campaign of the Assyrian King Sargon II.

ultu ālānī dan-nu-ti ša ^{kur}Sa-an-gi-bu-te at-tu-muš, a-
na ^{kur}Ar-ma-tal-li-i na-gi-i aq-ṭi-rib. ^{uru}Bu-bu-zi ber-
tu, ^{uru}Ḫu-un-du-ur ša 2 dūrānī la-mu-ú..., ^{uru}Ayya-le-
e, ^{uru}Ṣi-ni-iš-pa-la-a, ^{uru}Ṣi-ni-ú-nak, ^{uru}Ar-na, ^{uru}Sar-
ni-i, 7 ālānī dan-nu-ti a-di 30 ālānī ša li-mi-ti-
šu-nu ša i-na šēpī ^{kur}Ú-bi-an-da šadê na-du-ú, se-ḫer-šu-
nu ap-pul-ma qaq-qa-riš am-nu. gušūrī ta-aṣ-lil-ti-šu-
nu i-na gīri aq-mu-ma di-tal-li-iš ú-še-mi. qe-ra-a-te-
šu-nu na-kam-a-ti ú-pat-ti-ma uṭṭas-su-nu ma-'a-at-tu
ša la ni-i-bi um-ma-ni ú-ša-a-kil ebūra tuk-lat nišī-šú
u ^{ú}pu-e nap-šat bu-li-šu ab-ri-iš a-qu-ud-ma ar-bu-ti-iš
ú-sa-li-ka ta-mer-tu-uš, kirātī-šú-nu a-kis-ma qišātī-šú-
nu ak-šiṭ, nap-ḫar ^{giš}gup-ni-šu-nu a-na qù-ru-un-ni aq-
ru-un-ma i-na gīri aq-mu. i-na me-taq-ti-ya a-na ^{uru}Ar-
bu āl bīt abī-šu ša ^{m}Ur-sa-a ù ^{uru}Ri-ya ar ālī-šú ša
^{md}Ištar-dur a-lik, 7 ālānī ša li-mi-ti-šu-nu ša aḫḫī-
šú zēr šarrūtī-šú i-na lib-bi-šu-nu šu-šu-bu-ma dun-nu-
nu ma-ṣar-tu, alānī šu-a-tu-nu ap-pul qaq-qa-riš am-nu,

bīt ^{d}Ḫal-di-a ilī-šu ab-ri-iš a-qu-ud-ma ú-šal-pi-ta sa-ạ-gi-šu.

[1]20.4

Lesson 24

24.1 Old-Akkadian   The language of the Old-Akkadian Inscriptions (0.6) is distinguished from Old-Babylonian chiefly in phonetic structure (24.4, 24.11, Note), the declension of the determinative pronoun (24.6), the formation of the third person singular and plural feminine of the prefixed tenses (24.9), the formation of the Subjunctive in -a (24.15), and in the use of the preposition in for ina (24.18).

24.2 The Orthography of Old-Akkadian   In Old-Akkadian inscriptions, the signs for voiceless and voiced consonants are not distinguished. For that reason there appears, for example, the sign GU in the combination GU-ti-û (read Gu-ti-û) the Guteans. It also appears in i-la-GU (read i-la-ku_8), they went, and in li-il-GU-ut (read li-il-qû-ut), may he destroy. The sign DA appears twice in one word with two different readings: lu DA-na-DA-nu (read tá-na-da-nu), you will certainly give. The sign TI appears in i-TI-na (read i-dì-na), he gave, (Subj.), (24.10, 24.15).

The length of vowels remains (almost always) unexpressed in the orthography. Similarly, double consonants are generally unexpressed (i-dì-šum for iddiššum < iddin + šum, he has given to him. However, when -ma is added to a word with mimation, the resulting mm is expressed in the orthography: a-na-lim-ma (< ana ālim + ma), to the city and... The writing of $\underline{iš_x}$-ar-ru for iš'aru, he conquered (Subj.) is to be understood as an addition of -u to the formation $\underline{iš_x}$-ar (read $\underline{iš_x}$-a(r)-ru.) Cf. im-ḫu(r)-ru for imḫurū.

24.3 Vowels Adjacent vowels are never contracted in Old-Akkadian:

tiamtum, sea

iśniā (Old-Babylonian išniā or išnâ, 6.4)

Nabium, (Old-Babylonian Nabûm)

24.4 Sibilants Old-Akkadian possesses a sibilant ś (0.12) which has merged in Old-Babylonian with š. This ś appears in the Old-Akkadian forms of the anaphoric pronoun: śū, (Old-Babylonian šū), the pronominal siffix in the third person -śu, śum, (Old-Babylonian -šu, šum), the terminative ending -iś: maḫriś (Old-Babylonian maḫriš), before.
And as the stem-forming element of the Š-stem: uśamqit (Old-Babylonian ušamqit), he felled, śuta'rib (Old-Babylonian šuterrib), lead in again and again, (24.11). Finally, the ś occurs in roots of words:

śaplum (šaplum), lower

śaduum (šadûm) mountain

karāśum (karāšum), camp

na'śum, (nêšum), life

qiāśum, (qâšum), to bestow, to make a gift

24.5 The Anaphoric Pronoun In combination with -ma (8.14), the anaphoric pronoun (Old-Akkadian, śū, śī), has the meaning he himself:

> _šarram šūma_ _isbat_, he personally seized the king

The Akkadian singular masculine is _śua_ (Old-Babylonian, _šuāti_), the Akkadian plural masculine _śunūti_:

> _ištum tāhāzi śunūti iš'aru_, after he had victoriously waged those battles

24.6 Determinative Pronouns The determinative pronoun _ša_ (3.12), which serves also to introduce relative clauses (7.5) is originally the Akkadian singular of the determinative pronoun which is still declined in Old-Akkadian: _šu_, _ši_, _ša_ (the fem. sing. is _šat_; the masc. pl. is _šūt_, the fem. pl. is _šāt_). These forms agree in gender, number, and case with the forms which govern them:

> Nom. Sing. _Ilum-dān šu Gugu_ Ilum-Dān who (is the deputy) of Gugu
>
> Gen. Sing. _in bītim ši uštābila_, in the house in which I decided
>
> Nom. Masc. Pl. _enū Nabium šūt Qīśum ilqiam_ these are the materials of Nabium which Qisum took.

24.7 Pronominal Suffixes The suffixes of the third person occur in Old Akkadian with an _ś_:

> -_śu_, his, -_śum_, to him, -_śunu_, to her

In place of -_śunu_, one sometimes finds -_śuni_

> _in ālī-śuni_, in their cities

24.8 The Universal Relative As universal relative pronoun, the unchangeable _ša_, whoever, is used:

šá tuppam šúa ušassakūni, whoever causes this tablet to be cast down (24.15)

24.9 Conjugational Prefixes and Suffixes The prefix of the third person singular masculine is i- (1.4):

ip-te, he opened, im-ḫur, he received

Sometimes the third person singular masculine is written:

i-ik-mi, he bound, bandaged

Such writing as the above may be an effort to reproduce a pronunciation: *yikmi. One finds some forms written with the prefix e-:

en'ar, he cast down

The prefix of the third person singular feminine is ta- (20.11)

tamḫur, she received

The third person feminine plural is formed with the suffix -ū (instead of Old-Babylonian -ā, 3.6):

10 amātū ... illakū, ten female slaves ..., they will go.

24.10 The Root-vowel Some verbs have a different root-vowel in Old-Akkadian than in Old-Babylonian:

'arāšum (a/u) they sow, Old Babylonian erēšum (i) (24.11)

nadānum, to give, Pres. Old-Akkadian inaddan, but Old-Babylonian inaddin, he will give, Pret. always is iddin

24.11 Verbs I Aleph The a of the Old-Babylonian e-class (I Aleph verbs (4.6) has not yet shifted to e: 'arāšum (Old-Babylonian, erēšum), to sow:

Pret. a-ru-uš (a'ruš; Old-Babylonian ēriš, 24.10)
I sowed

Imp. 'à-ru-uš ('aruš; Old Babylonian eriš), sow!

'arābum, to enter

Pret. Š u-ša-rí-ib (uša'rib, Old Babylonian ušērib), cause [someone] to enter

Imp. Štn šu-tá-rí-ib (šuta'rib; Old-Babylonian šuterrib), he causes [someone] to go in again and again.

All of the proto-Semitic larygeals and pharyngeals have coalesced in Old-Babylonian with the glottal stop. [In other Semitic languages, the proto-Semitic $'_1$ = ', $'_2$ = h, $'_3$ = ḥ, $'_4$ = ᶜ, and $'_5$ = ǵ.] The weakening of $'_{3-5}$ changes a neighboring a to e (4.6). For example, $'_1$ is the substratum of abum, father, (Cf. Hebrew 'āb), $'_2$ is the same for alākum, to go, (Cf. Hebrew hālak), $_3$ for erēšum (Old Akkadian 'arāšum), to sow, (Cf. Hebrew ḥāraš, to cut into, engrave, $'_4$ for elûm (Old-Akkadian 'alā'um, to go up, (Cf. Arabic ᶜalā), $'_5$ is in erēbum (Old-Akkadian 'arābum, to go up, enter (Cf. Arabic ǵaraba, to rise [of the sun].

Since the transition from a to e has not yet occurred in Old-Akkadian, at least two of these sounds were distinguished, but the distinction is not visible in the script.

24.12 Verbs II Aleph The e-class verbs II Aleph of Old-Babylonian (9.6), maintain in Old-Akkadian both aleph and a-vocalisation:

en'ar (Old-Babylonian, inēr), he killed (24.9)

iš'ar (only Old-Akkadian), he conquered

uška'en (Old-Babylonian, uškēn), he threw himself to the grounds (19.6)

ura''iš, he threw down

The primitive pharyngeal of na'ārum, to kill, is $'_3$; cf. Arab. naḥara, to slaughter.

24.13 Verbs III Aleph Similarly in verbs III Aleph, Old-Akkadian maintains the a:

idā'um, to know; ti-da (tīda', Old-Babylonian tīde)

24.14 Verbs I w In Old-Akkadian, along with the verb tamā'um, to swear, another verb wamā'um is used. This verb has the identical meaning:

Pres. umma (ù-má), I swear

The Pret. Š of waṣā'um to go out, is found in Old-Akkadian as:

ušūṣi (Old-Babylonian ušēṣi, 12.4), he broke out

24.15 Subjunctive The Subjunctive ending in Old-Akkadian is -u (7.4), or -ūni:

Šarru-kīn...ᵈEnlil māḫira lā iddinūšum, Sargon... gave to Enlil no opponent of equally [noble] birth

ša tuppam šua ušassakūni, whoever causes this tablet to be thrown down

or in an oath:

umma...in ramānika lū tanaddanu, I swear (24.14)... certainly you yourself will give [it].

But pari-passu there is a Subjunctive formed in -a:

šu ana Šunītum addina, what I have given to Šunītum

in bītim ši uštābila, in the house where I decided

24.16 Prohibitive In Old-Akkadian, the Prohibitive (13.6) is formed with the Vetitive-particle (20.14) ay (written a, in Old-Akkadian) and the second person of the Preterite:

a taq-bi, you may not say [that]!

24.17 Particles To indicate direct speech, one may use enma, as follows, thus. It is from this form that the Old-Babylonian umma is derived:

šībūt enma Mannu ana Kinūnû, witnesses thus Mannu to Kinūnû = witness that Mannu said to Kinūnû

In addition, the enclitic particle -me may be attached to a particular word which one wishes to emphasize in a sentence:

Gutiummame eqlam ula a'ruš, The Guteans are here [so] I have not prepared the field

24.18 Prepositions Especially characteristic of Old-Akkadian is the preposition in, in, on (20.9), instead of the Old-Babylonian ina. Other Old-Akkadian prepositions include adi, adīma, until, up to, and ištum, ištumma, from.

24.19 Subordinating Particles Such particles in Old-Akkadian are ištum, after, since, and kī, if:

ištum tāḫāzi šunūti iš'aru ($iš_x$-ar-ru Cf. 24.2), after he had victoriously waged these battles

kī stands before the Predicate:

anālimma kī allakạn, if I come to the city

READING PASSAGE FROM OLD-AKKADIAN ROYAL INSCRIPTIONS

1. Šar-ru-kīn šar mātim ^{d}En-líl ma-ḫi-ra la i-dì-nu-śum, ti-a-am-tám a-lí-tám ù śa-pil-tám ^{d}En-líl i-dì-nu-śum.

2. a-dì-ma pu-ti ti-a-am-tim 'alappāt Me-luḫ-ḫa 'alappāt Má-gan^{ki} 'alappāt Tilmun^{ki} in kà-rí-ím ši A-ga-dè^{ki} ìr-ku-us. Šar-ru-kīn šarrum in Tu-tu-li^{ki} a-na ^{d}Da-gan uś-kà-en, ik-ru-ub; ma-tám a-li-tám i-dì-śum.

3. ù 50 iššiakkī ù śarram śú-ma iṣbat ù in Na-gur$_{8}$-za-am^{ki} tāḫāzam iś-ni-a-ma iś-ku$_{8}$-na-ma iš$_{x}$-ar ù in Urim^{ki} uś-tá-li-śa-ma im$_{x}$-tá-aḫ-ṣà-ma iš$_{x}$ -ar.

4. Rí-mu-uš šar Kiš in tāḫāzim Urim^{ki} ù Umma^{ki} iš$_{x}$-ar; ù 8040 eṭlūtim u-śa-am-qí-it. ...ù Ka-kug šar Urim^{ki} iṣbat, ù Ki-ba-íd iššiakki Lagaš^{ki} iṣbat, ù āl-śu-ni in'ar, ... ù in ālī-śu-ni 5985 etlūtim u-śu-ṣí-am-ma a-na kà-ra-śi-im iś-kùn.

5. Na-ra-am-^{d} Sîn da-núm šar ki-ib-ra-tim ar-ba-im, ša-ir 9 tāḫāzī in šattim 1; iš-tum tāḫāzī śú-nu-ti is$_{x}$-ar-ru,ù šar-rí-śu-nu i-ik-mi-ma maḫ-rí-iś ^{d}En-líl u-śa-rí-ib. in u-mi-śu Li-pi$_{5}$-it-ì-li mara'-śu iššiakki Marad^{ki} bīt ^{d}Šar-Marad in Marad^{ki} ib-ni. ša ṭuppam śú-a u-śa-sà-ku-ni ^{d}Šamaš ù ^{d}Šar-Marad išdī-śu li-sú-ḫa ù zar..'-śu li-il-qù-ṭa.

6. ^{d}Nergal pá-da-an ^{d}Na-ra-am-^{d} Sîn[1] da-nim$_{4}$ ip-te-ma Ar-ma-nam^{ki} ù Eb-la^{ki} i-dì-śum ù A-ma-nam śa-dú erēnim ù ti-a-am-tám a-lí-tám i-qí-iś-śum-ma in kakki ^{d}Da-gan mu-śa-ar-bí-ì šar-ru$_{x}$-ti-śu ^{d}Na-ra-am-^{d} Sîn da-núm Ar-ma-nam^{ki} ù Eb-

la^{ki} en-ar. ù iš-tum-ma pu-ti Purattim nārim a-dì-ma Ú-li-si-im^{ki} ni-śi$_x$ ša-at ^{d}Da-gan eššiś i-qi-šu-šum u-ra-iś ...

II. FROM AN OLD-AKKADIAN LETTER

7. en-ma Iś-ku-un-^{d}Da-gan a-na Lugala-ra: eqlam 'à-ru-uš ù būlam ù-ṣú-ur! a-pu-na-ma Gu-ti-um-ma-me eqlam ù-la a-ru-uš, a taq-bi. ... būlam a-na ālim śu-tá-rí-ib! ... kaspam a-na-da-kum. e-ni na-'à-aś ^{d}Šar-kà-lí-šar-rí^1 ù-má: šum-ma būlam Gu-ti-ù it-ru-ù, in ra-ma-ni-kà lu tà-na-da-nu. a-na-lim-ma ki a-la-kam kaspam a-na-da-nu-kum ù at-tà būlam ù-la tà-na-ṣà-ar. iš-pí-kí kí-nu-tim a-rí-iš-kà, mu-bi lu ti-da.

III. OLD-AKKADIAN LEGAL DOCUMENTS

8. (After an enumeration of items including 6^{túg}bar-ru šu-ut ra'śim, 3^{kuš}maš-li-a-tum, 2^{giš}sú-sú-la-an, There follows:) e-nu Na-bí-um šu-ut Qì-śum il-qì-am-ma it-ba-lu. Na-bí-um bāb ^{d}Tišpak it-ma; ^{m}Ilum-āl-śu dayyānum, ^{m}Ilum-dān šu Gu$_4$-gu$_4$ ..., ^{m}E-ru-ru šu šībūt ālim, ^{m}I-ku$_8$-núm mār È-ni-um, 2 šībūt Qì-śum.

9. I-tá-ra-ak, Šu-um, Rē'ītum, Ma-šum, šībūt en-ma Ma-an-nu a-na Ki-nu-nu: in bītim si uś-tà-a-bí-la a-na si-tim šīmī lu-uš-qú-ul-kum! al-kam! ...

10. 3 qa qam'im: 1 qa Gallābum, 1 qa Kaspū-śa, 1 qa Agālum, šu a-na Šu-ni-tum a-dì-na.

11. x kur še'am ^{m}Ilum-ba-ni im-ḫur, 6 kur še'am ^{m}Uršanum im-ḫur ... 1 kur še'am ^{m}Da-mi-iq-tum tám-ḫur ...

12. ^{m}Um-ma-ma,^{m}...[2], ^{m}Ša-ru-uš, ^{m}Mi-na-mu mar'atum, ^{m}Puzrū-śa, ^{m}Gi-ti-bu, ^{m}I-bu, ^{m}Me-er-tu-gag-ga, ^{m}A-li-ú-tá, ^{m}Bu-bu-tum; napḫar 10 amātū; a-na Ga-súr^{ki} i-la-ku$_{8}$.

[1]The names of some kings of Akkad are often written with divine determinatives.

[2]Personal name not legible.

Lesson 25

GRAMMAR

25.1 Old-Assyrian The language of the Old-Assyrian legal documents and letters (0.8) is distinguished from Old-Babylonian largely by the fact that several of the characteristic Babylonian vowel changes have not entered into the language (25.3 - 25.4, 25.11 - 25.13). Old-Assyrian has special pronominal formations (25.5 - 25.7) and a special formation of the Voluntative (25.18), Precative, (25.19), and of the Subjunctive (25.20).

25.2 The Orthography of Old-Assyrian Doubled consonants remain unexpressed in the text (as in Old-Akkadian, 24.2):

a-ta (atta) you

šu-ma (šumma), if

Long vowels are occasionally indicated by a repetition of the vowel:

a-ḫe-e (aḫḫē), brothers

On the other hand, one sometimes finds plene (full) writings like the above for vowels which are short; but apparently secondarily lengthened:

a-ḫu-ú (aḫu) Aguza, the brother of Aguza (25.8)

ša...i-ša-qú-lu-ú (išaqqulu), what he will pay (25.4)

For i-šu-ú (išu), to be well off, Cf. 25.13

25.3 Vocalic contractions Adjacent vowels are, in Old-Assyrian as in Old-Akkadian (24.3) generally not contracted:

uṣṣiū (Old-Babylonian *uṣṣû*), they come out

ku'ā'um (Old-Babylonian *kûm*, your (25.7)

itūar (Old-Babylonian *itûr* or Old Assyrian *itūwar* 25.14) he returns

Two identical vowels may be contracted when adjacent:

manân (< **manā'ān*) two minas

ašî (< **aši'ī*) my meteorite iron

išû (< **išu'ū*), they are well off

Two identical vowels will *not* be contracted if they are separated from one another by a morphologically doubled aleph (Cf. 16.4).

uqa''a, I wait

da''ānē, of the judges (Gen. Pl.)

These differences are not expressed in the script: *ašî* is written *a-ši-i*; *išû* is written i-šu-ú like *išu*, (Cf. 25.1) *uqa''a* is written *ú-qa-a*.

25.4 Vowel Harmony   A short unstressed *a* in an open syllable changes to harmonize with the vowel of the following syllable. The singular cases then of the Babylonian *aššatum*, wife, take the following forms in Old-Assyrian:

aššutum, *aššitim*, *aššatam*

Cf. also *aššitī*, my wife, and *qaqqurū* (Old-Babylonian *qaqqarū*), land. In the verb, the root-vowel *a* and the Present vowel *a* and the infix -*ta*- all submit to this vowel-harmonization:

iṣbat, he seized, but *taṣbitī*, you (feminine) seized and *iṣbutū*, they seized

ša...*išaqqulu* (Old-Babylonian *išaqqalu*), what he will pay

ītiṣi (Old-Babylonian *ītaṣi*), he went out

ilteqe (for *iltaqe, 25.13), Old-Babylonian ilteqe, he took

Cf. leqeānim (< *laqeānim), take for me

In the Preterite of the N-stem (10.3), the i before the middle consonant (which results from vowel harmony) continues even in the forms which have endings:

ikkinik (Old-Babylonian ikkanik) was sealed; Pl. ikkinkū (Old-Babylonian ikkankū

25.5 Personal Pronouns In Old-Assyrian, the anaphoric pronoun takes the form:

šūt (Old-Babylonian šū, 11.10), the one [just] mentioned

šīt, she, šunu, šina, they

The accusative of attā, you, is kuāti (Old-Babylonian kâta).

25.6 Pronominal Suffixes The singular suffixes correspond to those of Old-Babylonian (5.8, 5.9, 13.10). The plural suffixes -kunūti, -kināti, -sunūti, -šināti are used in Assyrian for the dative but in Babylonian for the accusative:

umme'ānam lušazzizakkunūti, he shall have the contributor come in to you (25.17)

As accusative suffixes one finds: -kunu, -kina, -šunu, -šina:

kasapkunu lušabbikunu, I shall satisfy you with your money.

-niāti can be accusative and dative (Old-Babylonian accusative -niāti, dative -niāšim)

iṣbutūniāti, they have seized us (25.4)

taddanniāti, you will give to us

The possessive suffixes -šunu and -kunu are shortened after a to -šnu and -knu:

šuqultašnu, their weight

25.7 Independent Possessive Pronouns Along with possessive suffixes, Old-Assyrian also has the accented possessive pronouns (6.8):

yā'um, my, ku'ā'um, your, šu'ā'um, his, ni'ā'um, our

Alaḫim ni'ā'im, our Alaḫum

25.8 Special Construct State Forms Old-Babylonian mārum, son, takes the Old-Assyrian form mer'um. The construct state is mera('), in the Nominative and mer'i in the Genitive:

The construct state of abum, father and aḫum, brother, is abu, aḫu, (Old-Babylonian abi, aḫi):

aḫu Aguza, the brother of Aguza

25.9 Formation of the Plural The Nominative plural in Old-Assyrian ends in -ū and the Genitive-Accusative in -ē:

aḫḫū, aḫḫē, brothers

mer'ū, mer'ē, sons

25.10 The Prefix of the Feminine Singular Third Person The Old-Assyrian prefix, if it has to deal with feminine personal subjects, is ta- (tu-, te-) (20.11, 24.9):

taṣbatanni, she has seized me

tuka''il she has in possession (25.14)

but if it is a feminine noun dealing with things, the prefix is i- (u-, e-):

ṭuppum...ša ellianni, the tablet which will appear

25.11 The Un-prefixed D- and Š- Forms In Old-Babylonian, in the prefixed forms, an *a* vowel appears after the first consonant in the D stem as well as after the stem-indication Š in the Š stem. In un-prefixed forms, it is *u* (11.3, 12.3).

Assyrian, on the other hand, shows an *a* in un-prefixed forms:

danninā (Old-Babylonian *dunninā*), strengthen!

šašqil (Old-Babylonian *šušqil*), let [him] pay

ḫabbulāku (Old-Babylonian *ḫubbulāku*) I am guilty, blamed, in debt

šabbu, he is satisfied

dammuqum (Old-Babylonian *dummuqum*) well made, restored

ta''urrum (Old-Babylonian *turrum*, 11.5) to return

25.12 Verbs I Aleph In Old-Assyrian *i'* shifts to *ē* (Old-Babylonian to *ī*, 4.6), *i'a* to *e* (Old-Babylonian i):

ēḫuz, (Old-Babylonian *īḫuz*), he took

eḫḫaz (*e-ḫa-az*, Old-Babylonian *iḫḫaz*), he takes

ētaḫaz (Old-Babylonian *ītaḫaz*), he has taken

In the e-class, there is no harmonization of *a* to *e*:

erābum (Old-Babylonian *erēbum*), to enter

ētarab (Old-Babylonian *īterub*) he has entered

In Old-Assyrian the present form of the verb *erābum* is *errab* (Old-Babylonian *irrub*) and the Perfect is *ētarab* (Old-Babylonian *īterub*).

25.13 Verbs III Vowel In verbs which are III *ē* (Final '), there is no harmonization of *a* to *e* (6.3).

tašamme (Old-Babylonian *tešemme*) you listen

<u>aštanamme</u> (Old-Babylonian <u>eštenemme</u>), I listen again and again

When a vocalic ending follows the root-vowel, no contraction takes place:

<u>ilaqqeū</u>, they take

But sometimes the root-vowel is squeezed out:

<u>itmū</u> (for <u>itmaū</u>), they swear

The root-vowel, when it is final, frequently does not shorten:

<u>i-šu-ú</u>, he is well off

<u>uš-ta-ba-a</u>, he will be satisfied (Cf. 25.2)

25.14 <u>Verbs Middle Vowel</u> The G Stative of verbs which are Middle <u>I</u> has the vowel <u>ē</u>:

<u>kēn</u>, is true cf. the interjection <u>kēna</u>, yes!

The vowel sequence <u>ua</u> is frequently changed to <u>uwa</u> in verbs which are Middle <u>ū</u>; this is by reason of a secondary "diphthongal" formation.

<u>adi tuwār Idī-^dAdad</u>, until the return of Idī-Adad

The formation of the D-stem of verbs Middle Vowel follows, in Old-Assyrian, the pattern of verbs Middle Aleph (11.6):

Inf. <u>ta''urum</u>, to return

Pret. <u>ša...tuka''ilu</u>, who has in possession

Only the D Preterite is formed as in Old-Babylonian:

<u>utār</u>, he turns back, Plural <u>utarrū</u>

25.15 <u>Verbs I w</u> For the most part in the Present and Preterite of the D-stem of verbs which are I <u>w</u>, (11.7) the <u>-wa-</u> drops:

lū <u>nuššer</u> (< <u>nuwaššer</u>) we wish to release

25.16 <u>Verbs I n</u> The Imperative of verbs I <u>n</u> (13.3) is formed in

Old-Assyrian without the prosthetic vowel i:

dinam, give!

Only the imperative of na'ādum, to pay attention, (16.4) is also in Old-Assyrian:

i'id, pl. i'dā

From nadānum, to give, (24.10) the Old-Assyrian forms are:

Pres. iddan, pl. iddunū (25.4)

Pret. iddin

Perf. ittidin

25.17 The Š-stem of izuzzum The Old-Assyrian Š-stem of the irregular verb izuzzum, to stand, is formed differnetly from the Old-Babylonian (21.13):

Pres. ušazzaz, he places, sets forth

Pret. ušazziz

Perf. uštazziz

Imper. šazziz (25.11)

25.18 The Voluntative To build the voluntative (18.8) in Old-Assyrian one places an l- before the first person singular of the Preterite:

lašqul (Old-Babylonian lušqul), I will pay, I wish to pay

lēpuš (Old-Babylonian lūpuš), I wish to do

lušabbi (same in Old-Babylonian), I wish to give satisfaction

In place of the Cohortative (19.9), the Voluntative of the first person plural is used. This is formed with lū and the first person plural of the Preterite:

lū nuššerka, we wish to let you go free (25.15)

25.19 The Precative The Precative (13.5) is formed in Old-Assyrian by placing an l- before the third person singular of the Preterite:

lizziz, he may stand, let him stand

lušazziz (Old-Babylonian lišziz, 21.13), he wishes to cause [someone] to move

25.20 The Subjunctive In verbal forms without endings, the Subjunctive (as in Old-Babylonian, 7.4) is formed by adding a -u:

wašib, he dwells

ša wašbu, who dwells

To forms with endings, one adds -ni:

ṭuppum ša ellianni (< elli + am + ni), the tablet which appears

In forms with a pronominal suffix, the subjunctive ending comes after the suffix:

ša ta''uram utarrakkani (< utār + am + ka + ni) who is responsible for aiding your return, (25.14).

25.21 Prepositions The preposition ina, in or on, appears in Old-Assyrian generally in the Old-Akkadian form in (24.18), whose n is assimilated to the initial consonant of the following word (20.9):

illibbīka (< in libbīka) in your possession

Before a vowel and sometimes before a consonant the preposition may appear as ina:

ina itti erāšim, at the end of your sowing

ina tuārīšu, at his return

ana, to or for can likewise be assimilated to the following consonant (although it is much less common than that of ina):

aqqātīšu (< an(a) qātīšu) to his hand

Other prepositions are adi, unto, until, maḫar, before, ištī, with, and ṭeḫi, close by, near

25.22 Prepositional Expressions   Prepositional expressions are formed from in and an(a):

sērum, back issēr, as a burden

libbum, middle, illibbi in possession of

šumum, name, aššumi, with regard to

Cf. also:

ammala (<*anamala) corresponding to

barī- (for Old-Babylonian birī), between in

ana barīšunu, between them, common to them

25.23 Negations   For negation Old-Assyrian uses lā, not, in main clauses, ula, not, is also so used.

READING EXERCISE - OLD-ASSYRIAN LEGAL DOCUMENTS

1. (Betrothal Document) kunuk E-na-na-tim[1] mer'i Tí-tí-na-ri, kunuk Šu-Sú-in mer'i Ili$_5$-mì-tí, kunuk ^{d}Adad-damiq mer'i Pì-lá-aḫ-Ištar. -- ^{d}Adad-damiq a-ša-tám ṣú-ḫa-ar-tám mer'at Ištar-na-da e-ḫu-úz. a-ša-tám ša-ni-tám ú-lá e-ḫa-az. šu-ma a-ša-tám ša-ni-tám e-ta-ḫa-az 1 ma-na kaspam[2] i-ša-qal. šu-ma a-na waraḫ 2^{kam} lá i-tal-kam ù da-tám ša a-ší-tí-šu lá iš-ta-al ṣú-ḫa-ar-tám a-na mu-tim ša-ni-im i-du-nu ...

2. (A matter of inheritance) A-mur-^{d}Šamaš a-ḫu-ú A-gu$_5$-za, A-šùr-rabi mera A-gu$_5$-za, Šu-Ištar A-šùr-ṭāb me-er-ú A-gu$_5$-za ù a-ḫa-sú-nu gu$_5$-ba-

[1]Proper nouns can be declined in Old-Assyrian

[2]For the construction of units of measure like manā'um, šiqlum, and uttatum, cf. būrum and kurrum 14.12.

áb-tum ni-iš A-lim[ki] it-mu-ú. a-na bé-tí-im ša Kà-ni-iš ša A-šùr-rabi wa-áš-bu ù ší-ma-at a-bi-šu-nu ù a-na mì-ma šu-um-šu A-mur-^{d}Šamaš a-na A-šùr-rabi ù a-ḫe-šu me-er-e A-gu$_5$-za ú-lá i-tù-ar. ù me-er-ú A-gu$_5$-za a-na A-mur-^{d}Šamaš ù me-er-e-šu a-na mì-ma šu-um-šu ú-lá i-tù-ru. qá-qú-ru ša ṭé-ḫi-i bēt I-dí-A-šùr mer'i Ku-bi$_4$-dí a-na ba-ri-šu-nu i-za-zu. maḫar Ku-ku-wa, maḫar Ili$_5$-ba-ni, maḫar ...[1], maḫar A-šùr-lá-ma-sí.

3. (A matter of inheritance) Lá-bar-ša Lá-ma-sí ù Šu-bi-ša-am-nu-ma-an i-zu-zu-ma ù Lá-bar-ša iš-tí bé-tim i-tí-ṣí. a-ḫu-um a-na a-ḫe-e la i-tù-wa-ar. ša i-tù-ru 5 ma-na kaspam i-ša-qal ... three witnesses.

4. (A promise of servitude.) Four seals. 18 šiqil kaspam[2] i-ṣé-er Ḫa-na ù Be-tí-a-na-al-kà Ḫu-ma-da-šu ù I-lá-li-iš-kà i-šu-ú[4]. kaspam i-na i-tí e-ra-ší-im i-ša-qá-lá[2]. [é]be-tám a-na ša-pár-tim ú-kà-lu. kaspam i-ša-qá-lá-ma ú i-na [é]be-tim ú-ṣí-ú.

5. (Payment of a debt) x[3] ma-na kaspam i-na ṭup-pì-a ḫa-ar-mì-im ša a-na Puzur-A-šur ḫa-bu-lá-ku-ni áš-qúl. Two witnesses.

6. (guarantee) 14 ma-na weri'am dammuqam i-ṣé-er Ša-lim-be-lí A-šur-re-ṣi i-šu-ú. šu-ma i-na ba-áb-tim ša Ša-lim-be-lí A-šur-re-ṣí weri'am il$_5$-té-qé i-na ḫu-bu-li-šu ša Ša-lim-be-lí uš-ta-ba-a. ... Three witnesses.

7. (receipt) 17 ma-na weri'um ša A-ma-a a-na Puzur-Ištar i-ḫi-ib-lu. weri'am Puzur-Ištar ša-bu. a-na A-ma-a lá i-tù-ar. ṭup-pu-um ša 17 ma-na werîm ša ḫu-bu-ul A-ma-a ša e-li-a-ni sà-ar[4] One witness.

[1] Proper name erased from the tablet

[2] To distinguish between the two parties, the debtor is referred to as plural and the creditor as dual.

[3] numbers not preserved

[4] 9.5

8. (an accounting) 2/3 šiqil 15 uttat kaspam[3] a-na gu$_5$-ba-áb-tim ša a-ni-qí ša A-na-aḫ-Ištar tù-kà-i-lu áš-qúl. 2 šiqil kaspam i-na tap-ḫi-ri-im ša Be-lim bēt A-la-ḫi-im ni-a-im áš-qúl.

9. (minutes, record) Ma-li-wa-aḫ-ší ta-aṣ-ba-ta-ni-ma um-ma ší-it-ma: kasap Ennum-Aya i-li-bi$_4$-kà. um-ma a-na-ku-ma: ke-na, i-li-bi-a i-ba-ší. um-ma ší-it-ma: kaspam dí-nam; a-na a-wa-at Ennum-Aya ma-ṣa-ku. kaspam áš-qúl, a-šu-mì Ennum-Aya Ma-li-wa-áš-ḫa ta-aṣ-ba-at-ma áš-qúl. Two witnesses.

10. (legal record) Ú-ṣú-ra-num ù A-mur-Ištar ... a-na Puzur-A-na iṣ-bu-tù-ni-a-tí-ma um-ma šu-nu-ma: ša qá-ta-tim ša ta-ú-ra-am ú-ta-ra-kà-ni ša-zi-iz-ma lu nu-šé-er-kà! um-ma Puzur-A-na-ma: a-ma, Šu-mì-a-bi-a li-zi-za-ku-nu-tí! um-ma Ú-ṣú-ra-num ù A-mur-Ištar-ma: a-na kaspim la e-pá-al-ni-a-tí, a-na ta-ú-ri-kà le-pu-ul-ni-a-tí-ma a-ma-lá dí-in kà-ri-im Kà-ni-iš^{ki} [4] nu-ša-sà-aḫ-kà ù kaspam ù ḫurāsam ta-da-an-ni-a-tí-ma ú-lá ni-lá-qé ku-a-tí-ma ni-ra-dí-kà. um-ma Puzur-A-na-ma: mì-šu-um a-na Kà-ni-iš ta-ra-dí-a-ni? e-er-ba-ma kasap-ku-nu lu-ša-bi$_4$-ku-nu ... um-ma šu-nu-ma: a-na kaspim ù ḫurāṣim ú-lá ni-li-kam ...

FROM ASSYRIAN BUSINESS LETTERS

11. a-na A-šùr-na-da qì-bi-ma um-ma A-šùr-i-dí-in-ma: ... áš-ta-na-me-ma[5] ^{d}Amurru-ba-ni a-na Kà-ni-iš e-ta-ar-ba-am ù kaspum 1 manā'um ù 2 manân a-qá-tí-šu pá-qí-id; a-ḫi a-ta! ṣa-ba-sú-ma kaspam ša-áš-qí-il$_5$-šu ...

12. um-ma Im-dí-ilum-ma: a-na E-nu-be-lim Ḫu-ra-ṣa-nim I-dí- ^{d}Adad ù A-mur-ilī qí-bi$_4$-ma: a-dí tù-wa-ar I-dí- ^{d}Adad sí-ki ú-kà-lu. I-dí-^{d}Adad ú-qá-a. a-ḫu-ú-a a-tù-nu! a-na u$_4$-um e-ṭa-ri-im eṭ-ra-ni-ma i-na

[3]cf. 14.12

[4]Kānis^{ki} is in apposition to kārim

[5]I hear again and again that..., I hear constantly that...

u_4-mì-im ša I-dí-^{d}Adad e-ra-ba-ni a-na té-er-tí-a i'-da-ma mì-ma 3 ṭup-pé-e-a ù ší-bé-e-a da-ni-na-nim-ma u_4-ma-kál lá i-bi-a-at. $ṭur_4$-da-ni-šu ù ṭup-pá-am iš-tí kà-ri-im ša 20 ma-na kaspam a-na ni-kà-sí-šu áš-qu-lu le-qé-a-nim. ...

13. a-na Puzur-A-šur Ša-lim-Ištar ù I-ku-pí-A-šur qí-bi-ma: um-ma Sà-ba-zi-a-ma a-na Puzur-A-šur qí-bi-ma: a-bi a-ta, be-li a-ta! i-'ì-id-ma a-wi-tí iš-tí Puzur-Ištar mer'i A-šur-ta-ak-lá-ku gu_5-mu-ur. ... ḫi-ri-iš-na-na ù ša e-mu-qí-im 1 1/2 manā'ē 5 šiqlē šu-qú-ul-ta-áš-nu ú-ka-al. I-ku-num mera E-la-ni iš-pu-ra-am, um-ma šu-ut-ma: šu-up-ra-ma a-ší-i li-dí-nu-ni-ma a-ma-lá dí-in da-a-ni kaspam lá-áš-qu-ul! i-na dí-in da-a-né 11 2/3 ma-na kaspam i-na A-lim^{ki} i-ša-qal-ma ù a-ší-áš-nu i-na Kà-ni-iš i-la-qé-ú. a-ma-kam um-me-a-nam lu-ša-zi-za-ku-nu-tí. ša a-ma-lá dí-in da-a-né kaspam šál-ma-am i-na A-lim^{ki} i ša-qú-lu-ù[1] kaspum li-ki-ni-ik-ma a-ší-a-am wa-šé-ra-šu-um! ...

14. a-na Puzur-A-šùr qí-bi_4-ma: um-ma Ili_5-we-da-ku-ma: a-bi_4 a-ta, be-li a-ta! i-na u_4-mì-im ša ṭup-pì ta-ša-me-ù i-'ì-id-ma ... a-wi-tí bu-tù-uq-ma a-na té-er-tí-kà lá-ak-nu-uš-ma ḫa-ra-ni le-pu-uš. 1 ma-na kaspam lu i-a-am lu ku-a-am qá-ti ú-kà-al. ...

[1]Which he, according to the decision of the judge, will pay in complete silver=the whole silver which he according...

Lesson 26

GRAMMAR

26.1 Middle-Assyrian The language of the Middle-Assyrian laws, decrees, proclamations, letters and rituals differs from that of Old-Assyrian (25.1). To some extent, the difference parallels the development of Middle-Babylonian (21.1) from Old-Babylonian, e.g., the dropping of mimation (26.3), the shift of št tc lt (26.5) the use of the enumerative pronoun gabbu (26.5). In addition to these, Middle-Assyrian is characterised by several special vowel changes (26.4 - 26.5) and pronominal formations (26.6 - 26.7).

26.2 The Orthography of Middle-Assyrian In opposition to Old-Assyrian, Middle-Assyrian frequently expresses the doubling of consonants in its script:

šum-ma, if

at-ta-ma-nu (attamannu) each, every

Long-vowels are more often written in plene-writing:

šu-ú-ut, he, the one mentioned (26.6)

har-ra-a-na, a journey

Plene-writings are also to be found with short vowels, which apparently admit of secondary lengthening:

šu-ú-a (šua) him

ša-a- (ša), who, the one who

e-ep-pu-ú-šu-uš (eppušū-šu), they deal with him (16.8)

The indication of the glottal stop at the beginning of a word (by means of a vowel sign before a Vowel + Consonant sign (3.13) occurs in Middle-Assyrian more widely than in verbs First Aleph (4.6):

i-id-dan (*iddan*) he gives

i-it-ti-ka-an-ni (*ittikanni*), he has slept with me

26.3 *Mimation* As in Middle Babylonian (21.2), Middle-Assyrian shows mimation only if it is supported by a -*ma* or a suffix:

šu-a-am-ma (as) his own

The Genitival ending -*im* shifts to *e* with the dropping of mimation:

ša šarutte, of the Kingdom

Similarly, the dative pronominal suffix changes from -*šim* to -*še*:

iddinašše(*ni*)<*iddin* + *am* + *šim* (+ *ni*) he has given to you

The dative pronominal suffix -*šum* (5.9) changes to -*šu*:

utta''erūniššu, they have reported to him (25.14)

26.4 *Changes of m and n* In Middle-Assyrian, an *m* between vowels frequently changes to *'*.

a'īlu (<*amīlu* (21.3) <*awīlum*) man, human being

ahā'iš (<*ahamiš*) one another

da'iq (<*damiq*) is good

a-na īne (<*ana mīnim*), why?

n between vowels can also go to *'*.

ša ki'āte (<*ša kinātim*), the name of a month

At the beginning of a word, *wa*- changes to *u*-:

usbat (26.5, Old-Babylonian and Old-Assyrian *wašbat*, Middle-Babylonian *ašbat*), she dwells

urkiš (<*warkiš*), later

26.5 Changes in Certain Consonantal-groups Before Dentals and Sibilants, as in Middle-Babylonian (21.5), š changes to l:

iltēn (< ištēn), one, a

iltuḫur (<*ištaḫur), he returned, he turned around (25.4)

Before the t of the feminine ending, z also changes to l:

mazzaltu (<*mazzaztum), place

The t of the infixes -ta- and -tan- changes to ṭ after q, 23.11:

uqṭanarrubū (< uqtanarrabū), they bring closer and closer

Before Labials, š changes to s:

usbat (Old-Babylonian and Old-Assyrian wašbat), she dwells

laspur (Old-Babylonian lušpur) I wish to send (25.18)

The shift of št to lt does not occur in the preposition ištu, with, (26.12) and the subordinating particle ištu, after, (26.13).

26.6 Personal Pronouns In the Nominative singular, the anaphoric pronoun takes the Old-Assyrian form šūt, he, the one mentioned: (25.5):

The Dative singular of the personal pronoun:

ana kuāša, to you (Middle-Babylonian kâša, 21.7)

ana šuāšu (or šuāša), to him

Gen.-Acc. Sing. šua (24.5) or šuātu (Middle-Babylonian šâtu), him

The form of the Dative singular is also used as Gen.-Acc.:

eqle šuāšu, of this field

For the Accusative plural (Old-Babylonian šunūti, Middle-Babylonian šâtunu) the new formations šunātunu, šinātina are used:

mā'ē šunātunu of this water

26.7 Determinative and Relative Pronouns To express certain specific ideas, Middle-Assyrian frequently combines the determinative pronoun _ša_ (7.5) often written _ša-a_, (26.2), with a Genitive:

ša-a sinnilte, the (property) of the woman

Expressions like _ša rēš šarre_, that of the head of the king, royal personnel, eunuchs (cf. Old-Babylonian _šūtrēšim_) are often found not as mere genitival combinations but as new word unities with a declension of their own:

šarēššarrānū, the (individual) eunuchs (10.8)

The universal relative pronoun in Middle-Assyrian is generally _ammar_ (for the Old-Babylonian _mala_):

ammar naṣṣatūni, whatever she brings with her [dowry] (22.10)

26.8 _Enumerative Pronouns_ To serve this function with _things_, _gabbu_, everything, (22.8) is used:

gabbu ša sinnilte everything of the woman [property]

gabbē ḫiṭṭānē, all sins, faults

But with _persons_, there is used either _yamattu_, each, every or _attamannu_ (whoever you are =) each.

26.9 _The Prefix of the third person singular of the feminine_ Middle-Assyrian uses the prefix _ta-_ (_te-_, _tu-_) not only with persons (25.10) but also with things:

ṭuppu..ašar tellianni, the tablet, where it appears

26.10 _The Stative naṣ_ A masculine Stative _naṣ_ is derived from an irregular verb with the root _*naṣṣ_, to bear, carry, to bring with. The feminine is _naṣṣat_, she brings with.

26.11 *The Subjunctive* The Subjunctive ending in Middle-Assyrian (in forms without endings) is -*ū*-*ni*:

> *kī*...*iddinūni*, as soon as he has given

Even in the third person feminine singular of the Stative, the ending -*u*-*ni* appears: *ammar* *naṣṣatūni*, as much as she brings with her (26.10).

A pronominal suffix can interpose between the -*ū*- and the *ni*:

> *šumma* *ušāḫizūšini*, If I have had her captured...

The Subjunctive ending is -*ni* after verbal forms that end in -*ū* or -*ā* or the Ventive ending -*a*(*m*) or -*ni*(*m*); also here a pronominal suffix can stand before the -*ni*.

> *ištu*...*uqarribūni*, after they had sacrificed
>
> *ša* *mussa* *iddinaššeni* (*iddin* + *am* + *šim* + *ni*, 26.3), which her spouse had given to her

In nominal clauses, (-*ū*) *ni* is added to the last word of the clause:

> *kī* *aššat* *a'īle*-*ni* *īde*, that she is the wife of a free man, he knows

26.12 *Prepositions and Prepositional Expressions* The preposition *išti*, with, (20.10) is found in Middle-Assyrian as *ištu*. In suffixed forms it is always *iltē*-:

> *ištu* *aḫā'iš*, with one another (26.4)
>
> *iltēša* *idabbub*, he speaks with her

Prepositional Expressions are formed from:

muḫḫu, scalp: *ana* *muḫḫi* ... in this direction

pānu, front: *ana* *pān*, before, (*ana* *pān* *Aššur* before [the god] Assur).

ina *pān*, before (*ina* *pān* *šarre*, before the king)

libbu, middle, heart: ina libbi, in, between

ṣēru, back: ana ṣēr, with regard to

One should not confuse Middle-Assyrian ištu, with, and the subordinating particle ištu, after, (26.13).

26.13 Subordinating Particles Noun clauses can be introduced with kī, that, (Old-Babylonian kīma, (17.8):

kī aššat a'īle-ni, that she [is] the wife of a citizen

Comparative clauses begin with kī, as:

kī...ēpušūni...eppušūš, as they... have dealt, so will men deal with him (16.8).

Temporal clauses are introduced by ištu (Middle-Babylonina ultu, 21.15) or kī, when, if:

ištu namurātē ana šarre uqarribūni, after they had presented the ceremonial gifts to the king

kī a'īlu bitqāte . . . iddinūni, if he has replaced the deficit

26.14 Particles for Direct Address Before a direct quotation of speech or a letter, Middle-Assyrian uses mā, as follows, thus (Middle-Babylonian ummā, 21.16).

mā še'am šēbila! mā ṭuppa alṭaṭar, As follows: Let the grain be brought to me! So have I written on the tablet.

26.15 Oaths An oath is written in the form of a conditional sentence introduced by šumma, if, and the subjunctive. A negation is implied rather than directly expressed:

šumma ušāhizūšīni means, I certainly have not had someone take it. Literally: If I have had someone take it...[may I perish!].

26.16 <u>Combining of Sentences and Clauses</u>   Sentences, clauses and phrases which are logically joined are, in Middle-Assyrian, rarely connected with -<u>ma</u> (1.9). For the most part, they are simply placed one after another without connecting particles:

<u>šūt iltuḫur iltēša idabbub</u>, he has turned around [and] he speaks with her

But -<u>ma</u> is often used to emphasize a given word (8.14)

<u>mamma šaniumma lā išaqqi</u>, no other may give [them] to drink, irrigate

READING EXERCISE FROM THE OLD-ASSYRIAN LAWCODE

1. šum-ma aššat a'īle i-na bēt a'īle ša-né-e-ma mīm-ma tal-ti-ri-iq, a-na qa-at 5 ma-na anneke tu-ta-at-ter, bēl šur-qé i-tam-ma, ma-a: šum-ma ú-ša-ḫi-zu-ši-ni, ma-a: i-na bētī-ya še$_{20}$-er-qí! -- šum-ma mu-us-sa ma-ge-er, šur-qa id-dan ù i-pa-aṭ-ṭar-ši; uz-né-ša[1] ú-na-ak-ka-ás. šum-ma mu-us-sa a-na pa-ṭa-ri-ša la-a i-ma-ag-gu-ur, bēl šur-qé i-laq-qé-e-ši ù ap-pa-ša i-na-ak-ki-is.

2. šum-ma aššat a'īle la-a a-bu-ša la-a a-ḫu-ša la-a mar-ša a'īlu ša-ni-um-ma ḫar-ra-a-na ul-ta-aṣ-bi-si, ù ki-i aššat a'īle-ni la-a i-de i-tam-ma-ma ù 2 bilāt anneke a-na mu-ut sinnilte i-id-dan. šum-ma ki-i aššat a'īle-ni i-de bi-it-qa-a-te id-dan i-tam-ma, ma-a: šum-ma a-ni-ik-ku-ši-ni, ù šum-ma aššat a'īle taq-ti-bi, ma-a: i-it-ti-ka-an-ni, ki-i a'īlu bi-it-qa-a-te a-na a'īle id-di-nu-ú-ni, a-na nāre il-lak; ri-ik-sa-tu-šu la-áš-šu. šum-ma i-na nāre it-tu-ra, ki-i mu-ut sinnilte aššas-su e-pu-šu-ú-ni a-na šu-a-šu[2] e-ep-pu-ú-šu-uš.

[1]Dual

[2]<u>ana šuāšu</u>, to him, with reference to him

3. šum-ma sinniltu i-na bēt a-bi-ša-ma us-bat mu-us-sa e-ta-na-ra-ab, mim-ma nu-du-un-na-a ša-a mu-us-sà id-di-na-aš-še-ni šu-a-am-ma[1] i-laq-qé; a-na ša bēt a-bi-ša la-a i-qa-ar-ri-ib.

4. šum-ma [mí]al-ma-at-tu a-na bēt a'īle te-ta-ra-ab, mi-im-ma am-mar na-sa-tu-ú-ni gab-bu ša-a mu-ti-sa; ù šum-ma a'īlu a-na muḫḫi sinnilte e-ta-rab, mi-im-ma am-mar na-aṣ-ṣu-ú-ni gab-bu ša-a sinnilte.

5. šum-ma mā'ū i-na lìb-bi būrē ša a-na ši-i-qe a-na ša-ka-a-ni il-lu-ku-ú-ni i-ba-áš-ši, bēlē eqlātī iš-tu a-ḫa-iš iz-za-zu; a'īlu a-na ṣè-er eqlī-šu ši-ip-ra e-ep-pa-áš eqil-šu i-ša-aq-qí. ù šum-ma i-na lìb-bi-šu-nu la-a ma-ag-ru-tu i-ba-áš-ši, ma-ag-ru ša lìb-bi-šu-nu dayyānē i-ša-'a-a-al, ṭup-pa ša dayyānē i-ṣa-bat ù ši-ip-ra e-ep-pa-áš. mā'ē šu-na-a-tu-nu a-na ra-mi-ni-šu i-laq-qé eqil-šu i-ša-aq-qí. ma-am-ma ša-ni-ú-um-ma la-a i-ša-aq-qí.

FROM THE "HAREM-LAWS" OF TIGLATH PILESAR I FOR EUNUCHS AND COURTIERS

6. šúm-ma sinniltu ša é-kál-lè lu-ú ta-za-mu-ur ù lu-ú ṣa-al-ta iš-tu me-ḫe-er-ti-ša ga-ar-'a-at ù šu-ú-ut[2] iz-za-az il-ta-nam-me, 100 im-maḫ-ḫa-aṣ, iltēn uzun-šu i-na-ki-su.

7. šum-ma sinnilti é-kál-lè naglabā-ša pa-at-tu-a [túg]ḫur-da-ba-áš-še[3] la-a ka-at-tu-ma-at a-na ma-zi-iz pa-ni tar-tu-gu-um, ma-a: ...[4] la-áš-pur-ka ù šu-ú-ut il-tu-ḫu-ur il-te-e-ša i-da-bu-ub, 100 im-maḫ-ḫa-aṣ; a-me-ra-an-šu qu-zip-pe-e-šu i-laq-qí ù šu-ú-a šagāt qablī-šu i-ra-ku-su.

[1]as his own

[2]one of the eunuchs or courtiers

[3]Accusative singular (with the loincloth). As a foreign word it does not fit the Akkadian declension-

[4]break in text.

8. šúm-ma ma-zi-iz pa-ni iš-tu sinnilti é-kál-lè i-da-bu-ub 7 e-ber-ta^{meš} a-na muḫ-ḫi-ša la-a i-qar-ri-ib. ...

9. šúm-ma ša rabi é-kál-lè qe-pu-tu-šu^{meš} a-na ši-id-di é-kál-lè la-a iṭ-ṭu-lu, ḫi-ṭa-a-né^{meš} la-a ut-ta-e-ru-ni-šu ur-ki-iš šarru ḫi-i-ṭa il-te-me, gab-bé ḫi-ta-a-né^{meš} rabi é-kal-lè e-mi-du-šu-nu.

A MIDDLE-ASSYRIAN LAND-TITLE

10. kunuk ^{m}Ú-bar-ya. 3 ikû 1 ku-ma-ni 3 šēpē eqlu ad-ru ù qa-qar āle e-^{3}ṣu ù ma-du būru zitta-šu ... ugar āl ša ^{m}Ili$_{5}$-it-ti-lu, i-na ši-a-ma-at ^{m}I-ga-ya-e a-bi a-bi-šu a-na ši-mé a-na ši-im ga-me-er a-na 50 ma-na anneke ^{m}Ú-ba-ri-ya mar A-ma-zi-ya mar I-ga-ya-e a-na ^{m}Ki-din-^{d}Adad mar I-din Ku-be i-din-ma ... tu-a-ru ù da-ba-bu la-aš-šu. annaka šīm eqlī-šu ad-re qa-qar āle ù būre ^{m}Ú-ba-ri-ya ma-ḫe-er a-pil za-ku. eqla ad-ra qa-qar āle būra ú-zak-ka i-na a-šal šarre i-ma-da-ad ù ṭup-pa dannata a-na pa-ni šarre i-ša-ṭar. ṭup-pu dannutu ša eqle šu-a-šu a-šar te$_{9}$-li-a-ni a-na ^{m}Ki-din-^{d}Adad-ma za-ku-at. kunuk ^{d}Adad-da-iq. maḫar ^{d}Šamaš-pāṭer mar ^{d}Šamaš-na-da, maḫar ^{d}Adad-da'iq mar ^{d}Šamaš-ilum, maḫar ^{d}Šamaš-tukultī ṭupšarru mar A-pil-Ku-be. urḫu A-bu-šarrānī ūmu 6^{kám} li-mu ^{m}Ibašši-ilum mar ^{d}A-šur-bēl-aple.

FROM A MIDDLE-ASSYRIAN LETTER

11. a-na ^{md}A-šur-ták-lak qí-bi-ma: um-ma ^{m}Ki-din-^{d}Gu-la-ma: ul-ta-ka-in; a-na ku-a-ša bētī-ka pa-ḫi-ti-ka gab-be lu-ú šul-mu! ma-a a-na i-né i-na bu-bu-a-te a-mu-at , ma-a še-am še-bi-la ma-a ṭup-pa al-ta-ṭa-ar. ù ^{f}Ú-ša-na-me-su a-na ^{d}Šamša-i-qí-ša a-ti-di-in. a-na muḫḫi-ka ul-te-bi-la-ši. ...urḫu ša ki-a-te ūmu 15^{kám} li-mu ^{md}Be-er-šuma-li-šer.

FROM A MIDDLE-ASSYRIAN ROYAL RITUAL

12. i-na kussê ša šarrutte ú-še-šu-bu-šu. nārū i-za-am-mu-ru rabiānū šarēššarrānū i-na pān šarre ul-ta-na-ak-na-nu šēpē ša šarre ú-na-šú-qu. ... šul-ma-na-te a-na šarre uq-ṭa-na-ru-bu; šul-ma-na pa-ni-a ša a-na šarre ú-qar-ri-bu-ni a-na bēt Aššur ub-bu-lu, a-na pān Aššur i-ša-ku-nu; ma-al-qi-tu ša šangê rabê. iš-tu na-mu-ra-a-te a-na šarre ú-qár-ri-bu-ni šukkalu rabiu šukkalu šaniu ḫattē a-na pa-an šarre i-kar-ru-ru, rabi ur-ta-a-né ki-si-šu rabi za-ma-re sa-am-me-šu ù at-ta-ma-nu bēl pa-ḫe-te ša ú-kal-lu-ni. ma-za-al-ta-šú-nu uš-šu-ru. ... šarru i-qa-bi-a-šu-nu; ma-a: ya-ma-tu pa-ḫa-su lu-ka-il! uš-ka-nu iq-qá-ra-ru i-qar-ri-bu, ya-ma-tu i-na ma-za-al-te-šú iz-za-az.

Lesson 27

GRAMMAR

27.1 *Neo-Assyrian* The language of the Neo-Assyrian vassal-treaties, legal documents, and letters (0.8) is distinguished from Middle-Assyrian (26.1) by peculiarities which correspond, to some extent, to the development of Middle-Babylonian into Neo-Babylonian (22.1). These include consonantal and vowel changes (27.6, 27.7) and the partial blurring of case distinction in declension (27.8). Moreover in Neo-Assyrian, the influence of Aramaic begins to be felt (27.20, 27.25). Neo-Assyrian has some orthographic peculiarities (27.2, 27.3), the development of characteristic sound-changes (27.5 - 27.7), and a special formation of the G perfect of verbs I *w*. Neo-Assyrian also shows special prepositions (27.20, 27.21) and subordinating particles (27.23), as well as the formation of temporal clauses with *kīma* (but without the subjunctive ending (27.24).

27.2 *The Script of Neo-Assyrian* Doubling of consonants is expressed in the script only occasionally.

it-tal-ka (*ittalka*), he has come

but *a-sa-pá-ra-šu* (*assaparaššu* < *aštapar* + *am* + *šu*) I have sent him away

Long vowels are so indicated (through *plene* writing) only in open syllables:

ki-i (*kī*), as

a-de-e (*adê*), oath of fidelity

i-qab-bu-u-ni (as soon as) he commands

In closed syllables, the vowel-length is either left unindicated:

da-an (*dān*), he is strong

or the syllable is opened by the insertion of an additional vowel:

ṭa-a-ba (or *ṭa-ba* for *ṭāb*), is good

27.3 The Writing of Vocalic Endings on the Verb As in Neo-Babylonian (22.10), vocalic endings are added to the verb in a somewhat freer manner:

ta-šá-kan-a-ni, (if) you dwell

ša...*e-pu-uš-u-ni*, who...makes

iš-pur-an-ni, he wrote to me

Still, this is probably only a peculiarity of the *script* and these forms are to be read *tašakkanāni*, *eppušūni*, *išpuranni* (and not **tašakkan'āni* etc.)

Still, one does occasionally find normal writings:

la ta-ta-ba-ka-a-ni (if) you do not pour out,

Sometimes, when the ending is a vowel, the preceding consonant is doubled:

tu-še-šab-ba (*tušeššabā*), you cause them to sit down, settle

lā ta-na-ke-er-ra-ni (*tanakkerāni*) (if) you do not become hostile

lā tu-ḫal-laq-qa-a-ni (*tuḫallaqāni*) (if) you do not destroy

27.4 Vowels The vowels *e* and *i* are distinguished in Neo-Assyrian only at the beginning of a word:

e-pu-šu (*eppušu* < *eppašū*, 25.4), they do, make

i-du-ak (*iduāk*), he kills

At the end of a word and in the middle of a word, signs containing e- and i- (e.g., te and ti, še and ši) are used indiscriminately:

šim-te as well as šim-ti, of destiny

ep-ši-tu (epšetu), the deed, activity

27.5 Contraction of Vowels In a departure from Old- and Middle-Assyrian, (25.3), Neo-Assyrian contracts many adjacent vowels; ai (ae), for example, always shifts to ê:

šamê (∠ šamāʾī) of the sky, heaven

However, ia, iu, and ua do not contract at the end of a word:

bikiā, weep!

anniu, this

quluā, burn!

But if one or more syllables follows ia, iu, or ua, generally a contraction takes place

iqbâkanûni (∠ iqbi + am + kunu + ni), (the one who) has spoken to you, (27.10).

annûte (∠ *anniūte)this

šanûmma (∠ *šanium + ma) another

With ia there may be no contraction:

šaniāte, others

With verbs that are Middle Vowel, ia and ua are not contracted.

iṭiab, he becomes good

iptuag, he has plundered

tuāru, to return

27.6 Sound-changes in Consonantal Groups The combination št which changes to lt in Middle-Babylonian (21.5) and Middle-Assyrian (26.5) shifts in Neo-Assyrian to ss:

ussēsâkkunu (∠ *uštēsi + am + kunu) I have led you out

assaparaššu (*aštapar + am + šu), I have sent him away

issi (∠ išti) with (27.20)

In Neo-Assyrian, lt may shift to ss even in circumstances where the lt was not originally an št.

isseqe (∠ iltaqe) he has taken

Assimilation of a d to an n occurs (as in Neo-Babylonian) (22.3) in some forms of the verb nadānu, to give:

ittanna (∠ ittadna), he has given

27.7 Sound-changes of m and w An m between vowels often shifts (as in Middle-Assyrian, 26.4) to '.

di'ātu (∠ dimātu), tears

de'iqtu (∠ damiqtu) Feminine of damqu, good

But if an m between vowels goes back to an older w, it may in Neo-Assyrian shift to b:

Old-Assyrian awutum (Old-Babylonain awātum) Middle-Assyrian amutu

But Neo-Assyrian abutu, word, command; abat šarrim, command of the king

An m before š (as in Neo-Babylonian, 22.3), shifts to n:

šulanšunu (∠ šulamšunu), their well-being

At the beginning of a word, wa- (as in Middle-Assyrian, 26.4), shifts to u, but wā shifts to ā:

urdu (∠ wardu) servant

āšibūte (∠ wāšibūte), the inhabitants

27.8 Case-Endings   Neo-Assyrian distinguishes only two case-endings in the singular; Nominative and Accusative take the ending -*u* and the Genitive takes the ending -*i* (-*e*):

Nominative *ūmu anniu lā ṭāba*, this day is unsuited (27.2)

Accusative *ipšu bārtu abutu lā ṭābtu lā de'iqtu teppašāniššūni*

if you carry out against him an evil deed (27.17)

Genitive *ana šimti* (*šimte*, 27.4) for destiny

In the Plural, for all cases the ending is -*ē* or -*ī*: -*ānī*, -*ūte*, (-*ūti*), -*āte* (-*āti*), -*ēte* (-*ēti*):

adê, promise of fidelity

ilānī rabûti āšibūte, the great gods who dwell

27.9 The Noun with Suffixes   In the Nominative and Accusative singular, the possessive suffixes (3.7) are added to the construct state of the noun (3.8):

ṣupuršu, his finger nail

In Neo-Assyrian, a few nouns whose root ends in two different consonants have a connecting vowel inserted between the root and the suffix (similarly, nouns which end in doubled consonants, cf. *muḫḫu*, 3.8). The connecting vowel is generally *a*, but it is subject to vowel harmony (25.4):

liptušu (< *liptašu*), his exhaustion

urdaka, your servant

urdušu, his servant

With the addition of the suffix -*šunu* to the connecting vowel *a*, vowel harmonization does not always take place. This may be due to a shift in accent:

dul-la-šú-nu, their ritual

27.10 Pronominal Suffixes The Accusative pronominal suffixes of the second and third person plural -kunu and -šunu (25.6) can also be used for the Dative in Neo-Assyrian (Old-Assyrian -kunūti, -šunūti). Before the Subjunctive suffix -ni, -kunu and -šunu shift to -kanu and -šanu.

Dative ša ukallimūkanūni iqbâkkanūni, whom he introduced to you (and about whom) he spoke to you

Accusative ussēṣâkkunu (∠ uštēṣi + am + kunu), I have led you out

27.11 The Anaphoric, Demonstrative, and Indefinite Pronoun The Nominative of the anaphoric pronoun šūt, šīt (25.5), he, the one just mentioned, is replaced in Neo-Assyrian to some extent by the Accusative šuātu, šiāti (11.10).

amēlu šuātu ṣarip, that man is purchased

The demonstrative pronoun anniu, this, is frequently written ḫanniu in Neo-Assyrian.

akkī annîma along with akkī ḫannîmma, with the meaning: likewise (27.22)

As an indefinite pronoun, memēni, somebody, something, is used. With the negative particle lā it means, nobody, nothing:

memēni issīya lā idbub, no one has disputed with me

27.12 Interrogative Pronouns and the Universal Relative mannu, who?, and mīnu, what?, are used as the interrogative pronouns:

mannu šarru ša akkī annî, who is a king like this one?

ayyu, which, can also be used substantivally:

ayyu bēl ṭābti ša akkī annî, who (is) a friend like this one?

The Universal relative of Neo-Assyrian is *mannu ša*, whoever

mannu ša...*ubta''ūni* whoever...shall strive

27.13 The Perfect G of Verbs I *w* The G Perfect and the similarly formed Gt Pret. of verbs I *w* (*ittabal*, 9.3) are formed in Neo-Assyrian with the root-vowel *i* and with *ū* after the doubled *t*:

ittūbil, he has brought

27.14 The G Perfect of Verbs Middle Vowel The G. Perfect and the similarly formed Pret. Gt of verbs which are Middle Vowel (*iktūn*, *ištīm*, 9.3) are formed in Assyrian, as is the Present (7.2), through the insertion of an *a* after the root vowel:

iptūag, he has plundered

27.15 The Verb *udā'u* Instead of *idûm* (*yd'*), to know, (16.6), Neo-Assyrian uses the verb *udā'u* (*wd'*), with the same meaning. The Present *udda*, he knows, serves also as the Stative. (Prefix stative, 11.9).

27.16 The Cohortative As in Neo-Babylonian (22.12), in Neo-Assyrian the first person plural of the Preterite (without the particle *i*) serves as the Cohortative (19.9):

nušaṣbit, let us get ready!

27.17 The Subjunctive In Neo-Assyrian (as in Middle-Assyrian, 26.11) the Subjunctive is formed by adding -*ūni* to verbal forms which are otherwise without endings:

> <u>ša</u>...<u>šumšu</u> <u>izkurūni</u>, whose name he had named

Between <u>ū</u> and <u>ni</u> a pronominal suffix can be inserted:

> <u>ša</u> <u>ukallimūkanūni</u>, whom he presented to you (27.10)

For verbal forms that end in -<u>ū</u>, -<u>ā</u>, and Ventive-endings -<u>a</u>(<u>m</u>), -<u>ni</u>(<u>m</u>), the Subjunctive ending is simply -<u>ni</u>. Here, too, a pronominal suffix can precede the -<u>ni</u>. (26.11):

> <u>šumma</u>...<u>lā</u> <u>taṣabbatāni</u>, if you do not seize
>
> <u>šumma</u>...<u>teppašānišsūni</u>, if you make a move against him

27.18 <u>Imperative Forms with šumma</u> In vassal treaties, commands and prohibitions are expressed in the form of a conditional sentence with <u>šumma</u>, the Present, and the Subjunctive ending (26.15). In a prohibition then, no negative is expressed, and in a command <u>lā</u> is expressed:

> <u>ina</u> <u>šarrūti</u> <u>māt</u> <u>Aššur</u> <u>šumma</u> <u>tunakkarāšūni</u> From his royal throne over the land of Assur, you shall not remove him (literally, if you remove him...[may you die].
>
> <u>šumma</u> <u>attūnu</u> <u>ana</u> <u>Aššur-bāni-apli</u>...<u>lā</u> <u>tanaṣṣarāni</u>

You shall protect Assur-banipal (27.20). Literally: if you do not protect Assurbanipal...!

Normally, conditional sentences in Assyrian as in Babylonian do not take the Subjunctive. (15.9)

> <u>šumma</u> <u>mAššur-aḫu-iddina</u>...<u>ana</u> <u>šimte</u> <u>ittalak</u>, if Esarhaddon dies.

27.19 <u>The Use of Tenses</u> Past time is expressed in Neo-Assyrian (in non-negated main clauses) through the use of the perfect: (21.14) ikkaru iḫtesi bēssu imtaša' eqlu iptūag, he mistreated the peasant, plundered his house and took away the land.

The Preterite occurs only in negated main clauses and in dependent clauses:

memēni issīya lā idbub, no one has argued with me

ša šarru išpuranni, what the king has written to me

For the Perfect after kīma, as soon as, cf. 27.24

27.20 Prepositions In place of ana, to, sometimes the Aramaic preposition la, to, (22.13) is used in Neo-Assyrian:

la māt Barḫalzi, to the land of Barḫalzi

The preposition ana is used sometimes in Neo-Assyrian for the specification of the Accusative:

šumma attūnu ana Aššur-bāni-apli mar šarri rabiu ša bēt redûti...

lā tanaṣṣarāni, if you do not protect Assurbanipal, the heir to the throne...(27.18)

dNabiu u dMarduk ana šarri bēlīya likrubu, Nabiu and Marduk--

may they bless the King, my Lord! (22.13)

Other Neo-Assyrian prepositions are:

issi (< išti, 27.6) with (with suffix, issīkunu, with you)

issu (< ištu) from, out of

akkī, as

kūm, and ina kūm, instead of, for; dāmē kūm dāmē, blood for blood

(with suffix, ina kummušu, in place of him)

27.21 Prepositional Expressions To some extent, Neo-Babylonian prepositional expressions have meanings different from those of Neo-Babylonian

(22.14). These are formed, for example, from *muḫḫu*, scalp:

ana muḫḫi, thither (26.12)

ina muḫḫi, with regard to, by reason of

from *pānu*; front

ina pān, before, alongside (26.12)

issu pān, from, out of

from *libbu*, heart, middle

ana libbi, against, for

issu libbi, from, out of

27.22 *Adverbs* To specify time, Neo-Assyrian uses the following:

umā, now

ina šerte, tomorrow

ina ši'āri, tomorrow

ina lidiš, the day after tomorrow

ina urkiš, later

ina matēma, sometime

to specify manner:

addanniš, very

akkī (ḫ)*annîmma* (27.11) likewise, just so

27.23 *Subordinating particles* Comparative clauses and phrases are introduced by *akkī ša*, just as, so as;

akkī ša abu ana marēšu eppušūni, as a father deals with his sons

Object clauses are introduced by *kī*, that, (26.13); causal sentences with *nēmel*, because:

nēmel ina rēšuššu azzizūni, Because I am to him as a head, leader (20.2).

Temporal clauses are introduced by issu bēt, since, adu, as long as, or immat, when:

issu bēt nišē ibbišūni, since there have been men

adu šamê qaqquru dārûni, as long as heaven and earth last

immat šarru ... iqabbūni, when the king commands

Akkī can also be used as a temporal conjunction:

akkī dabābu aniu...ašmûni, as I heard this word

27.24 Sentences with kīma In Neo-Assyrian, the Perfect, without subjunctive ending, follows the particle kīma, as soon as, if;

kīma mAššur-aḫu-iddina...ana šimti ittalak, as soon as Esarhaddon dies...

kīma ittabši when [the child] appears

27.25 Word-order Under the influence of Aramaic, Neo-Assyrian (as Neo-Babylonian 22.17) sometimes changes its normal (1.8) word-order:

šarēši ittūbilanni ana bēt mDāni, the official brought me to the house of Dani

1. FROM CONTRACTS OF ESARHADDON WITH THE MEDEAN PRINCES

1. a-de-e šá mAššur-aḫu-iddina $šar_4$ māt Aššur ina pān ilānī rabûti šá šamê qaqqiri is-si-ku-nu iš-ku-nu-u-ni, ina muḫḫi mAššur-bāni-apli mar šarri rabê šá bēt redûti mar mAššur-aḫu-iddina $šar_4$ māt Aššur bēlī-ku-nu,šá a-na mar šarrūti šá bēt redûti šùm-šú iz-kur-u-ni ip-qi-du-šú-u-ni. ki-ma mAššur-aḫu-iddina $šar_4$ māt Aššur a-na šim-ti it-ta-lak, mAššur-bāni-apli mar šarri rabiu šá bēt redûti ina kussī šarrūti tu-še-

šab-ba! šarrūtu bēlūtu šá māt Aššur ina muḫ-ḫi-ku-nu up-pa-áš. ...
šum-ma at-tu-nu a-na ^{m}Aššur-bāni-apli mar šarri rabiu ša bēt redûti, šá ^{m}Aššur-aḫu-iddina šar māt Aššur ú-kal-lim-u-ka-nu-ni, iq-ba-ka-nu-ni, a-de-e i-na muḫ-ḫi-šú is-si-ku-nu ú-dan-nin-u-ni iš-ku-nu-ni, la ta-na-ṣar-a-ni; anà lìb-bi-šú ta-ḫa-ṭa-a-ni, qātātē-ku-nu a-na lem-net-ti anà lìb-bi-šú tu-bal-a-ni, ip-šú bar-tu a-bu-tú la ṭābtu la de'iqtu te-ep-pa-šá-ni-šú-u-ni; ina šarrūti māt Aššur tu-nak-kara-šú-u-ni; issu lìb-bi aḫḫē-šú rabûti ṣeḫrūti ina ku-mu-šú kussī māt Aššur tu-šá-aṣ-bat-a-ni; šarru šanûm-ma bēlu šanûm-ma ina muḫ-ḫi-ku-nu ta-šá-kan-a-ni; a-na šarri šanîm-ma bēli šanîm-ma ma-miti ta-tam-ma-a-ni! ...
šum-ma ^{m}Aššur-aḫu-iddina šar$_{4}$ māt Aššur ina ṣa-ḫa-ri šá marē-šú a-na šim-te it-ta-lak, lu šá-ziq-ni lu šarēši a-na ^{m}Aššur-bāni-apli mar šarri rabiu šá bēt redûti i-du-ak, šarrūtu šá māt Aššur it-ti-ši; šum-ma at-tu-nu is-si-šú ta-šá-kan-a-ni, a-na urdānūtī-šú ta-tu-ra-a-ni; la ta-bala-kàt-a-ni la ta-na-ke-er-ra-ni; mātāti šá-ni-a-ti is-si-šú la tu-šam-kar-a-ni[1], la ta-ṣab-bat-a-ni-šú-u-ni, la ta-du-ka-šú-u-ni ù mar ^{m}Aššur-bāni apli mar šarri rabiu šá bēt redûti kussiu šá māt Aššur la tu-šá-aṣ-bat-a-ni!
šum-ma at-tu-nu ina pān ^{mí}a-ri-ti šá ^{m}Aššur-aḫu-iddina šar$_{4}$ māt Aššur ù aššat ^{m}Aššur-bāni-apli mar šarri rabiu šá bēt redûti la ta-da-gal-a-ni; ki-ma it-tab-ši, la tu-rab-ba-a-ni; kussīu šá māt Aššur la tu-ša-aṣ-bat-a-ni; e-pi-šá-nu-ti šá bar-ti la ta-ṣab-bat-a-ni la ta-du-ka-a-ni, šùm-šú-nu zēr-šú-nu ina māti la tu-ḫal-laq-qa-a-ni; da-me ku-um da-me la ta-ta-ba-ka-a-ni! ...

II. FROM NEO-ASSYRIAN LEGAL DOCUMENTS

2. (Pledge of Indentured Servitude) de-e-nu ša ^{md}Šamaš-nāṣer issi

[1] for tušakkarāni (∠ *tusankārani)

$^{f\ uru}$Arba-ìl-ḫa-mat sinnissī-šú ša ^{m}Sa-na-a-nu issi ^{md}Nabiu-erība marī-šá, napḫar 2 issu libbi āli ša marat šarri, ina muḫḫi ḫi-bil-te-šú ina muḫḫi nikkassē-šú ig-ru-u-ni, ma-a:

1 ma-na kaspi ina muḫ-ḫi-ki uḫ-te-bil[1]; ma-a: issu bēt šarēši ša šarri ú-se-ṣa-ku-nu; ma-a: qātātē-ku- u ša 50 emār uṭṭati ša epinni ša alpi, 12 1/2 ma-na kaspi a-taḫ-za. $^{f\ uru}$Arba-ìl-ḫa-mat ^{md}Nabiu-erība iq-ṭi-bi-u, ma-a: ina ku-um nikkassē an-nu-te ni-pa-laḫ-ka. -- ^{f}Arba-ìl-ḫa-mat, ^{md}Nabiu-erība, ^{f}Bēl-le'i, ^{f}Aḫātu-la-mur, ^{f}Šùl-mu-i-tú, napḫar 5 napšāti ana ^{md}Šamaš-nāṣer i-pal-lu-ḫu. man-nu ša ina še-er-te ina li-di-iš lu aḫū-šá lu šakin-šá de-e-nu idabbubūni, nikkassē an-nu-te a-na ^{md}Šamaš-nāṣer iddan. ...

3. (Slave Purchase) ku-um kunukki-šú ṣu-pur-šú iš-kun. ṣu-pur ^{m}Aššur-nāṣer bēl amēli. ^{m}Aḫī-li-i'-ti urdu-šú ú-piš-ma ^{md}Šamaš-abu-uṣur issu pān ^{m}Aššur-nāṣer anà lìb-bi 50 ma-na erê i-se-qè. kas-pu gam-mur ta-din-ni[2]. amēlu šu-a-tú ṣa-rip la-qì. tuāru de-nu dabābu la-šú. man-nu šá ina ur-kiš ina ma-te-ma lu ^{m}Aššur-nāṣer lu marē-šú lu aḫḫē-šú lu bēl pāḫas-su, man-nu šá de-nu dabābu issi ^{md}Šamaš-abu-uṣur mar-šú mar marē-šú ú-ub-ta-a'-u-ni[3], 10 ma-na kaspi 1 ma-na ḫurāṣi ina bur-ki ^{d}Adad bēl ^{uru}Kak-zi išakkan. ...

III. NEO-ASSYRIAN LETTERS

4. a-bat šarri a-na ^{m}Man-nu-ki-i-māt-Aš-šur: ^{md}Adad-ēriš a-na pa-zu-ur-ti a-na muḫ-ḫi-ka a-sa-pá-ra-šu. ...

[1] for uḫtabbil

[2] for tadin; writing with a superflouous vowel

[3] for ubta''ūni (bu''u), cf. 19.12.

5. a-bat šarri a-na ^{m}Man-nu-ki-māt-Aš-šur: at-ta nišē mātī-ka 3 umē ina pa-an ^{d}Adad di-at pa-ni bi-ki-a, sa-ri-ra! māt-ku-nu ú-ga-ar-ku-nu ka-pi-ra! ma-aq-lu-a-te qu-lu-a! ...

6. a-na šarri bēlī-ya urda-ka ^{m}Ištar-šumu-ēriš: lu šul-mu a-na šarri bēlī-ya! ^{d}Nabiu u ^{d}Marduk a-na šarri bēlī-ya lik-ru-bu! ūmu 20^{kám} ūmu 22^{kám} ūmu 25^{kám} a-na šá-ka-ni ša a-de-e ṭa-a-ba. im-ma-at šarru be-li i-qab-bu-u-ni nu-šá-aṣ-bi-it liš-ku-nu.

7. a-na šarri be-lí-ya urda-ka ^{md}Adad-šumu-uṣur: lu-u šùl-mu a-na šarri bēlī-ya! ^{d}Nabiu u ^{d}Marduk a-na šarri be-lí-ya lik-ru-bu! ina muḫḫi 2 ša ina bēti ešši ù ina muḫḫi ^{md}Sîn-per'u-ukīn, ša šarru be-lí iš-pur-an-ni, ma-a: a-lik a-mur-šú-nu! ú-ma-a šarru be-lí ú-da: šarēši it-tu-bi-la-an-ni a-na bēt ^{m}Da-ni-i; i-na muḫḫi ma-ar-i-šú dul-lu e-ta-pa-áš; li-ip-tu-šú da-an, ma-ri-iṣ a-dan-niš. né-me-el i-na re-šu-uš-šú az-zi-zu-u-ni, u_4-mu an-ni-ú la ṭa-ba a-na a-la-ki; ina ši-'a-a-ri al-lak, a-mar-šú-nu, šulan-šú-nu a-na šarri a-qab-bi; mašmaššē ú-pa-qá-da dul-la-šú-nu e-pu-šu.

8. a-na šarri bēlī-ya urda-ka ^{md}Marduk-šumu-uṣur: lu-u šùl-mu a-na šarri bēlī-ya! ^{d}Nabiu ^{d}Marduk a-na šarri bēlī-ya lik-ru-bu! abū-šú ša šarri bēlī-ya 10 emār zēri ina māt Ḫa-laḫ-ḫi it-ta-na 14 šanāti eqlu a-ta-kal, me-me-ni is-si-ya la id-di-bu-ub[1]. ú-ma-a bēl pāḫete la māt Bar-ḫal-zi it-tal-ka; ikkaru iḫ-te-se, bēt-su im-ta-šá-a', eqlu ip-tu-ag. šarru be-lí ú-da ki-i muš-ke-nu a-na-ku-u-ni; ...šarru be-lí de-e-ni le-pu-uš! ina bu-bu-ti lu la a-mu-at!

9. a-na šarri be-lí-ya urda-ka ^{md}Adad-šumu-uṣur: lu-u šùl-mu a-na šarri be-lí-ya! Aššur ^{d}Nin-lil ^{d}Sîn ^{d}Šamaš ^{d}Adad ^{d}Marduk ^{d}Zar-pa-ni-

[1] artificial lengthening of <u>idbub</u>

tu$_4$ ^{d}Nabiu ^{d}Taš-me-tu$_4$ ^{d}Ištar ša Ninua ^{d}Ištar ša ^{uru}Arba-īl ^{d}Nin-urta ^{d}Nergal ^{d}La-aṣ ilānī rabûti ša šamê qaqqiri u ilānī rabûti a-ši-bu-te māt Aššur mat Akkade a-na šarri be-lí-ya a-dan-niš a-dan-niš lik-ru-bu! ṭu-ub lìb-bi ṭu-ub šīrē ūmē arkūti še-be-e li-tu-ti pa-le-e šá nu-uḫ-ši a-na šarri be-lí-ya li-di-nu! šumu u zēru per'u lil-li-du a-na šarri be-lí-yá li-ib-ši! šur-šu-ka li-iš-mu-ḫu li-rap-pi-šú! ... ša šarru bēl šarrānī be-lí iš-pu-ra-an-ni, ma-a: ú-ma-a lìb-ba-ka li-ṭi-ib-ka! ... -- a-ki šá abu a-na marē-šú e-pu-uš-u-ni, šarru be-lí a-na urdānī-šú e-ta-pa-áš. issu bēt nišē i-bi-šú-u-ni, man-nu šarru šá a-ki an-ni-i a-na urdānī-šú de'iqtu e-pu-uš-u-ni? ù ayyu-ú bēl ṭābti šá a-ki an-ni-i a-na bēl ṭābti-šú ṭa-ab-tu ú-ter-ru-u-ni? a-ki ḫa-an-ni-ma ilānī rabûti šá šamê qaqqiri ṭa-ab-tu de-iq-tu a-na li-ip li-pì ša šarri be-lí-ya a-du šamê qaqquru da-ru-u-ni le-pu-šú! a-ki da-ba-bu an-ni-ú ṭābu ep-ši-tu an-ni-tu de-iq-tu ša ša ru be-lí e-pu-uš-u-ni áš-mu-u-ni a-mur-u-ni lìb-bi i-ṭi-ba-an-ni ib-tal-ṭa. ...ki-i an-ni-ma i-na libbi da-ru-te ša šarri be-lí-yá šarru be-lí lu-pa-ar-ši-man-ni, a-ki šá issi šarri be-lí-yá ki-na-ku-u-ni. ina mu-ti šim-ti la-mu-ut! ... a-na mārē-yá šarru be-lí ki-i an-ni-ma ṭè-mu liš-kun; šarru be-lí mar marē-šú-nu lu-par-ši-im! ...

GENERAL INDEX — PART I

A

B

C

Q

R

S

T

W

Y

PART II

AN AKKADIAN GRAMMAR

GENERAL VOCABULARY

A Translation of Riemschneider's

Lehrbuch des Akkadischen

by

Thomas A. Caldwell, S.J.
John N. Oswalt
John F. X. Sheehan, S.J.

Marquette University Press
Milwaukee, Wisconsin 53233
United States of America

Copyright © 1975 by
John F. X. Sheehan, S.J.

ISBN 0-87462-440-1

Second Printing, 1976
Third Printing, 1977
Fourth Printing, 1978

All rights reserved. No part of this publication may be reproduced, stored in a retrieval system or transmitted in any form or by any means, electronic, mechanical, photocopying, recording, or otherwise without the prior written permission of the copyright owner and publisher.

Printed in the United States of America
by
Marquette University Press
Milwaukee, Wisconsin, U.S.A.

General Vocabulary

The student would be well advised to study the following: the alphabetical order in this vocabulary is a b d e g h i y k l m n p q r s ṣ š t ṭ u w z. The glottal stop (') and mimation (m) are ignored in the alphabetical order.

A

â, particle of forbidding, cf. ay

abālu (Mid. Bab.) cf. wabālu(m)

[abātu(m)] cf. nābutu(m)

abbuttu(m), slave mark, Old Bab. Hairstyle of slave, Young Bab., a metal band for the hair; an abnormality in omens

abnum, stone, hail

abru, a wooden goad, abriš, as a wooden goad

abullu(m), gate, city-gate, "gate" as term describing a liver-phenomenon, part of liver

abutu (Neo-Ass.) cf. awātu(m)

adāru(m) (a/u) G to be afraid, to fear
Gtn to be constantly afraid;
N to be afraid

addaniš, very, extremely, in high degree addanniš addanniš, in the highest degree

ituAddārum, Adar, name of the 12th month

adê (Pl., Neo-Ass.) oath of allegiance

adi Neo-Ass. adu, prep., until; adi inanna, until now; (as subordinating particle), while, so long as, until

adīma (Old-Akk.) until

adirātu(m) (Fem. Pl.) fear

adru, threshing-floor

adu (Neo-Ass.) cf. adi

adû[1] (Neo-Bab.), now

adû[2] cf. adê

agāru(m) (a/u) G to hire, rent

agû[1] (fem. agatu; Neo-Bab.) this; libbu aga'i, in such a way

agu(m)[2], flood

aḫā'iš (Mid-Ass.) cf. aḫāmiš

aḫāmiš Mid-Ass. aḫā'iš, together; Mid-Bab. itti aḫāmiš, Mid-Ass. istu aḫā'iš, in common, with one another

aḫātu(m), sister

aḫāzu(m) (a/u) G to take, seize; marry; aššatam aḫāzum, to take someone as wife. qātāte aḫāzu, to take bail, surety,
Š to have (someone) taken
dīnam šuḫuzum, to grant a legal process

ahītu(m), side; ahītam, at the side

ahu(m) (Pl. ahhū, ahhī), const. state
of Pl. ahhī, brother
ahum...ahum, the one...the other

a'īlu (Mid-Ass.) cf. awīlum

ay, Old-Akk. â particle of prohibition

ayyabu(m), enemy

ayyu, which?

ayyumma, someone, anyone

akālu (m) (a/u) G to eat, devour; enjoy; to suffer; karṣi akālu, to calumniate, eqlu akālu, to enjoy a crop; Gtn to keep on eating; karṣi atakkulum, to calumniate repeatedly, Š to have (something) eaten, to cause someone to eat

akanna[1], here; ana akanna, hither

akanna[2] (Mid-Bab.) so

akītu (m), New Year Festival; bīt akītim, house of the New Year's festival

akkā'i (Late-Bab.) how?

akkī (Neo-Ass.) preposition, as; akkī (h)annīmma, likewise, correspondingly

akkī ša (Neo-Ass.) Subordinating particle, just as

alaktu(m) caravan

alāku(m) (a/i) G go, (Ventive) come; Mid.-Ass. to be suited for, arbūtam alākum, to take up flight; Mid.-Bab. ana dinān... alāku, to make entreaty for someone, to sacrifice for someone
Gt to depart, Gt ventive to depart, to break up (camp) Gtn to go away repeatedly, to wander
Š to cause someone to go arbûtiš šuluku, to make a desert out of, to lay waste

alālu(m) G to hang (intr.); D to hang (trans

'alappu(m) (Old-Akk.) cf. eleppu(m)

āliku(m) going; ālik harranim, one on a journey, traveller, one who goes to the battlefield; ālik pāni ummānim, one who goes before the army

'alium (Old-Akk.) cf. elû (m)[1]

mialmattu, widow

alpu, ox, cattle, bull

ālu(m) (Pl. ālānū) city, dwelling, settlement
ša libbi ālim, inhabitant

amāru(m) (a/u) G to see, look at; examine test; experience; to read (a tablet) ṭuppi (unnedukkī)

ina amārīka, as soon as you have read my tablet; N to see one another, to meet , to be seen

amātu (Mid. and Neo-Bab., rarely Old-Bab.) cf. awātu

amēlu (Neo-Ass.) cf. awīlum

amīlu (Mid-Bab.) cf. awīlu

amēlutu (Young-Bab.) cf. awīlūtum

āmerānu, eye-witness

amma (Old-Ass.) well now! come!

ammaka(m), there

ammaki (Young-Bab.) subordinating part. instead of...

ammala (Old-Ass.) prep. on the grounds that...

ammar (Old-Ass.) so much as mimma ammar, everything which

ammīni(m), why?

amtum, female slave, servant

amūtum, liver, liver-omen, characteristic of the liver

ana, prep. to, for, against, toward, because of

anaku(m) Ass: annuku(m), tin, pewter

anāku, I

anēni (Late-Bab.) we

annanna, so-and-so

annaqu(m) (Old-Ass.): ring

annikīam, here

annītu, cf. annû(m)

annû(m)(Fem., annītum) Neo-Ass. anniu or hanniu, this
annītu (subst.) this thing, Mid-Bab. ana muhhi annītī in addition to this; Neo-Ass. (h)annîmma, likewise, corresponding

annuqu(m) (Old-Ass.) cf. annaqu(m)

anumma, now

anzû, mythical giant bird, eagle

apālu(m) (a/u) G to appease, to pay for Gtn continually to appease, to care for, N to be security for

apāniš (Young-Bab.) through the window (cf. aptu) or apāniš, as an apû (a small animal)

aplu(m), heir, aplum rabûm, eldest son

appārum(m), swamp, reeds

appu(m), nose, face, appi martim "nose" of the gallbladder, front-part of upper side of the gallbladder

appūnāma, moreover, besides

apputum, urgent

aptu, window

apu, reed, cane

'arābu(m) (Old-Akk.) cf. erēbu(m)

arādu (Neo-Bab.) cf. warādu(m)

arahu(m) (a) G to hasten, Štn continually to compell (someone) to hurry

arāru(m) (u) G to tremble

'arāšu(m)[1] (a/u) (Old-Akk.) cf. erēšu(m)[1]

'arašu(m)[2] (i) (Old-Akk.) cf. erēšu(m)[2]

'arba'u(m) (Old-Akk.) cf. erbû(m)

arbūtu[1], waste, destruction; arbūtiš šūluku, to leave as a desert

arbūtu(m)[2], flight, arbūtam alākum, to take flight

ardu (Mid. and Neo-Bab.) cf. wardu(m)

[mi]arītu, pregnant woman

arku(m), long

arû (Young-Bab.) cf. warû(m)

aslu(m), sheep

aṣû (Mid-Bab.) cf. waṣû(m)

ašābu (Mid-Bab.) cf. wašābu(m)

ašar, prep., in place of, subordinating part. where, whither, wherever

ašarēdu(m), one of the highest rank

ašarēdūtum(m), the highest rank (subst.); ašarēdūtam alākum, to assume the highest rank

ašaršani, in another place, to another place

āšibu (Mid-Bab., Neo-Ass.) cf. wāšibu(m)

ašiu(m) (Old-Ass.) iron, iron found in a meteor

ašlu, rope, cord for measuring

ašqulālu(m), storm-cloud, whirlwind

ašru(m), place, position; ašar ištēn, in one place

ašša (Neo-Bab.) that, thereupon

aššatu(m) Ass. aššutu(m), wife

aššum, Old-Ass. aššumi, prep. by reason of; aššumīya, for my sake, subordinating part., because

atappulu(m) (Inf. Gtn from apālu) responsibility, concern

atāru(m), cf. watāru(m)

attā, you (sing.)

attamannu (Mid-Ass.) each

attī (fem. sing.) you

attu- (Mid-Bab.) Possessive pronoun, attū'a, my, attūšu, his

attunu, you (plural)

awātu(m) Mid. and Neo-Bab. amātu, Old Ass. awutum, Mid. Ass., amutu Neo-Ass. abutu (Const. st. abat) word, command, affair, thing bēl awātim, awatam batāqum, to conclude an affair, Old-Ass., plaintiff, legal opponent

awīlu(m), Mid-Bab. amīlu, Mid. Ass. a'īlu, Neo-Ass. amēlu, man, free citizen, Mid-Ass. man, anyone

awīlūtu(m), Young-Bab. amēlūtu, mankind

awutu(m) (Old-Ass.) cf. awātu(m)

B

babālu(m) (variation of wabālum) G to bring, carry, N to be brought

babbanû, splendid, outstanding

bābtu(m), trading material, commodity

bābu(m), gate, entrance; bāb ekallim, "Palace-door" = technical term in liver-description

bā'iru(m) (Part. of bârum) fisherman, angler

bakā'u (Ass.) cf. bakû(m)

bakû(m) (bkī), Ass. bakā'u(m), G weep

balāṭu(m)[1], life, Neo-Bab. balāṭ, napšāti, health

balāṭu(m)[2] (u), Ass. balāṭu(m) (a), G to be healthy, to live, D to keep alive

balṭu(m), living; preserved, unharmed

balu, without; ina balīki, without you (fem

banû(m)[1], Verb-Adj., pretty, good, noble, beautiful

banû(m)[2] (bnī), Old-Akk. banā'um G to build, make, create, bring forth; N to be formed

banû(m)[3] (bnī), G to be friendly; Neo-Bab. pānū ibannû, the face will shine (with pleasure)

bānû, maker, creator

baqāmu(m) (a/u), G to shear, cut, Š to have cut

baqāru(m) (a/u), to dispute, vindicate, justify

barbarratu, she-wolf

barbaru(m), wolf

barī- (Old. Ass.) cf. birī-

tûgbarru(m), Old-Akk., a covering for the head, head-gear

bārtu(m), mutiny rebellion

barû(m)[1], cf. berû(m)

barû(m)[2] (brī) G to see, to look at Št šutebrûm, to be apparent; to last

bâru(m) (b'r), G to catch (fish)

bārû(m), Verb-Adj., seeing, looking; Seer, overseer of a sacrifice, diviner of entrails

bašā'u (Ass.) cf. bašû(m)

bāštu(m), dignity, majesty

bašû(m) (bšī), Ass. bašā'u, G to be present, to exist, Š to bring into existence, N to come to being, to result, to be in existence

batāqu(m) (a/u), G to cut through, to cut off, to break through; Old-Ass. awatam batāqum, to carry out a commission; to conclude an affair, D to cut off; Dt to be broken through

bâtu(m) (bīt), Old-Ass., to dwell, to spend the night

ba''û, Neo-Ass., cf. bu''û

[bazā'u(m)], cf. buzzu'u(m)

bēltu(m), mistress, lady

bēlu(m), Master, owner, bēl immerim, owner of the sacrificial lamb, bēl lumnim, opponent, bēl tērētim, deputy, bēl awātim, plaintiff, opponent, Mid. and Neo-Ass. bēl pāḫete, deputy, Neo-Ass. bēl ṭābti, benefactor, friend

bêlu(m) (b'l), to rule, to be the master

bertu, fortress, castle, citadel

berû(m), barû(m) (br'), to be hungry

bēt, issu bēt, Neo-Ass., cf. ištu

bētu(m), Ass., cf. bītu(m)

biblu(m), wedding present

biltu(m), tribute, booty, tax

birī-, Old-Ass. barī-, between; ina birīni, between us; Old-Ass. ana barīšunu, among them

bīšu(m), possession, property; bīš qātīšu, the possession of his hand = what belongs to him

bitiqtu, deficit, harm, loss

bitrāmu(m), colored

bītu(m), Ass. bētu(m), Old-Ass. also ebētum, house, temple; Mid-Ass. ša bēt abe, the (property) of the paternal house; Neo-Ass. bet redûti, succession-house = palace of the crown prince; mar šarri rabiu ša bēt redûti (great king's son of the succession-house = the crown prince) mar šarrūti ša bēt redûti, the son of the kingdom of the succession-house = the crown prince.

bu'āru(m), health, salvation, deliverance, well-being

bubūtu, Pl. bubū'ātu, hunger, famine

būdu(m), shoulder, side

bukru, first-born

bullû(m), destroyed, decomposed, dissolved

bulluṭu, D inf. of balaṭum, to live, to bring to life, so bringing to life; life

bulṭu(m), life, lifetime

būlu(m), animal, cattle

buqūmu(m), fleece; shearing

burku, lap

būru[1], (a surface measure)

būru[2], a well

bussurtu(m), report, embassy

buštīṭu(m), termite, beetle

būšu(m), possession, property

butuqtu(m), breach in a dike, rupture of the perineum

bu''û, Neo-Ass. ba''û, D to seek, to strive for

buzzu'u(m) (bz'), D to mistreat, Dtn to mistreat continually

D

da''ānu(m) (Old-Ass.) cf. dayyanu(m)

dabābu[1], word, legal complaint

dabābu(m)[2] (u) G to speak, to discuss, to make a legal complaint Mid-Bab. ṭābūta dabābu to come to a good understanding; Neo-Ass. dēnu dabābu to make a complaint

dadmū, dwellings

dagālu (a/u), G to look; to wait for, to await

dayyānu(m), Old-Ass. da''ānum, a judge

dakāšu(m) (a/u), G to break out, to swell up; Gt to swell up on two sides

dâku(m) (dūk), G to kill, to beat; Š to have killed; N to be killed

dâlu(m) (dūl), G to run around

damāqu(m) (i), G to be good, favorable; D to do good

damiqtu (Fem. of damqu), good

dammuqu(m) (Ass.) cf. dummuqu(m)

damqu(m) (Fem. damiqtum, Neo-Ass. de'iqtu) well, good

dāmu(m), blood, Mid-Bab. dāma turru, to avenge blood

danānu(m) (i), G to be strong, solid; D dunnunu(m), Ass. dannunu(m) to make firm to unite firmly; Rt to match one's strength with somebody dannatu(m), necessity, difficulty; citadel

danniš, very, very much

dannu(m) (Fem. dannatum) strong, hard, difficult; fortified; valid; Mid-Ass. ṭuppu dannatu, binding document

dânu(m) (dīn), G to judge, dīnam dânum, to proclaim justice, to render a verdict

dāpinu, powerful

dappu(m), drop, lump, clot

dāriš, cf. dārû(m)

dārītu(m), length, duration; ana dāriātim, forever

dāriu (Ass.) cf. dārû(m)

dārû(m), Ass. dāriu(m), lasting, eternal, dāriš ūmmim, forever

dārûtu, longlasting life

dâṣu(m) (d'ṣ), G to oppress

[dašû], cf. duššû

dātu(m) (Old-Ass.), cf. di'atu(m)

de'iqtu (Neo-Ass.), cf. damqu(m)

dēnu (Ass.), cf. dīnu(m)

[dešû], cf. duššû

di'atu(m), Old-Ass. dātu(m), knowledge, skill, information di'atam (dātam) šâlum, to inquire about

dīdu, an article of clothing

dimtu (Pl. dimātu, Neo-Ass. di'ātu) tears

dinānu, representation (Mid-Bab.) ana dinān...alāku, to intercede for someone, to make a sacrifice for someone

dīnu(m), Ass. dēnu(m), opinion, decision; legal process dīnam šŭhuzum, to render a verdict

dipāru, torch

dišu(m), grass

ditallu, ashes; ditalliš, as ashes

dudittu, breastplate, jewelry for the breast

dullu, work, service; cult, ritual

dummuqu(m), Ass. dammuqu(m), well-made, of good quality

dunnunu (St.D of danānu) strongly fortified

dūru(m) (Pl. dūrānū) wall; fortified settlement

duššû(dš'), D to permit to flourish, grow

duššupu(m), sweet, sweet as honey

E

ebbu(m), pure, clean; dependable, well-chosen, bright

ebēbu(m) (i), G to be clean, D to make clean

ebertu, step

ebūru(m), harvest

edēdu(m), G (only in the Stative) to be pointed

edēlu(m) (i), G to close; N to be closed

ederu(m) (i), to embrace, to surround

lúediku(m), basket-maker

egû(m) ('gū), G to be tired, to become negligent

ekallu(m), palace; bāb ekallim, "Palace-gate" = technical term for part of liver

ekēmu(m) (i), G to take away, to take prisoner, (with Acc.) to take someone away, to spoil, to despoil

ekletu(m), grayness, darkness

el-, cf. eli

elā'u (Ass.) cf. elû

elēnu(m), upward; ana elēnum, upwards

eleppu(m) (Fem. Pl. eleppātum), Old-Akk. 'alappum, ship

elēṣu(m) (i), G to rejoice, D to cause to rejoice

eli, prep. on, over, elīšu, on him, elīša, on her, elšunu = elīšunu, on them

eliš, above, from above

ellu(m), pure, clean

elû(m)[1] (Fem. elītum), Old-Akk. 'alium (Fem. 'alītum) upper

elû(m)[2] ('lī), Ass. elā'u, G to climb up, emerge, Neo-Bab. la qāti šarri elû, to slip away from the king's hand, Š to let someone come up

ēma (Young-Bab.) everywhere, wherever

emāru (Neo-Ass.) cf. imēru(m)

emēdu(m) (i), G (with Acc.) to put, place; Mid-Ass. hiṭṭa emēdu to impose punishment on someone (Acc.) N to depend on one another, to unite

emu(m), father-in-law

emû (Young-Bab.) cf. ewû(m)

emūqu(m), power, strength, Old-Ass. ša emūqim (a quality of material)

enēqu(i), G to suck, Š to suckle, to nurse

eni (Old-Akk.) an interjection of unclear meaning

enma (Old-Akk.) thus (speaks) cf. umma

enna (Neo-Bab.) now

ennetu(m), sin

enū (Pl., Old-Akk.) objects, things

ēnu(m) (Ass. and Neo-Bab.) cf. inu(m)

epāšu(m) (Ass.) cf. epēšu(m)

epēqu(m) (i), G to grasp, to put one's arms around, D to grow over, to grow together

epēšu(m) (u), Ass. epāšu(m) (a/u), G to make, to do, to deal with someone; to work (a field) to raise plants; Old-Ass. ḫarrānam epāšum to undertake a business trip; Neo-Ass. dēnu epašu, to decide a matter of law; D Neo-Ass. bēlūtu eppušu to exercise rule, uppiš...ilqe (isseqe) he has bought (the subject comes after uppiš) epinnu(m), a plow

ēpišānu, the maker, the one who has made

epšetu, Neo-Ass. deed, matter, an action

eqlu(m) (Pl. eqlētu, Ass. eqlātu) field; rēš eqlim, goal

erābu(m) (Ass.) cf. erēbu(m)

erāšu(m) (a/u) (Ass.) cf. erēšu(m)[1]

erbe, cf. erbûm[1]

erbu(m), income

erbû(m)[1] (Fem. erbettum) Abs. st. erbe Fem. erbet (Old-Akk.) 'arba'um four; ana erbīsu, four times, four-fold; šar erbettim, according to the four directions

erbû(m)[2], grasshopper; (as collective) grasshoppers, locusts

erēbu(m) (u), Old-Akk. 'arābum, Ass. erābu(m) (a/u) G to go in, to enter, ana libbim erēbum, to fit in, Gt to enter, to penetrate, Gtn to visit frequently, Š to let someone enter, to penetrate, Štn to let someone go in again and again

erēnu(m), cedar

erēpu(m) (u), G to become cloudy

erēšu(m)[1] (i) Old-Akk. 'arāšum (a/u), Ass. erāšu(m) (a/u), G to prepare, to sow, Gtn to cultivate, to plow and harrow

erēšu(m)[2] (i), Old-Akk. 'arāšum (i), a wish, demand

ēribu(m), the one who enters

erištu(m), wish, demand; erištum-, symptom (term in liver analysis)

errēšu, peasant, plowman, farmer

erru(m), intestine; Pl. errū, viscera

erṣetu(m), land, territory, earth

esēḫu(m) (i), G to divide, to allot, apportion

esēru(m) (i), G and D to enclose, Dt to be closed in

eṣēdu(m)[1], harvest

eṣēdu(m)[2] (i), G to harvest

eṣēnu (i), to smell; to tolerate

ēṣu (Ass.), cf. īṣu(m)

ês, whither?

ešēru(m) (i), G to be straight, to be in order, to flourish; ana pani ešērum, to come to (someone) Š to bring into order, to straighten out, Št to bring justice to somebody

eššu(m), new; eššiš, Old-Akk. eššiś, renewed

etēqu(m) (i), to travel, to go farther, to cross over, to jut out

eṭāru(m) (Ass.), cf. eṭēru(m)

eṭēru(m), Ass. eṭāru(m) (i), to save, rescue, deliver

eṭlu(m) (Pl. eṭlūtu), youth, young man; warrior

ewû(m) ('wī) Young-Bab. emû, G to become; Š to cause to become

ezēbu(m) (i), to abandon, to leave "in the lurch"

ezzu, enraged, furious

G

gabbu (Mid-Bab., Mid-Ass.) totality, all

gamālu(m) (i), to treat in a friendly manner, to be indulgent to

gamāru(m) (a/u), G to bring to an end, to complete, D gummuru(m), Ass. gammuru(m), to make complete, to make full

gamru(m), Verb-Adj., brought to an end, completed, ūmū gamrūtum, the days have elapsed, are completed; Mid-Ass. ana šīm gamer, for the full price

gapšu(m), huge, powerful

garā'u (Ass.), cf. gerû

gašīšu(m), stake; ina gašīšim šakānum, to impale on stakes

gašru, strong

gegunû(m), chief temple, temple-tower

gerru(m), journey, business trip

gerû(grī), Ass. garā'u, G to quarrel, to carry on a trial; Mid-Ass. ṣalta garā'u, to quarrel

gīru, fire

gubabtu(m) (Old-Ass.) priestess

gišgupnu, tree-trunk

gušūru, beam, rafter

H

ḫabālu(m)[1], force, oppression, violent deed

ḫabālu(m)[2] (a/u), G to commit a misdeed, D to harm, Dt to be harmed, to suffer injury

ḫabālu(m)[3] (a/u), G to borrow, to be in debt, D to put someone in debt, N to be liable, to fall into debt

ḫabātu(m)[1] (a/u), G to rob, to plunder; Dt to be kidnapped

ḫabātu(m)[2] (a/u), G to wander, to pass through

ḫābilu(m), evil-doer, robber

ḫadû(m)[1], joy, happiness

ḫadû(m)[2] (ḫdū), G to rejoice, Gtn to keep on rejoicing

ḫalāpu (u), to glide through, to slip in

ḫalāqu(m) (i), G to be destroyed, to be lost; D to destroy, wreck

ḫalāṣu(m) (a/u), to squeeze out, to extort

ḫallu(m), thigh

ḫalqu(m) (Fem. ḫaliqtum) lost; ḫaliqtum, lost property

ḫamāṣu (a/u), G to break away, to tear off, D ḫummuṣṣu, to rob, to deprive of ḫamiš, cf. ḫamšu(m)

ḫammû(m), a rebel

ḫamšu(m) (Fem. ḫamuštum; Abs. st. ḫamiš, Fem. ḫamšat), five, adi ḫamšišu, five-fold

ḫamṭiš, Mid-Bab. ḫanṭiš, quickly, in haste

ḫanāmu(m) (i), G to bloom, blossom

ḫanniu (Neo-Ass.), cf. annû

ḫanṭiš (Mid-Bab.), cf. ḫamṭiš

ḫapātu(m) (i), G to be powerful

ḫarāru(m) (a/u), G to plow, to dig, to hollow out

ḫarbūtu(m) = arbutu[1], devastation; ḫarbūtam alākum, to be devastated, destroyed

ḫarmu(m) (Old-Ass), to be enclosed in a sheath, wrapping; ṭuppum ḫarmum, double tablet, document

ḫarrānu(m), way, journey, business trip; caravan, campaign; ālik ḫarrānim, traveller, one who goes on the campaign

ḫasā'u (Neo-Ass.) cf. ḫesû

ḫašāḫu(m) (i), to need, desire, demand

ḫašālu(m) (a/u), G to pound, break, Gtn to grind grain

ḫašû(m), lung

ḫātu(m), panic, terror

ḫâtu(m) (ḫīt), G to watch over, Gtn to keep on watching over

ḫaṭā'u (Neo-Ass.), cf. ḫaṭû

ḫaṭṭu, staff, official staff, scepter

ḫaṭû (ḫṭī), Ass. ḫaṭā'u, G to sin; to neglect, ḫīṭa ḫaṭû, to commit a sin

ḫāwiru(m), admirer, fancier

ḫepû(m) (ḫpi), G to break, to smash; N to be broken in half

ḫerû (ḫrī), G to dig

ḫesû (ḫs') Neo-Ass. ḫasā'u, G mistreat

ḫibiltu(m), harm, damage

ḫidûtu(m), a happy occasion, festival

ḫirišnānu(m) (Old-Ass.) a quality of material

ḫiṣbu(m), yield, produce, profit

ḫiṭu, ḫiṭṭu (Pl. ḫiṭṭānū), transgression, failure, sin; punishment

ḫubullu(m), debt, tax, tribute

ḫumuṣṣīru(m), rat

ḫurāṣu(m), gold

tûgḫurdabašše (Hurrian) loin-cloth

gišḫuṣābu, twig, branch

ḫušaḫḫu(m), hunger, famine

I

i, (Cohortative particle)

ibru(m), associate, friend

idi (prep.) to the side of, at the side of

idu(m), arm, side

idû(m) (*yd'*) Old-Akk. and Old-Ass. *ida'um* (*ydā*, *yd'*) G to know

igāru(m), city wall, wall of house

ikkaru, peasant, farmer

ikû, a unit of surface measure

ilittu(m), posterity

ilku(m), vassalage

iltēn (Mid-Bab. and Mid-Ass.), cf. *ištēnu(m)*

iltu(m), goddess, demon (f.)

ilu(m) (Pl. *ilānū* or *ilū*), god

ilūtu, divinity

imēru(m) Ass. *emāru(m)* donkey; the burden of a donkey; an omer (unit of grain measure); Neo-Ass. *emār zērī* (unit of surface measure)

imitta(m), right, toward the right

imittu(m), right, right side

immat (Neo-Ass.) Subjunctive particle, when

immeru(m), sheep, sheep of sacrifice

imnu, right side

in, Old-Akk. and Old-Ass., cf. *ina*

ina, Old-Akk. and sometimes Old-Ass. *in*, in, on; by means of; some of

inanna, now; *adi inanna*, until now

inbu(m), fruit; sweetness, graciousness

īne in *ana īne* (Mid-Ass.), cf. *mīnu(m)*

inṣabtu, ring, earring

īnu(m) Ass. *ēnu(m)*, Neo-Bab. *ēnu*, eye well

inūma, subordinating particle; when, if, whenever, as

ipšu, deed, (Evil-) deed; *ipiš pim*, speech, word, expression

irīmu(m), a piece of jewelry

irtu(m), breast

isqu (Pl. *isqētu*), without land, apportioning of land

issi (Neo-Ass.), cf. *išti*

issu (Neo-Ass.), cf. *ištu*

isu(m), jaw, jawbone

iṣṣēr (<*in*(*a*) *ṣēr*) (Old-Ass.), cf. *ṣēru(m)*[1]

iṣu(m) (Fem. *īštum*), Ass. *ēṣu*, few in number

išariš, in a proper manner, justly

išaru(m), normal, correct

išātu(m), fire

išdu(m), (dual išdān) foundation, root, base, lower part; išdān, basis, foundation, dependability

išertu(m), temple, chapel

išpikū (Pl.) yield, harvest

iššiakku(m) (Old-Akk.) prince, sovereign, noble

iššu(m), woman, wife

ištaru, goddess

ištēn, cf. ištēnu(m)

ištēniš, ištīniš, in common, together

ištēnu(m) (Fem. ištētum), Abs. st. ištēn, Mid. and Neo-Bab., Mid-Ass. iltēn, Fem. ištiat, one

išti (ištī-), Mid-Ass. ištu (with Suffixes iltē-), Neo-Ass. issi, Prep. with, Mid-Ass. ištu ahā'iš, with one another

ištīniš, cf. ištēniš

ištu[1], Old-Akk. ištum, Mid and Young-Bab. ultu, Neo-Ass. issu, Prep. from, out of, since, Neo-Ass. issu libbi, from; Neo-Ass. issu pān, from

ištu[2], Mid-Ass., prep., cf. išti

ištu[3], Old-Akk. ištum(ma), Mid-Bab. ultu, subordinating part., since, after; Neo-Ass. issu bēt, since

ištum(ma), cf. ištu[3]

išû(m) (yšū), G to have; laššu, there is not, eli...išûm, to have money, to have something deposited with someone

itinnu(m), master-builder, architect

itti, with, with the agreement of; ittīya, with me

ittu(m), sign; point of time, endpoint; ina ittī...by such and such a time

itu (Mid-Bab.) with, at the side of

itû(m) (Fem., Pl. itâtum), boundary; itât, around

itūlu(m), to lie down, rest

izbu(m), abortion, the product of an abortion

izuzzu(m), G to stand, to receive something, Mid-Ass. barīšunu izzaz (stands between them) stand at the their service, Neo-Bab. ina libbi...ušuz, has entered; eli...izuzzum, to triumph over, prevail; Gt to come to a standstill; Š to set up; to let someone move

Y

yamattu (Mid-Ass.) each one

yānu (Mid. and Neo-Bab.) is not at hand, there is not

yā'u(m) (Old-Ass.) cf. yû(m)

yā'ūtun, cf. yû(m)

yû(m), Old-Ass. yā'um; yā'ūtun (Pl.) my

K

kabātu(m) (i), G to be difficult, to be heavy

kabtu(m) (Fem. kabittum) difficult, important, of high rank

kayyānu(m), normal; constant, lasting

kakku(m) (cons. st. kakki or kak) weapon, attack, fight; "weapon" (liver-term) kakki imittim, "weapon of the right", liver-term

[kalāmu] cf. kullumu

kalbu(m), dog

kališ, totally

kalu(m), totality; kal pānika, totality of your front = all that lies before you

kalû(m) (klā), G to hold back, N to be held back

[kâlu(m)] cf. kullu(m)

kamāru(m), a type of fish

kamāsu(m) (i), to bind together

kamû(m) (kmū, Old-Akk. kmī), to bind, to take prisoner, to fortify

kanāku(m) (a/u), G to sign, to seal, to correspond through sealed documents, N to be sealed

kanānu (a/u), G to roll up, to wrap up, Štn to bow deeply again and again

kanāšu(m) (u), G to bow, yield, to submit, Š to make someone submit, to overcome

kanīku(m) (Fem. Pl. kanīkātum), sealed document

kânu(m) (kūn), G to be solid, firm, true; Neo-Ass. issi... kuānu, to be bound fast with; D to confirm, ratify to prove something to somebody, to stabilize

kapāru (a/u), G to wipe off, D to clean cultically, to free from sin

kapāṣu(m) (i), to bend, flex, to fold in (of liver parts)

karābu(m) (a/u), G to pray; to bless someone

karānu(m), wine

karāru (a/u), to put, to put down

karāšu(m) (Old-Akk.) karāśum, camp

karṣū (Pl.) calumny; karṣi akālum, to calumniate

karšu(m), stomach, belly

kāru(m), wharf, harbor, embankment; trade-center

karû(m) (krī), G to be short

kaskasu(m), breastbone

kaspu(m), silver, money

kasû(m) (i), G to bind, D to fasten together

kašādu(m) (a/u), G to arrive at, reach

kašāṭu (i), to cut off

katāmu(m) (a/u), G to cover, D to clothe; to conceal, Dtn to conceal repeatedly

ka''ulu(m) (Ass.), cf. kullu(m)

kēna (Old-Ass.) it is true, yes, indeed

kerru(m), campaign

kī[1], prep. Mid-Bab. and Neo-Ass. as; Neo-Ass. kī annîmma, correspondingly, likewise

kī[2], Subordinating particle, when, if, as soon as; Late-Bab. if, in case, perchance; Mid and Neo-Ass., that

kīam, so, thus

ki'ātu, Mid-Ass., cf. kinātu

kibru(m), Fem. Pl. kibrātum, shore, edge, kibrātum, districts of the world; kibrāt ebrêm, the four corners of the world

kibsu(m), track, step, walk, gait, path

kīdu(m), the outer side; ana kīdi(m), toward the outside, on the outside, ina kīdi(m), outside

kīma[1], prep. as, according to

kīma[2], subordinating particle, as soon as; as; that

kinātu, employee, colleage, Mid-Ass. ša ki'āte = ša kināte, the name of a month

kīnu(m), solid, true, dependable, regular

kirû (Pl. kirâtu), garden, orchard

kīsu, bag, pouch

kišādu(m), neck

kišpū (Pl.), magic, witchcraft

kiššatu(m), world

kittu, truth

kû(m), Old-Ass. ku'ā'um, your

ku'ā'u(m) (Old-Ass.), cf. kû(m)

kubšu(m), cap

kullu(m) (kūl), Ass. ka''ulu(m), D to hold, to keep ready, to have at one's disposal; Old-Ass. ana šapartim ka''ulum, to have a pledge; Old-Ass. sikki... ka''ulum to hold the arrest of someone = to hold someone under arrest

kullumu, Ass. kallumu, D to cause something to be seen, to show, to present, to point out

kūm, Neo-Ass. prep., instead of, dāmē kūm dāmē, blood for blood; ina kūm (with suffix ina kummu-) instead of, in place of

kumānu (Mid-Ass.) a surface measure

kunukku(m), a seal; a (sealed) tablet, document

kurrum, a "kor", a grain measure

kurummatu(m), food, provision; kurummatim, a field in private use

kussīu(m) (Ass.) cf. kussû(m)

kussû(m), Ass. kussīu(m), throne

kuṣṣu(m), winter, cold

kutimmu, goldsmith

kuzbu(m), fullness

L

la (Neo-Bab. and Neo-Ass.), to

lā, not, lā...lā, neither...nor

la'ābu (i), G to grow weak through sickness

labāru(m) (i), G to grow old, Dt to be made old, to decline

labāšu (a), G to clothe, to equip

lamādu(m) (a), G to learn, to experience, ina lā lamādīšu without his learning of it; D to teach

lamānu, cf. lemēnu

lamassu(m), a protective divinity

lamû (Young-Bab.), cf. lawû(m)

lapāni (Neo-Bab.) before, opposite

lapātu(m) (a/u), G to disturb, attack, devour, destroy; to besmear, D to stop, Š to plunder

laqā'u, (Neo-Ass.) cf. leqû(m)

laššu = lā išu, there is not

lawû(m) (lwī), Young-Bab. lamû, G to enclose, to surround, N to be enclosed

lemēnu (i), G to turn bad; to treat badly

lemnu(m) (Fem. lemuttum), bad, evil

lemnettu, cf. lemuttu(m)

lemuttu(m) (Pl. lemnētu, Neo-Ass. lemnettu, evil, ana lemnetti, with evil intention

leqû(m), Ass. laqā'u(m), G to take, to take for oneself, to fetch, to harvest (grain); Gtn to take again and again

lētu, cheek, side; Neo-Bab. lēta nadû, (to let the cheeks fall = [to gape]) to be undecided, to tarry

letû(m) (lt'), G to split, N to be split; ana šena neltûm, to be divided, to fall into two groups

le'û(m) (l'i), G to be able

lē'u (Pl. lē'ānu), wooden tablet

libbu(m), heart, middle part, ša libbim, that of the body, embryo; libbišunu, among them, from them; Neo-Bab. ana libbi, thither; Neo-Bab. ina libbi, thereby, for that reason: Prepositional expressions: ina libbi, in; Old-Ass. illibi (<in(a)libbi), in the possession of; Neo-Ass. ana libbi, against; issu libbi from, out of

libbū, (Neo-Bab.) corresponding, libbū agā'i, in such fashion

libittu(m), brick, baked tablet

lidiš; ina lidiš, the day after tomorrow

lillidu, growth, the upcoming generation, the young of the herd

limītu, neighborhood, vicinity

līmu, year designation

lipištu(m), matter, pus, discharge

liptu, "touching" (through illness)

līpu, twig, sprout; līp līpi, posterity, descendants

lipû(m), fat, fatty tissue

lišānu(m), tongue; ša lišānīya, "the one of my tongue", my secret agent

littūtu, long life

lītu(m), administrative area

li'u(m), see lû(m)

lū, precative particle, "yea" lū...lū (lū...ūlu) whether it be...or...; either...or

lû(m) (<li'um), animal, bull

lumnu(m), evil, wickedness

luparšim, may he survive

lu''u, D to soil

M

-ma[1], and, and then; -ma u, and moreover, but

-ma[2], emphatic particle

mā, Mid. and Neo-Ass., particle introducing direct speech: Thus as follows:

ma'da, (Neo-Bab.), very much

madādu (a/u), G to measure

mādu(m) (Fem. mattum) Ass. and Young-Bab. mā'du (Fem. ma'attu), many, numerous

mâdu(m) (mīd), G to be many, to become many

magāru (u), G to be in agreement, to yield, to grant; Gt to get together

magrītu (m) (Pl. magriatu), animosity

magru (Mid-Ass.) one who is in agreement, ready

magrūtu, agreement, lā magrūtu, lack of unity, disagreement

maḫar, before, by; maḫrīka, before you ana maḫrīka, into your presence; Young-Bab. maḫarka = maḫrīka

maḫāru(m) (a/u), G to turn to someone; to receive, accept; Neo-Bab. ana pānīka maḫer (is received before you) is agreeable to you; Št to set oneself equal to

maḫāṣu(m) (a), G to beat; N to be beaten, to be beaten with rods

maḫīru(m), market price, value

māḫiru(m), equal opponent

maḫriš (Old-Akk.) before

maḫru(m), see maḫar

maḫrû(m) (<maḫrīum), first, prior

mayyālu(m), bed

mākālu, food

makkūru(m), treasure, possession

mala, as much as; ammala (Old-Akk.) according to

malāḫu(m), sailor

malālu(m)[1] (a), G to rob, plunder

malālu(m)[2] (i), cf. melēlu(m)

māliku(m), counsellor, adviser

malqētu, tax, levy

malû(m) (mlā), G to be full, to become full, Neo-Bab. ana ṣirê malû, to be full to the brim, to have enough, D to fill

māmītu, oath, sworn agreement

mamman, Neo-Bab.and Mid-Ass. mamma, somebody, someone; (with the negative:) no one

-man, enclitic particle, enclitic, like the English 'ever' as in whoever, somebody or other

manā'u(m) (Ass.) manû(m)[1]

mannu(m) which? who? Neo-Ass. mannu ša, whosoever

manû(m)[1], Ass. manā'u(m), a mine

manû(m)[2] (mnū), G to number, to count; Young-Bab. qaqqariš manû, to make like the earth = to flatten

manzāzu (Neo-Bab.) cf. mazzizu

maqātu(m) (u), G to fall; lunge; Gtn to fall again and again, Š to fell, to bring to a fall

maqlû (Pl. Ass. maqluāte), burnt offering

marāṣu(m) (a), G to fall sick, to be sick

mar'atu(m) (Old-Akk.) cf. mārtu(m)

marḫītu(m), concubine, wife

marṣātu(m), cf. marṣu(m), Verbal-Adj. sick; marṣātum (Fem. Pl.) trouble, problems, hardships

martu[1] (Neo-Ass), cf. mārtu

martu(m)[2] (Pl. marrātum) gall, gallbladder; reš martim, tip of the gall-bladder

mārtu(m) (Old-Akk. mar'atu(m), Old-Ass. mer'atu(m), Neo-Ass. martu, daughter

maru, mar'u (Mid. and Neo-Ass.), cf. māru(m)

māru(m) Old-Akk., mar'um; Old-Ass. mer'um; Mid. and Neo-Ass. mar'u, maru, son; mār(i) šiprim, messenger, emissary

maruštu(m), evil

maṣā'u(m) (Ass.) cf. maṣû(m)

masraḫu(m), beginning; masraḫ marti(m) bile-duct

maṣṣartu, watch

maṣû(m), Ass. maṣā'u(m), G to become as; Old-Ass. ana...maṣā'um, to intervene on behalf of

mašā'u, Neo-Ass., cf. mašû

maškanu(m), place

kušmašliu(m) (Pl. mašliātum, Old-Akk.) skin of an animal

mašmaššu, priest in charge of oaths and exorcisms

mašraḫu(m), splendor

mašû(m) (ms') Neo-Ass. mašā'u(a/u), G take away, hide

matēma (Neo-Ass.), cf. matīma

matīma, sometime; Neo-Ass., ina matēma, sometime

mātu(m) (Fem.; Pl. mātātum) land; mātum kalūša, the whole land

mâtu(m) (mūt), G to die

mā'ū (Mid.-Ass.), cf. mû

mazzaltu (Mid-Ass.) position, site

mazzāzu(m), site, place, position

mazzizu, Neo-Bab. manzāzu (part. from izuzzu) standing, Mid-Ass. mazziz pānī, courtier, official; Neo-Bab. manzaz pānī, courtier, official

-me (Old-Akk.) enclitic particle introducing direct speech

meḫru(m)[1], like, corresponding; an equal

meḫru(m)[2], an answer (to a letter)

melēlu(m) (i), G dance, jump

mēleṣu(m), joy, exultation

memēni (Neo-Ass.) somebody, something

mer'atu(m) (Old-Ass.), cf. mārtu(m)

mērešu(m), planting, cultivation

mer'u(m) (Old-Ass.) cf. māru(m)

mesû(m) (msī), G to wash

mētaqtu, continuation of the march

migru(m), favorite

milku(m), plan, counsel

millatu(m), pillage

mīlu(m), abundance; flood-tide; mīli irtim, courage, success

mimma, something; everything; mimma šumšu (everything which its name is =) each and every. (With the negative) nothing; Mid-Ass. mimma ammar, everything which

mimmāmu(m), each and every

mīnâ(mma) (Mid. and Neo-Bab.) why?

mīnu(m) what?; ana mīnim, Mid-Ass. ana īne, why?

mīnû (Mid-Bab.) what? which?

miqittu(m), fall, defeat

miqû(m), charm, attractiveness

^{is}mismakkannû, a tree

miṣru, territory, boundary

miššum (Old-Ass.) why?

mitgurtu(m), agreement

mitḫāriš, in equal parts

mû (Pl. Gen-Accus., mê), Ass. mā'ū, water; fluid; Neo-Bab. mû ēni, spring-water

mubi (Old-Akk.) exactly (?)

mudeššû, participle of duššû, causing to thrive

muḫḫelṣītu(m) (Fem. part. of neḫelṣûm) a slippery place

muḫḫu(m), upperside, skull; Mid-Bab. ana muḫḫi annīti, beyond that, still more; prepositional expressions: ana muḫḫi, for the purpose of, ina muḫḫi, because of, ina muḫḫīšu, for the reason (that)

mukillu(m) (Participle of kullum) limping, mukīl rēš lemuttim, he who protects evil (name of a demon)

multu (<muštu) (Young-Bab.) a comb

murīššu(m) (D participle of râšu) who causes jubilation, triumph

murṣu(m) sickness

mušallimu (D participle of šalāmu) causing health

mūšītu(m), night

muškēnu (Participle of šukênu) (description of a group of men that lived in a special dependence on the king); Neo-Ass., poor

muššuru (Mid. and Neo-Bab.) cf. wašāru(m)

muštu, comb

mūšu(m), night; urrī u mūšī, day and night

mutti*š*, before

mutu, husband; Mid-Ass. *ša mute*, the property of the husband

mūtu(m), death, a death

N

na'ādu(m) (i), G to pay attention, to heed, to bring to someone's attention, D to inform, Š to report

na'āru(m) (Old-Akk.), cf. nêru(m)

nabalkutu(m) (blkt), N to turn around; to revolt, to fall away, secede

nābutu(m) (i), N to flee, to run away

nadānu(m) (Pres. Old-Akk., inaddan, Old-Bab., inaddin, Neo-Bab., inamdin, Ass., iddan, Pret., iddin), G to give; distribute. ana kaspim nadānum, to sell; Mid-Ass., bitqāte nadānu, to make up a deficit; Mid-Ass., ana šime nadānu, to sell, give for a price; Gtn to give again and again; N to be given

nadītu(m), a kind of priestess (who must remain childless)

nadû(m) (ndī), G to cast (down) to lay (down); (Stat.) to lie; to pile up (grain); Neo-Bab. lēta nadû, to be irresolute, to delay; Š to have cast down; to neglect; ša libbim šuddûm, to cause an abortion; N to be cast down, to be accumulated; Ntn (Stat.) to be strewn with, to be dotted with

nâdu(m) (n'd), to praise; Dt to be praised

nagāšu(m) (i), Gtn to wander about continually

naggāru, carpenter, cabinet maker

naglabu, (Dual) naglabā, softness, nakedness

nagû, province

nahāsu(m) (i), G to yeild, fall back

nahrāru(m), help

nakaru(m), strange; an enemy

nakāru(m) (i), G to be strange, hostile, Gt to become an enemy; D nukkuru, Ass. nakkuru, to change, to put aside, Š Neo-Ass. issīsu šakkuru, to make someone an enemy of another

nakāsu(m) (i), to cut off, lop off

nakkamtu, store, treasure

nakru(m) (Stat. cons. nakir, Fem. nakartum, cf. nakarum) enemy; hostile

nâku (nīk), to sleep; to sleep with

namāšu (u), to get in motion, to set out

namkaru(m), irrigation ditch

namrā'u(m), fattened cattle

namriš, brilliantly, splendidly

namtarru (Fem. Pl., namtarrātu) destiny

namurru, fearful, awesome, brilliant

nāmurtu, a gift

nanmurtu(m), a meeting

nantallû(m), darkness

nanzāzu (Young-Bab.) position; courtier

napāḫu(m) (a/u), G to ignite, N to be ignited, Ntn to be ignited again and again

napālu (a/u), G to destroy

naparkû(m) (prkū), N to cease

naparqudu(m) (prqd), N to lie on one's back

napḫazu(m), totality; napḫar, together, all told

napištu(m) (Const. Stat., napišti or napšat) life, soul, person; Neo-Bab. balāṭ napšāti, health

naplastu(m) (left) lobe (of the liver)

naplāsu(m), glance; naplāsušša, at her glance = where she looks

naplusu(m), to look at, Ntn to look at again and again, to keep under surveillance

nappāḫu, a smith

naptanu, a meal

naqāru(m) (a/u), G tear down, destroy, N to be destroyed

naqû(m) (nqī), G sacrifice, Gtn to sacrifice again and again

narāmtu(m), beloved, favorite wife

narāmu(m), beloved (masc.)

na'ratu, singer (fem.)

narkabtu, war-chariot

nāru(m)[1], river, ordeal by water

nāru(m)[2], singer (masc.)

nasāḫu(m) (a/u), G to tear loose, tear away, dissolve; Old-Akk. išdī nasāḫum, to tear up by the roots; Š (Old-Ass.) to have transferred, N to be torn loose

naṣ (Fem. naṣṣat), he (she) brings along

naṣāru(m) (a/u), G to protect, guard; maṣṣarta naṣāru, to keep watch

našāqu (i), G to kiss, D to kiss

našā'u (Neo-Ass.), cf. našû(m)

našpaku(m) (Fem. Pl., našpakātum) a vat

na'šu(m) (Old-Akk.), cf. nêšu(m)[1]

našû(m) (nšī), Ass. nasa'u, G to lift up, carry; give attention to; Neo-Ass. šarrūtu našā'u, to seize hold of the kingship

naṭālu(m) (a/u), G to look at, gaze at, see; Gt to look at one another; to look away

naṭû(m) (ntū), G (only in Stat.) to be suited, fitted

nawāru(m) (i), to illumine, radiate

nawû(m), camp

nazāru(m) (a/u), G to deplore, curse, execrate

nazzāzu(m), position

neḫelṣû(m) (ḫlṣī), N to slide

nekurtu(m), enmity

nēmel (Neo-Ass.) because

nēmelu(m), profit, advantage

nepelkû(m) (plkī), N to be broad

nepû(m) (npī), G to take something as a pledge, to take someone into servitude as a result of debt

neqelpû(m) (qlpū), N to push downstream (intrans.); Š to lead downstream

nêru(m) (n'r) (Old-Akk.) na'ārum (a), G to kill, to destroy, to bring down

nēšu(m), lion

nêšu(m)[1], (Old-Akk.) na'šum, life

nêšu(m)[2] (n'š), G to be alive, D to bring to life

ni'ā'u(m) (Ass.), cf. nûm

nibu, the act of naming; ša lā nībī, countless

nidittu, gift, yield, output, tribute

nikkassu(m) (Old-Ass.) bill, account; (Neo-Ass.) account, a claim

nikpu(m), push, thrust

nīnu, we

niqû(m), sacrifice

nīru(m), yoke; also "yoke" as a liver-term

nišku(m), a bite

nišū (Fem. Pl.; Neo-Ass. Masc. Pl.) Old-Akk. nišū, people

nīšu[1], lifting up (of the hands)

nīšu[2], oath

nû(m) (Old-Ass.) ni'ā'um, our

nudunnû(m) (Mid-Ass.) nudunnā'u, dowry

nuḫšu(m), superfluity, abundance

nukaribbu(m), gardener

nukurtu, enmity

nūnu(m), fish

nūru(m), light

P

padānu(m), path; "path" as term of liver-description

pâgu (pūg), G to rob, plunder, take away

paḫāru(m) (u), G to gather (intrans.); D to assemble (trans.)

paḫû, cf. peḫû

pāḫutu (Mid. and Neo-Ass.) mandate, duty, obligation; bēl pāḫete, agent, official

palāḫu(m) (a), G to be afraid; to respect, Neo-Ass. to show respect; Gtn to fear repeatedly

[palāsum], cf. naplusum

palāšu(m) (a/u), G to penetrate, perforate

palû(m), Ass. palā'u, time of a given reign, a year of the reign

pān, cf. pānu

pānātu, front; Neo-Bab. ina pānāt, because of

pānī (Neo-Ass.), cf. pānu(m)

pānu(m) (Pl. pānū, Neo-Ass. pānī) front part of; pānū, face, countenance; front; pānū ana...šakānum, to make up one's mind to do something; Mid-Ass. mazziz pānī, courtier. Prep. expressions: Mid-Ass. ana pān, before, at; ana pānīka, before you; Neo-Bab. Mid and Neo-Ass. ina pān before, at, in view of. Neo-Ass. issu pān, from, out of

pānû, Ass. pānīu, earlier, prior

paqādu(m) (i), G to entrust; to supervise; Neo-Ass. to put in charge, D to appoint, to put in charge

paqāru(m) (a/u), G to dispute, to claim

parakku, throne, lofty seat

parāsu (a/u), G to cut, separate; to test; to decide, N to cease, to be held in abeyance

paršumu (Neo-Ass.) old, luparšim, may he live

pašāqu(m) (a/u), to be or become narrow, to be or become difficult

pašāru (a/u), G to sell, D to redeem, ransom, release

pašāšu(m) (a/u), G to spread over, smear with, cover

patālu(m), G (only in Stat.) to come together, to wind around

patā'u (Ass.), cf. petû(m)

paṭāru(m) (a/u), G to separate, to split; to dissolve; D to split, to release

pāṭu(m), border, borderland

pazzurtu, secret, secret mission

peḫû (pḫī), G to close, D to close, lock; Dt to be shut up

pertu, scalp, hair of the head

per'u, posterity, descendents, abundance of children

petû(m) (pt') Ass. patā'u(m), G to open; Gtn to open again and again; D to open, to lay bare; N to be opened

pilakku, spindle, shaft

pillurtu(m), cross

pilšu(m), hole, breach

pīqat, perhaps

pirištu(m), a secret

pitḫu, hole, opening

pitiltu(m), string, cord, a tangle

piṭru(m), chink, cleft

pû(m), mouth; ana pī ṭuppim, according to the wording of the tablet; Neo-Bab. ša lā pīya, against my order

puḫru(m), assembly

pūḫu(m), substitute, exchange

puluȟtu, fear, respect

purkullu, stone-cutter

pušqu(m), narrowing, narrow place

pūtu(m), front, forehead; edge

ú pū'u, chaff, fodder

Q

qa, a unit of volume-measure

qabaltu(m), middle

qabā'u (Ass.), cf. qabû(m)

qablu(m) (dual, qablān)

qablān, middle part, waist, hips

qablûm (<*qablīum) (adj.) middle

qabû(m) (qbī), Ass.: qabā'u, G to say, speak; command

qâdu (qūd), G to ignite

qalû (qlū) (Ass.) qalā'u, G to burn

qam'u(m) (Old-Akk.), cf. qēmu(m)

qamû (qmū), G to burn

qannu, clothing

qâpu(m)[1] (qīp), G to trust; to entrust

qâpu(m)[2] (qūp), G to become dilapidated

qaqqadu(m), head; total capital

qaqqaru(m), Ass. qaqquru(m), earth, ground, piece of land; Neo-Ass. earth, soil; Young-Bab. qaqqariš, like the earth, qaqqar āle, settled area

qarābu (Mid.-Ass.), cf. qerēbu(m)

qarānu (u), G to pile up, accumulate

qararu(m) (u), G to roll up, N to be crooked, Ntn to meander

qarrādu(m), hero

qaštu(m), a bow

qâšu(m) (qīš), to bestow, to give

qatānu(m) (i), G to be thin, narrow

qātu(m) (Fem.; dual qātān, pl. qātātu Neo-Ass. qātāte) hand; qātātu guarantee, ša qātātim, warrantee, guarantee; Mid-Ass. ana qāt 5 mana anneke utturu (wtr), to cause someone to hand over payment of 5 minas

qatû(m) (qtī), G to be at an end; Dt to be brought to an end

qa''û(m) (Ass.) cf. qu''û(m)

qebēru(m) (i), to bury

qēmu(m) Old-Akk. qam'um, meal, flour

qēpu (Pl. qēpūtu) (Mid-Ass.), the one commissioned, delegated

qerâtu, cf. qerītu

qerēbu(m), Ass. qarābu(m) (i), G to be near; to get near, to come close; Mid-Ass. ana... qarābu, to get near to a thing, to touch something; D to bring something near, to bring up something, Dtn to bring up something again and again

qerītu (Pl. qerâtu), storage container; banquet

qibītu, command, order

qinnatu(m), hindquarters, anus, buttocks

qištu, grove, a wood

qīštu(m), present, gift

qitrubiš, in a scuffle, in hand-to-hand combat

qû(m), thread, cord

qūlu(m), lamentation, agonized silence

qurunnu, heap, pile

qutrinnu (Young-Bab.) smoke

qu''û(m) Ass. qa''û(m), D to await, wait for

quzippu, clothing

R

ra'āšu(m) (Old-Akk.) D ru''ušum, to cast down, beat down, put down

rabā'u(m) (Ass.), cf. rabû(m)[2]

rabiānu(m), chief official of a city

rabiu(m) (Ass.), cf. rabû(m)[1]

rabû(m)[1] (Fem. rabītum) Ass. rabiu(m) great, the Great One; Mid-Ass. rabi ekalle, the palace-inspector; rabi urtānē, master of the treasury, (?) rabi zammārē, music-master

rabû(m)[2] (rbī), Ass. rabā'u(m), G to be great; D to make great, to rear, bring up; Š to make great

rabûtu(m), greatness, worth; kīma rabûtīka, according to your greatness; graciously

radā'u(m) (Ass.), cf. redû(m)[1]

rādu(m), thunderstorm

ragāmu (u), G address, speak, call to

rahāsu(m) (i), G to knock down, lay low, destroy

rā'imu(m), the beloved

rakābu(m)(a), G to ride; Gt to ride toward one another

rakāsu(m) (a/u), G to bind, to anchor (ships); D to bind up, connect

rakbû(m), message, messenger

rākibu(m), the one who rides; rākib imēri, donkey-rider

ramāku(m) (u), G to wash oneself, bathe

ramānu(m), Ass. ramunu(m), self, ina kasap ramānīšu, at (his, her, its) own cost, Old-Akk. in ramānika, in your person, you yourself; Mid-Ass. ana raminīšu, for himself

râmu (r'm), G to love

ramû(m) (rmī), G to camp, settle; dwell

rapāšu(m) (i), G to be broad, wide; D to spread out

rapšu(m) (Fem. rapaštum) wide, spacious, extended

raqāqu(m) (i), G to be thin

râqu(m) (rīq), G to be empty; (Late-Bab.) to have time

rašāšu(m), an official

rašbu(m) (Fem. rašubtum), commanding respect

ra'šu(m) (Old-Akk.), cf. rēšu(m)

rašû(m) (ršī), G to have; to acquire, Š to cause someone to have; pānam šuršûm, to cause the front to be taken = to establish

râšu (rīš), G to exult, jubilate; D to cause jubilation

rebû(m) (Fem. rebūtum), fourth

redû(m) (rd') (Ass.) radā'u(m), G to lead; to follow; to overtake, to accompany

rēdû(m), soldier

redûtu, succession, following

rēmēnû, merciful

rēmūtu, donation, gracious gift

rēqu(m), distant: ūman rēqam, on a distant day, in the future

rêqu(m) (r'q), G to be distant

rēqūtu(m), distance; rēqūssa, in the future

rēšu(m) Old-Akk. ra'šum, head, point, rēš eqlim, goal; rēšam kullum, to hold up the head, to protect, support; Neo-Ass. ina rēšuššu (loc.-adverb) at its head, Neo-Ass. šarēši, eunuch, official

re'û(m) (r'i), G to pasture

rē'û(m), shepherd

rigmu(m), cry of woe, lament

rikiltu (Mid-Ass.), cf. rikistu

rikistu Mid-Ass. rikiltu, an agreement

riksu, assemblage, union, league

rišātu(m) (Pl.) jubilation

ru'āmu(m), charm, attractiveness

rubû(m) (<rubā'um), prince

rubûtu(m), rule, dominion

ruḫû, saliva; sorcery, casting of a hex

S

sābītu(m) (Fem.) wine-drawer

sagû, temple, shrine

saḫāru(m) (u) Mid-Ass. šaḫāru, G to turn to, to care about, to seek

salīmu(m), offer of peace, treaty of peace, peaceful conclusion

sammu, harp (?)

sāmtu, carnelian (gem, stone)

sâmu(m) (sīm), G to be reddish brown

sanāqu(m) (i), G to be narrow; to test; to arrive, happen; D to control, to investigate, to limit, hem in

sapāḫu(m) (a/u), G to destroy, to lay-waste; D to destroy; N to be destroyed, to be broken up sarāru(m)[1], G (Stat. only) to be false

sarāru[2]] cf. surruru

sarruru (Ass.), cf. surruru

sâru(m) (sūr), dance, romp, be wild

sebe, cf. sebû(m)

sebû(m) (Fem. sebettum; Abs. state, sebe, Fem. sebet) seven

seḫru, environs, neighborhood

sikku(m), custody, arrest, confinement

simānu(m), propitious time, right time; ^{itu}Simānum Siman, name of the third month

simēru, ring, circle

simtu(m), form, members, ornamentation

sinniltu (Mid-Ass.), cf. sinništu(m)

sinnissu (Neo-Ass.), cf. sinništu(m)

sinništu(m) Mid-Ass. sīnniltu, Neo-Ass. sinnissu, woman, wife; Mid-Ass. ša sinnilte, the (property) of the wife, Mid-Ass. sinniltu ša ekalle, sinnilti ekalle, woman of the palace

sippu(m), door-frame

siqru(m), order, command

sisû, horse

sittu(m), remnant, remains

suluppu(m), date

sūmu(m), red spot, black and blue mark

sunqu(m), need, famine

sūnu(m), lap

surruru (Ass.) sarruru, D to pray

^{giš}sussulu(m), basket

Ṣ

ṣabātu(m)(a), G to take, seize, grasp, to overtake, pānī... ṣabātum (to take the front) to put oneself at the head of; šēpi ṣabātu(m), to grasp the feet, to submit oneself; Old-Ass. to summon someone, to take someone to court; Gt to pounce on one another; to grow together; D to compell someone to grasp, Š to cause someone to grasp. Mid-Ass. ḫarrāna šaṣbutu, to have someone undertake a journey; Neo-Ass. to prepare. Neo-Ass. kussiu šaṣbutu, to have someone mount the throne. Št to have one another grasp. itti...šutaṣbutum to ally one person to another. N to be taken, to be included

ṣābitu(m), restraining

ṣabtu(m), taken; the prisoner

ṣābu(m), group of people, workers, soldiers

[ṣabû(m)] cf. ṣubbû(m)

ṣaḫāru (Ass.), cf. ṣeḫēru

ṣalāmu(m) (i), G to be black, dark

ṣaltu, a quarrel; Mid-Ass. ṣalta garā'u, to quarrel, to wrangle, brawl

ṣamādu(m) (i), to harness

[ṣamāru] cf. ṣummuru(m)

ṣarāmu(m) (i), G to strive, to make an effort

ṣarāpu(m)[1] (a/u), to color red

ṣarāpu[2] (i) (Neo-Ass.) G to buy

ṣeḫēru(m) Ass. ṣaḫāru(m) (i), G to be small, to be a minor

ṣeḫḫerūtu (Pl.) little ones, servants

ṣeḫru(m), small; a child

ṣellu(m), cf. ṣēlu(m)

ṣēlu(m), ṣellu(m), rib, side

ṣēnū, "small-cattle", sheep and goats

ṣênu(m) (ṣ'n), to load, ship

ṣērāniš, cf. ṣēru(m)[2]

ṣērtu, cf. ṣīru

ṣēru(m)[1], back; backwoods, steppe; ša ṣērim (the one of the steppe=) steppe-dweller; ana ṣērīya, before me; Old-Ass. iṣṣēr (<in(a) ṣēr) on account of... Mid-Ass. ana ṣēr, with regard to

ṣēru(m)[2], a snake; ṣērāniš, as a snake

ṣibittu(m), prison

ṣibtu(m) (Pl. ṣibātum), increase, tax, "growth" = liver-term

ṣibûtu(m) (Pl. ṣibiātum) business, undertaking

ṣidītu, provisions, food for a journey

ṣīḫtu(m), laughter, joy

ṣillû(m), needle, pin

ṣimdatu(m), royal command, decree; decision

ṣirû, edge, brim, Neo-Bab. ana ṣirê malû, to be filled to the brim, to have enough, more than enough

ṣīru (Fem. ṣērtu) elevated, exalted

ṣītu(m), ascent, departure, exit, discharge; ana ṣītim šūṣûm to go out, leave

ṣubātu(m) (sing. and pl.) clothing

ṣubbû(m), to regard, look at

ṣuḫārtu(m), girl, maid-servant

ṣuḫāru(m), boy, lad, male slave

ṣulūlu, protection, shield

ṣummirātu(m), ṣummurātu(m) (Pl. Fem.) striving, yearning for, wish

ṣummû (Neo-Bab.) thirst; ina ṣummê from thirst, by reason of thirst ṣummirātu(m), ṣummurātu(m) (Pl. fem.) striving, yearning for, wish

ṣummû (Neo-Bab.) thirst; ina ṣummê from thirst, by reason of thirst

ṣummurātu(m) cf. ṣummirātu(m)

ṣummuru(m), D to strive for, to aspire to

ṣūmu(m), thirst

ṣupru, fingernail

Š

ša[1] (Old-Akk.) Nom. šu, Fem. šat; Pl. šūt, Fem. šāt; Gen. ši, Accus. ša, the one of, which

ša[2] (Old-Akk. and Old-Ass.) whoever, whatever

ša'ālu(m) (Ass.) cf. šâlu(m)

ša'āru(m) (a) (Old-Akk.) to do battle, to be victorious

šabā'u(m) (Ass.) cf. šebû(m)

šabāsu(m) G (Stat. only, šabus) to be angry

šabāšu (u), G to collect rent

šābulu(m), to be dried up, shrivelled

šabû(m) (Ass.) cf. šebû(m)

šadādu (a/u), G to draw, tug; delay

šadû(m) (Old-Akk.) śadu'um, mountain

śadu'u(m) (Old-Akk.) cf. šadû(m)

šagātu, belt, girdle, binding

šahāṭu(m) (i), G to leap, to attack

šahăru (Mid-Ass.) cf. sahăru

šahluqtu(m), destruction

šā'imu(m) (Partic. of šâmu[1]) purchaser

šakānu(m) (a/u), Old-Akk. śakānu(m), G to place, set; to celebrate (a feast) or to work (a field); Old-Akk. tăhāzam śakānum to have a slaughter take place; ṭēma šakānu, to impart a command; pānī ana ... šakānum, to resolve oneself to do something; ina gašīšim šakānum, impale; Neo-Ass. issi...šakānu, to do a common enterprise with someone; Gtn to set again and again; Š to have put, N to be put, placed, set, made

šaknu, representative, official, agent

[lû]šākû, steward, administrator

šalālu(m) (a/u), G to plunder, rob, "count as booty"

šalamtu(m), corpse, cadaver

šalāmu(m) (i), G to be well off, to thrive, flourish; D keep in good health, to save from harm; to offer a substitute, to make restitution

šalaš, cf. šalšu(m)

[śalāšu(m)] cf. šullušu(m)

šalbabu, powerful, mighty

šallatu(m), booty

šalmu(m), intact, complete

šalšu(m) (Fem. šalaštum; Abs. state šalaš, šalāšat) three; ana šalāšisu, threefold, three times

šâlu(m) (a), Mid-Bab. and Ass. šā'alu(m), G to ask, inquire; (with the accus.) to inquire about, after; di'atam (dātam) šâlum, to inquire about; Gtn to ask again and again

šamā'u(m) (Ass.) cf. šemû(m)

šamāḫu (u), G to flourish, to sprout

šamāru (a), G to respect; Gt to respect permanently, perpetually

šamaššammu, sesame

šamê (Neo-Ass.) cf. šamû[2]

šamnu(m), oil

šamru, stormy, wild

šamû(m)[1], rain

šamû[2] (Pl. of šamûm), Neo-Ass. šamê (<šamā'ī) sky, heaven

šâmu(m)[1] (š'm), G to buy

šâmu[2] (šīm), G to decide

šanānu(m), G to quarrel, Gt to quarrel with one another

šanātu(m) cf. šattu(m)

šanā'û(m), another, the other; an opponent

šandabakku, chief official of Nippur

šangû, a priest

šaniu, cf. šanû(m)[1]

šanû(m)[1] (Fem. šanītum), Ass. šanī'u(m), another, the other, the second; šanûm šumšu, a second meaning (of an omen)

šanû(m)[2] (šnī), Old-Akk. śanā'um, G to be otherwise, to be second; Old-Akk. to do something for the second time. Gt to do something permanently, to change something permanently; Gtn to be changed repeatedly; D to do something for the second time, to repeat; Št to double

šapālu(m), G to be below, under, D to go down

šapartu(m), pledge, security

šapāru(m) (a/u), G to write, to send

šaplānu(m) below; ana šaplānum, downwards

šapliš, below

šaplû(m) (Fem. šaplītum), Old-Akk. śaplum, (Fem. śapiltum) lower

šaptu(m) (Du. šaptān) lip

šaqālu(m) (a/u), G to weigh, Š to have (someone) weighout, N to be weighed out, to be scarce, suspended

šaqā'u (Mid-Ass.) cf. šaqû[1]

šaqû[1] (šqī), Ass. šaqā'u, to water, to irrigate

šaqû(m)[2] (šqū), G to be high, to become high, to become important; D to move up, to bring upwards šarāku(m) (a/u), G to bestow a present, to give

šarāqu(m) (i), G to steal, to rob; Gtn to steal again and again

šarēši (Neo-Ass.) (that of the chief=) castrated court official, eunuch (Assyrian palace-official) cp. šaziqni

šarēššarru (Pl. šarēššarrānū; Mid-Ass.) eunuch

šarhu(m), magnificent, splendid

šarru(m) (Pl. šarrū or šarrānū) king

šarruttu (Mid-Ass.) cf. šarrūtu

šarrūtu(m), Mid-Ass. šarrattu, kingship

šāru(m) wind, direction; šār erbettim, according to the four directions

šat (Fem.) determinative pronoun, cf. ša[1]

šāt (Fem. Pl.) determinative pronoun cf. ša[1]

šatāqu(m), G (stat. only) to crush, squeeze (?)

šattammu(m), administrator

šattu(m) (Pl. šanātu, Neo-Ass. šanāti) year; šattam, in this year

šatû (štī), G to drink

šaṭāru (a/u), G to write

šaziqni (Neo-Ass.) that of the beard (ziqnu) = courtier, Assyrian palace official; cp. šarēši

šēbu (Ass.) cf. šību(m)

šebû(m) (šb'), Ass. šabā'u(m), G to be full, satisfied, (with the accus.) to be satisfied with; D to satisfy, to bring to satisfaction; Dt to be satisfied, filled, to become satisfied, to satisfy oneself

šēbultu(m), shipment, goods that are shipped

šēdu(m), a protective deity

šegû(m) (šg'), G to be mad, insane

šemû(m) (šm'), Ass. šamā'u, G to hear, (of a tablet) to have read out, Gtn to hear repeatedly; to eavesdrop

šena, two (Fem. šitta); ana šenīšu, twice, two-fold

šēnu(m), shoe

šēpu(m) (Fem.; dual šepān) foot, and "foot" (liver term); Neo-Bab. šēpi ṣabātu, to seize the feet, to submit oneself

šērtu, ina šērte (Neo-Ass.) tomorrow

še'u(m), grain, barley

šī (Fem.) anaphoric pronoun, cf. šū

šiamātu, article of purchase, sale; merchandise

ši'āru, ina ši'āri (Neo-Ass.) tomorrow

šibšu, lease of a field, rent, fee

šību(m) (Pl. adj. šibūtum, Pl. substant. šibū) Neo-Ass. šēbu, old, venerable, of great age; šibūtum, elders, (Old-Akk. also witnesses); šībū, witnesses šiddu, area, surface

šiḫtu(m), leap, attack; rage

šiliḫtu, canal, branch of a canal

šīlu(m), small hole, aperture

šimtu(m)[1], destiny, determination; affair; ana šimti alākum, to go to destiny, to die

šīmtu(m)[2], color (?)

šīmu(m), price, purchase-price; Mid-Ass. ana šīm gamer, for the full price; Mid-Ass. ana šime nadanu, to give for a price, to sell

šinnu(m) (Fem.) tooth; šinnān (dual) teeth

šipātu, wool

šipru(m) (Pl. šiprātum) embassy, craft, message; work; mār šipri, messenger, exchange of messengers

šiptu, oath, formula of swearing

šiqlu(m), shekel

šīqu, watering place, oasis

šīru, meat, flesh

šišītu(m), membrane, film

šīt (Fem.;Ass.) anaphoric pronoun, cf šū

šit'aru(m), glittering, shiny, radiant

šitta (Fem.) cf. šena

šu (Old-Akk.) Determinative pronoun, cf. ša

šū (Fem. šī, pl. šunu, fem. šina) Old-Akk. śū (fem. śī) Ass. šūt, (Fem. šīt) anaphoric pronoun, he, she, the one just mentioned, Old-Akk. šuma, he himself

šû(m), Ass. šu'ā'um, possessive pronoun, his

šubtu(m), dwelling

^{mi}šugītu(m), priestess

šuḫatinnu(m)^{sar}, a kind of plant

šukênu(m), Old-Akk. śuka''unum, Ass. šuka''unu(m), to submit oneself

šukkalmaḫḫu(m) Grand Vizier

šukkalu(m), messenger, delegate; vizier

šullušu(m), Old-Akk. śulluśum, D to do something for the third time

šulmānu (Pl. šulmānāte) present, gift

šulmu, health, well-being; as a greating: "Hail!"

šulušā, three each, three times

šumēlu(m) left side, the left one; šumēlam, to the left; ana šumēlim, toward the left

šumma, if

šumu(m) name; Neo-Ass. bearer of the name, heir; šanûm šumšu, second meaning (of an omen)

šunātunu (Mid-Ass.) Gen. Accus. of šunu

šunu (Pl.) anaphoric pronoun, cf. šū

šuquitu(m), weight, value

šurinnu, stem, trunk, staff

šurqu, the thing stolen

šuršu, root; Neo-Ass. šursukka, from your root, to your root

šupû (wpī), visible, brilliant

šuqallulu(m) (šqll), to hang up, suspend

šūṣû(m), Verb-Adj. banned; the one banned

šūt[1] (Ass.) anaphoric pronoun, cf. šū

šūt[2](Pl.) Determinative pronoun, cf. ša[1]

šutāpu, companion, associate

šutā'û(m), Št to be idle, lazy unemployed

šutebrû(m) cf. barû(m)[2]

šuteṣbû(m) (ṣb'), Št to carry out according to plan

šutlumu(m), to give, to grant

šūtrēšim (those of the head =) courtiers

T

tabāku(m) (a/u), G to pour out (blood), to shake off, throw away

tabālu(m) (a), G to carry away, bring away, put aside

tabû(m), cf. tebû(m)

tadānu (Mid. and Neo-Ass.) secondary verbal form of nadānu(m)

taḫāzu(m), slaughter, massacre

takālu (a), G to trust, have confidence in

takāpu(m), G (stat. only) to be spotted

[talāmu(m)], cf. šutlumu(m)

tallu(m)[1], diaphragm, midriff

tallu[2], door-post, drapery

tamāḫu(m) (a/u), G to grasp, seize

tāmertu, field, meadow, irrigated land

tamkāru(m), merchant

tamû(m) (tmā), Old-Akk. and Ass. tamā'u(m), G to swear; (with the accus.) to swear by; D to affirm by oath

tanzimtu(m), complaint

tapḫaru(m), Ass. tapḫurum, treasure

tappû(m), colleague, fellow-member of a treaty, one under pledge

tarāku(m), G (stat. only) to be dark

tarbaṣu(m), fold, pen

tarṣu, the other side; ana tarṣi to the other side

tarû(m) (trū), Old-Akk. tarā'um, to take away, to bring, to take

târu[1], Mid. and Neo-Ass. tuāru, resumption of a legal-process târu(m)[2] (tūr), G to turn, to turn around, turn back, come back to, return; ana mādim târum, to become much, numerous; Old-Ass. ana...tuārum to come back to; Mid-Ass. ina...tuāru, to come back from; D turru(m), Ass. ta''uru(m), to turn back, bring back, exchange, to drive (the enemy) back, to render an account, to make good an account; Mid-Bab. dāma turru, to avenge spilt blood

taṣliltu, roofing

tebû(m), tabû(m) (tb'), G to rise up, to get up, to be under way, to be walking, on the march

terḫatu(m), bride-price

têrtu(m) direction, instruction; bēl têrētim, the one commissioned, deputy, agent

teslītu(m), entreaty, prayer

tešītum, disorder, perplexity

tešmû(m), favorable hearing, granting a request

ti'āmtu(m) (Old-Akk.) sea

tuāru (Neo-Ass.) cf. târu[1]

tību(m), assault, charge

tibûtu(m) uprising, revolt; tibût erbim, plague of locusts

tillu(m), a tell, a heap of ruins

tīru, watchman, gate-keeper

tizqaru, prominent, notable

tukultu, trust, reliability

tultu(m), worm, grub, maggot

tulû; dual, tulâ, breasts

Ṭ

ṭābtu, salt

ṭābu(m), good, beautiful, satisfied; friendly; lā ṭābu, ugly, hateful, repulsive

ṭâbu(m) (ṭīb), G to be good, to be satisfied, to be suited; D to do well; to provide tranquillity, to pacify

ṭābūtu, (Mid-Bab) well off, prosperous

ṭarādu(m) (a/u), G to send

ṭebûm (tb'), G to sink; D to cause to sink, to submerge

ṭeḫi, prep. (Old-Ass.) close by, near

ṭeḫû(m) (ṭḫī), G to come near, D to cause to come near

ṭeḫḫû(m), border-territory

ṭēmu(m), report, command, information, authority

ṭubbu, well-being; ṭūb libbi, psychological well-being; ṭūb šīrē, physical well-being ṭuppu(m)[1], tablet, clay tablet, document; Old-Ass. ṭuppum ḫarmum, "double-document." (a tablet inside a "case" which is inscribed with the same text as the tablet); Mid-Ass. ṭuppu ša dayyānē, legal proclamation. Mid-Ass. ṭuppu dannutu, valid document.

ṭuppu[2], Stative, he is enrolled

ṭupšarru, scribe

U

u, and, and then, also, or

ubālu (Ass.) cf. wabālu(m)

ubānu(m) (Fem.) finger; "finger" (as liver-term); ubān ḫasî qablītum, middle "finger" of the lung

udā'u (Pres. udda, Pret. udi), G to know (Neo-Ass.)

udû, implement, sack, sac

ugaru(m), field, open country, meadow

ul, not; ul...ul, neither...nor

ula, not

ullû, that, that one

ulluṣu(m) (D infin. of elēṣum) jubilation

ultu (Mid-Bab.) cf. ištu

ūlu...ūlu, either...or

ūmâ, (Neo-Ass.) now

ūmakkal, a single day, a particular day

ūmišam, daily

umma...-ma, thus (speaks so-and-so...)

ummā (Mid-Bab.) thus, so; ummā...-ma (speaks) as follows

ummānu(m) army, troop; ālik pānī ummānim, the one who goes before the army

ummeātu(m), summer

ummi'ānu(m) Old-Ass. umme'ānum, creditor, financier, contributor; craftsman, master

ummu(m) (Pl. ummātum), mother

umšu(m), heat

ūmu(m) day; ūm 4^{kam} four days long; ina ūm 20^{kam} on the 20th day; ana ūm 10^{kam} within ten days; Old-Akk. in ūmīšu, at that time; Mid-Bab. ina ūmēšu, later; ūmam rēqam, on a distant day, in the future; dāriš ūmim, forever; Neo-Ass. ūmu anniu, the present day, today

unnedukku(m), letter

unqu(m), ring

upšāšû (Plural) (magical) intrigues

urdānūtu (Neo-Ass.) service, the status of a slave

urdu (Neo-Ass.) cf. wardu(m)

urḫu (Mid-Ass.) cf. warḫu(m)

urkiš (Mid. and Neo-Ass.) later; ina urkiš, later

urru, day, light, urrī u mūšī, by day and by night

urtānu (Mid-Ass.) an official; rabi urtānē, higher official, treasurer(?)

usukku(m), cheek

usā'u (Neo-Ass.) cf. waṣû(m)

uṣurtu, sketch; plan, intention

ušābu (Mid. and Neo-Ass.) cf. wašūbu(m)

ušumgallu, dragon, demon, (as description of the king:) all powerful; ušumgal kališ parakkī sovereign over all thrones = king of kings

ušuzzu (Neo-Bab.) cf. izuzzu(m)

utāru (Mid-Ass.) cf. watāru

utru, (Late-Bab.) surplus, excess

utukku(m), (good) spirit; demon

uṭṭetu(m) (Ass.) uṭṭatu(m), grain, barley; Old-Ass. a "standard" (a unit of weight)

uznu(m) (Dual uznān) ear

W

wabālu(m) (a/i), Mid-Bab. abālu, Neo-Ass. ubālu, G to raise, bring, carry, carry away, ana libbim wabālum, to bring in, to fit in, Neo-Ass. qātāte ana lemnetti ina libbi... ubālu, to lift the hands against someone; Gt to take away, Š to have brought, to have forwarded, Št to decide; to ponder

wadā'um (wd') cf. udā'u

waklu(m) foreman; wakil 10 ṣābim, overseer over 10 men

walādu(m) (a/i), to give birth, to bear

wamā'u(m) (wmā) (Old-Akk.), G (with accus.) to swear by

wapû (wpī), G to become visible, Š to make visible

warādu(m) (a/i), Neo-Bab. arādu, to go down, to draw towards

warāqu(m) (i), G to be green, yellowish

wardu(m), Mid and Neo-Bab., ardu, Neo-Ass. urdu slave, servant

warḫu(m), Mid-Ass. urḫu, month

warkānu(m), later

warkatu(m), back; situation, concern warkat behind

warkû(m) (<warkīum) that which is behind, later, warkīka, after you, ištu warkīšu since he is dead, since his death

warû(m) (wrū), Neo-Bab. arû, G to lead; Gtn continually to lead, to fetch again and again; Š to have (someone) lead

wâru(m) (w'r), G to go, to set out, attack, D to cause to to, to send

waṣû(m) (wṣī), Mid. and Neo-Bab. aṣû, Old-Ass. waṣā'um, Neo-Ass. uṣā'u, G to come out, to go away, to pull out; to go to meet; Š to have someone come out toward, Gt to go forth, to haul away; to have (liquid) pressed out, to betray (a secret); ana ṣītim šūṣûm, to leave; Štn to divulge (secrets) repeatedly, to chatter wāṣû(m) (Part. of waṣûm) the one (the thing) going out

waṣûtu(m) departure, waṣûtam alākum, to depart, to take one's exit

wašābu(m) (a/i), Mid. and Neo-Bab. ašābu, Mid and Neo-Ass. ušābu, G to settle, to sit, to dwell, to be in a place, Š šūšubu(m) (Pres. Bab. ušešseb, Ass. ušeššab) to let oneself be put, placed to settle down

wašāru(m) (a/i), Mid-Ass. ušāru, G to be loose, slack; to abandon (a place); D wuššuru(m), Mid. and Neo-Bab. muššuru, Old-Ass. waššurum to set free, loosen, to surrender, give up; Dt, to be set loose, set free

wāšibu(m), Mid. and Neo-Bab., Neo-Ass. āšibu, dwelling, sitting

watāru(m) Ass. utāru, G to be enormous; D to make (something) colossal. Mid-Ass. ana qāt...utturu, to cause someone to exceed the payment of...

watû(m) (wtā), G to find

weri'u(m), (Ass.) copper

wildu(m), posterity

Z

zabālu(m) (i), G to deliver, to betray (a secret)

zakāru(m) (a/u), G to name, to speak; Neo-Ass. ana... šumšu zakāru, to name ----to----.

zakû (zkū), Ass. zakā'u, G to become clean, free (of obligations); Mid-Ass. ana...zaku, is free for...., D to make free (of obligations)

zamāru(m) (u), to sing, praise (in song)

zammāru, singer; rabi zammāre, music conductor

zanānu(m) (u), G to rain

zânu(m) (z'n), G (Stat.) to be decorated

zaqātu(m) (a/u), G to stick, poke, sting

zar'u (Old-Akk.) cf. zēru(m)

zâzu(m) (zūz), G to divide; ana sena zâzum, to divide into two parts

zēru(m) Old-Akk., zar'um, seed, sperm, seed-corn; successor, descendant, sprout, scion. Neo-Ass. emār zēri, a unit of surface measure

zêru (z'r) G to hate

zibbatu(m), tail

ziḫḫu(m), blister, pimple

zikaru(m), male; lad, man

zinnu(m), rain, downpour

zittu(m), portion, inheritance

zumru(m), body

zuqiqīpu(m), scorpion

Proper Nouns

1. Names of gods

dAdad, weather-god

dAya, consort of Šamaš

dAmurru(m), god of the nomadic people

Annunītum, epithet of Istar

Antu(m), consort of the sky-god Anum

Anu(m), Sky-god, supreme god of the Pantheon

dAššur, City-state god of Aššur

dBau, City-state goddess of Lagaš

dBēltu, "Lady", title for various goddesses

dDagan, West-Semitic god

dDamu, god of well-being

dEa, god of wisdom

dEnlil, Chief-god of the Sumerian pantheon

dGula, goddess of well-being

dḪaldia, Ḫaldi, National god of the Urarti people

Igigū (Pl.), Collective name for the major gods

dIštar, most important goddess of the pantheon; goddess of love, revered also as goddess of war

dKabta, god of brick-making

Kūbu, demon of miscarriage, used apotropaically in personal names

Lamaštu, fever-demoness

dLaṣ, consort of Nergal

dMarduk, city-state god of Babylon

dNabû(m), Ass. dNabiu, god of wisdom, protective patron of scribes

dNanāya, about the same as Ištar, goddess of love

dNergal, god of the underworld

dNingal, consort of the moon-god Sîn

dNinsianna, the planet Venus, identified with Ištar

dNinšubur, messenger and companion of Ištar

dNinlil, spouse of Enlil

dNinurta, orginally a god of vegetation, later a war-god

dNudimmud, epithet of Ea

dNusku, "Vizier" of Enlil

dSataran, town god of Dēr

dSîn, moon-god

dŠamaš, sun-god

dŠar-Marad, town-god of Marad

dTašmētu, spouse of Nabû

dTišpak, town-god of Ešnunna

dUrmašum, ?

dZarpanītu, consort of Marduk

Geographical Names

^{uru}Ayyale, a place in Urartu

^{uru}Akka, Akko

Akkade, Capital city at the time of the dynasty of Akkad

Akkayyu, a man from Akko

Ālum^{ki}, "the city," a place on which the Assyrian commercial colonies in Asia Minor were dependent (probably Assur)

Amanum^{ki}, Amanus

Apišal, a city, probably in the upper Euphrates area

^{uru}Arbu, a place in Urartu

Armanum^{ki}, a city, probably in the upper Euphrates district

^{kur}Armatalli, a district in Urartu

^{uru}Arna, a place in Urartu

Aššur, Aššur

Bābilu(m), Babylon

^{id}Banītu, Banitu canal

^{kur}Barḫalzi, a district in upper Mesopotamia

^{uru}Bubuzi, a place in Urartu

Ebla^{ki}, a city in northern Syria

Eridu, a city in southern Mesopotamia

Gasur^{ki}, an old-Akkadian settlement in the neighborhood of modern-day Kirkuk

^{uru}Gunātum, a place in Babylonia

Gurasimmu, Aramaic tribe of nomads in southern Babylonia

Ḫalaḫḫi, ?

^{uru}Ḫinnatuni, a city in Canaan

^{uru}Ḫundur, a place in Urartu

Yabliya^{ki}, ?

^{uru}Kadukū, a district in Mesopotamia

^{uru}Kanzi, a place in Urartu

Kāniš, a city in Asia Minor, modern-day Kültepe

^{kur}Kara-Duniyaš, Babylonia in the time of the Kassites

^{kur}Kar-^{d}Bēli, a district in Babylonia

^{uru}Kinaḫḫi, Canaan

Kiš, A city in central Mesopotamia

Lagaš, A city in southern Mesopotamia

Larsam, A city in southern Mesopotamia

Magan^{ki}, a coastal region near the Indian Ocean

Marad, a city in Central Mesopotamia

^{uru}Medûm^{ki}, a district in southern Mesopotamia

Meluḫḫa, the western Indus region

^{kur}Miṣru, Egypt

Nagurzam^{ki}, a place in southern Mesopotamia

Nippur, a city in southern Mesopotamia

Nippurayyi, an inhabitant of Nippur

Purattu, the Euphrates

^{uru}Riyar, a place in Urartu

^{kur}Sangibute, a district in Urartu

^{uru}Sarni, a place in Urartu

Sippar, a city in central Mesopotamia

Sippar-Yaḫrurum, a district in the city of Sippar

^{uru}Ṣinišpala, a place in Urartu

^{uru}Ṣiniunak, a place in Urartu

Šankanum, ?

^{uru}Širimtum, ?

Tilmun^{ki}, Bahrain

Turukkūtum, the Turukki folk (name of a mountain people)

Tuttul^{ki}, a place on the Euphrates, probably modern-day Hit.

^{kur}Ubianda, a mountain in Urartu

Ullisum^{ki}, a region probably in Syria

Umma, a city in southern Mesopotamia

Urim, Ur, city-state in southern Mesopotamia

Uruk, biblical Erech, a city-state in southern Mesopotamia

3. <u>Names of Temples</u>

E-engurra, Temple of Ea in Eridu

Ekur, Temple of Enlil in Nippur

Emaḫtila, a part of the temple of Ezida in Borsippa

Esagil, Temple of Marduk in Babylon

Ezida, Temple of Nabû in Borsippa

4. <u>Personal Names</u>

The names which follow are identified by nationality (Sumerian, etc.) where they are not Akkadian. The Akkadian names are given a translation. Because of the complexity of the problems, not all the translations would be acceptable to all scholars. In some cases, even no worthwhile educated guess can be made. Those names are left untranslated.

Abu-šarrānī, Father of Kings

^{d}Adad-da'iq (Mid-Ass.) = ^{d}Adad-damiq

^{d}Adad-damiq, Adad is good

^{md}Adad-ēriš, Adad has claimed, wished, demanded

^{md}Adad-šumu-uṣur (Neo-Ass.) Adad, protect the heir

Agālum, wild horse

Agūza, Cappadocian

Aḫam-arši, I have obtained a brother

^{f}Aḫātu-lāmur (Neo-Ass.) May I see a sister

^{m}Aḫī-li'tī, My brother is my strength

Aḫu-kīnum, true brother

Aḫum, brother

Aḫum-waqar (the brother is dear) (Stat. of <u>waqar</u>, cf. 19.10)

Aḫūni, our brother

Aḫūnīya, my Ahuni

Aḫūšina, their brother

Aḫu-ṭāb(u), the brother is good

Akuki, West-Semitic

Alaḫum, Cappadocian

^{m}Ālī-ūta, I have found my city

Amar-^{d}Su'enna, (Sumerian); King of the 3rd dynasty of Ur, 2045-2037

Amazīya

Amīlīya, my man

Amīl-^{d}Marduk, friend of Marduk

Ammā, Cappadocian

Ammīditana, (West-Semitic) King of Babylon, 1683-1647

Ammīṣaduqa, (West-Semitic) King of Babylon, 1646-1626

Āmur-īlī, I have seen my god

Āmur-Ištar, I have seen Ištar

Amurrum-bānî, Amurru is my maker

^{d}Amurru-karābī-išme, Amurru has heard my prayer

Āmur-^{d}Šamaš, I have seen Šamaš

Ānaḫ-Ištar, I have become tired, Ištar

Apil-ilīšu, heir of his god

Apil-Kube, heir of Kubu

Aplum, heir

Appa-Daraḫ, (unusual writing for Tappa-^{d}Daraḫ)

f ^{uru}Arba'il-ḫammat the city-state Arba'il is the lady

^{m}Aššur-aḫu-iddina (Neo-Ass.) Aššur has given me a brother; Asarhaddon, King of Assyria, 681-669

^{m}Aššur-bāni-apli, Aššur is the producer of the heir; Aššurbanipal, King of Assyria 669-631

^{m}Aššur-bēl-aple, Aššur is the master of the heir

Aššur-iddin, Aššur has given

Aššur-lamassī, Aššur is my protective-god

Aššur-nādā, Aššur be praised

Aššur-nāṣer, Aššur is protector

Aššur-rabi, Assur is great

Aššur-rēṣî, Assur is my helper

^{md}Aššur-taklāk(u), I trust in Aššur

Aššur-ṭāb, Aššur is good

Awīl-^{d}Adad, man, servant of Adad

Awīl-^{d}Amurrim, man, servant of Amurrum

Awīl-^{d}Ninurta, consort, man, servant of Ninurta

^{m}Baba, abbreviated name

Balmunamḫe, Sumerian

^{m}Balumme, West-Semitic

Baqqum, gnat

Bēlānum, lord, master

^{md}Bēl-ibni, Bel has accomplished

^{f}Bēl-le'i, Bel can do all things

Bēlšunu, their lord

Bēlum, lord

^{md}Bēl-usātī, Bel is my help

^{md}Bēr-šuma-līšer, May Ber prosper the name-(bearer)

Betianalka, Cappadocian

Bītum-rabi, the temple is great

^{m}Bubūtum, hunger

Burraburiyaš, (Kassite) King of Babylon 1375-1347

^{m}Damiqtum, The Good

^{m}Dāni

Elani, Cappadocian

Enanatum, Sumerian

Enium, Old-Akkadian
^{d}Enlil-damiq, Enlil is gracious
Ennum-Aya, See, there is Aya

Ennu(m)-bēlum, See, there is the master

Enki-dug, (Sumerian), Enkidu, hero, friend of Gilgamesh

^{d}Enlillušaga, Sumerian

^{d}Enlil-muballiṭ, May Enlil keep in life

Eruru, Old-Akkadian

Gallābum, barber

^{d}Giš, Gilgameš

^{m}Gitibu, Old-Akkadian

Gugu, Old-Akkadian

Ḫammurapi, (West-Semitic) King of Babylon, 1792-1750

Ḫana, Cappadocian

Ḫuraṣānum, the golden

Ḫumadašu, Cappadocian

^{m}Ḫuzalu, gazelle

Ibašši-ilum, There is a god

Ibbâ-šarrum, The king has given me the name

Ibbatum

^{m}Ibbi-^{d}Ninšubur, Ninsubur has named

Ibbi-^{d}Sîn, Sîn has named (King of the 3rd dynasty of Ur, 2027-2003)

Ibni-^{d}Sîn, Sîn has made

^{m}Ibu, Old-Akkadian

Iddin-yattum, My (goddess) has given

Idī-^{d}Adad, My strength is Adad

Idī-Aššur, My strength is Aššur

Iddin-Kube, Kubu has given

^{m}Igayae, Hurrian

^{m}Igmil-^{d}Sîn, Sîn has exercised grace

Ikūnum, (short-form for) Ikun-pī-.

Ikūppī-Aššur (<Ikūn-pī-Aššur) the word of Aššur became true

Ilališka, Cappadocian

Ilī-emūqî, My god is my strength

Ilī-imitti, My god is my protection

Ilī-imguranni, My god has heard me

Ilī-iqīšam, My god has granted me (a son)

Ilī-wēdāku, My god, I am alone

^{m}Ilšu-ibbīšu, His god has called him by name, named him

^{m}Iliittilu

^{m}Ilum-āl-šū, (Old-Akkadian) God is his city-state

^{m}Ilum-bānî, God is my maker

^{m}Ilum-dān, God is constant

Imdī-ilum, My protection is god

^{m}Imgur-^{d}Sîn, Sîn has received, accepted

^{m}Imguru, (short form of <u>Imgur-^{d}...</u>

^{md}Innin-šumī-uṣur, Innin, protect my name

Ipiq-annunītum, Protection (?) of <u>Annunītum</u>

Ipiq-Ištar, Protection (?) of Ištar

Iškun-^{d}Dagan, (Old-Akkadian) Dagan has established

Iškurgalbi, Sumerian

^{md}Ištar-dur, Sardur II of Urartu (760-730)

Ištar-illassu, Istar is his relative

Ištar-nādā, praise Ištar

^{m}Ištar-šumu-ēriš, Istar has produced the heir

Itarak, Old-Akkadian

Kakug, Sumerian

Kaspū-ša, Old-Akkadian, her ransom

^{m}Katarsaḫ, Kassite

Kiba'id, Old-Akkadian

Kidin-^{d}Adad, Protection of Adad

^{m}Kidin-^{d}Gula, Protection of Gula

Kinūnû, born on the Kinunu festival

Kubaba, heroic female figure

^{m}Kubbulu, the bound, the twisted, muzzled

Kubi-idī, Kubu is my strength

Kukuwa, Cappadocian

Kurgalamaḫani, Sumerian

Labarša, Cappadocian

Lamassī, my protective divinity

Lipit-ilī, the work of my god

Lipit-Ištar, the work of Ištar

Luga, Sumerian

Lugalara, Sumerian

^{d}Luḫušum, (an heroic figure)

Maliwašḫi, Cappadocian

Manna-šī, "who is she?", "what is it?"

Mannu, abbreviated name, "Who...", "What..."

^{m}Mannu-kī-māt-Aššur, "What is like the land of Aššur

^{m}Marduk, abbreviated name

^{m}Marduk-kašid, Marduk overwhelms

^{d}Marduk-lamassašu, Marduk is his protective divinity

^{d}Marduk-nāṣer, Marduk is protector

^{d}Marduk-šākin-šumi, Marduk establishes my name

^{md}Marduk-šumu-uṣur, (Neo-Ass.) Marduk, protect the heir

Māšum, twin

Māti-bēlum, When, O Lord

^{m}Mattatum, woman's name, perhaps for *Mārtatum, little daughter

^{m}Mertugagga, Old-Akkadian

^{m}Minamu, Old-Akkadian

Muḫaddûm, He causes to rejoice

Nabi-^{d}Gula, named by Gula, called by Gula

Nabi-^{d}Sîn, named or called by Sîn

^{md}Nabiu-erība, Nabû has replaced

Nabium, the one called or named

^{md}Nabium-atpalam, Nabum, intercede for me

^{md}Nabû-šumi-iškun, Nabu has established my name

Naḫiš-šalmum, It prospers the healthy child

Napḫu'ruriya (Egyptian: nfr-ḫpr.w Re) Amenophis IV, 1364-1347

Narām-^{d}Sîn, Favorite of Sîn (King of the Dynasty of Akkad, 2259-2223)

Nidnat-^{d}Sîn, gift of Sîn

^{d}Ninurta-ašarēd, Ninurta is the most noble

Nīšī-īnīšu, the lifting of his eyes

Nūr-ilīšu, the light of his god

Nūr-^{d}Kabta, the light of Kabta

^{m}Nūr-^{d}Šamaš, the light of Šamaš

^{f}Qaqqadānītu, She of the large head

Qīšum, gift

Qīš-^{d}Nunu, gift of Nunu

Qurdi-Ištar, the great deed of Ištar

Pilaḫ-Ištar, Fear Ištar

Puzrū-ša, (Old-Akkadian) her refuge

Puzur-Anna, the security of Anna

Puzur-Aššur, the security of Aššur

Puzur- Ištar, the security of Ištar

^{m}Rabi-^{d}Sataran, Great is Sataran

Rē'ītum, shepherdess

Rīmuš, King of the dynasty of Akkad, 2284-2275

Sabazia, Cappadocian

Samsuditana, West-Semitic; King of Babylon, 1625-1594

Samsuiluna, West-Semitic; King of Babylon, 1749-1712

^{m}Sanānu

Sāsīya, my moth

^{d}Sîn-abūšu, Sîn is his father

^{d}Sîn-aiyabāš, Sîn--may I not be foiled

^{md}Sîn-dīnī-epuš, Sîn--obtain for me my due

^{d}Sîn-idinnam, Sîn has given to me

^{md}Sîn-imguranni, Sîn has yielded to me, has accepted me

^{md}Sîn-īriš, Sîn has requested

^{md}Sîn-mušallim, Sîn keeps (one) in health

^{md}Sîn-per'u-ukīn, Sîn has firmly planted the sprout (scion)

^{d}Sîn-pilaḫ, Fear Sîn

^{d}Sîn-šamuḫ (Sîn is magnificent, Stat. šamuḫ, 19.10)

^{md}Sîn-uballiṭ, Sîn has kept alive

Ṣillī-^{d}Adad, My shield is Adad

^{m}Šadî-aḫḫū'a, My refuge is my brothers

Šalim-bēlī, My Lord prospers

Šalim-Ištar, Ištar prospers

Šamaš-abu-usur (Neo-Ass.) Šamaš, protect the father

^{d}Šamaš-garri, Šamaš is my...?

^{d}Šamaš-ḫāzer, Šamaš is helper

^{d}Šamaš-ilum, Šamaš is the god

^{d}Šamaš-liwwir, May Šamaš be radiant

^{d}Šamaš-nādā, Praise Šamaš

^{md}Šamaš-nāṣer, Šamaš is protector

^{md}Šamaš-pāter, Šamaš redeems (from evil)

^{d}Šamaš-tukultī, Šamaš is my trust

^{d}Šamaš-iqīša, Šamaš has bestowed gifts on me

^{m}Šarātu, West-Semitic

^{d}Šar-kal(i)-šarri, King of Kings; King of the dynasty of Akkad, 2223-2198

Šarru(m)-kīn, The King is the true one; King of the Dynasty of Akkad, 2340-2284

^{m}Šaruš, Old-Akkadian

Šubišamnuman, Cappadocian

Šū-Ištar, the servant of Ištar

Šulgi, (Sumerian) King of the 3rd dynasty of Ur, 2093-2046

^{m}Šulmu-itu

Šum, (Old-Akkadian) Master?

^{m}Šumadda, West-Semitic

Šumi-abīya, Name(-bearer) of my father

^{m}Šumma-ilum, If a god...

Šunītum, Old-Akkadian

Šū-Su'in, the (servant) of Sîn

^{m}Šutatna, West-Semitic

Taddin-Nūnu, Nunu has given

Tamlatum

Tappa-^{d}Daraḫ, (West-Semitic), opponent of Šulgi

Titinari (or Titinatal), Cappadocian

^{m}Ubarru, stranger

^{m}Ubar = ^{m}Ubarru

^{m}Ubarīya, my stranger

^{m}Ummama, Old-Akkadian

^{m}Ursa, Urartian

^{m}Uršānum, hero

^{m}Ur-^{d}Utu, (Sumerian) perhaps to be read, *Warad-^{d}Šamaš*, servant of Šamaš

Uṣur-Anum, Heed Anum

^{f}Ušanamesu

Ūta-mīšaram, I have found justice

Warad-^{d}Gula, servant of Gula

Warad-^{d}Sîn, servant of Sîn

Zimri-eraḫ, West-Semitic